New Solutions for Cybersecurity

New Solutions for Cybersecurity

Edited by
Howard Shrobe, David Shrier, and Alex Pentland

connection.mit.edu

The MIT Press
Cambridge, Massachusetts
London England

© 2017 Massachusetts Institute of Technology

All rights reserved. No part of this book may be reproduced
in any form by any electronic or mechanical means (including
photocopying, recording, or information storage and retrieval)
without permission in writing from the publisher.

This book was set in Open Sans by GetSmarter. Printed and
bound in the United States of America.

Library of Congress Cataloging-in-Publication Data is available.

Portions of this work were previously published;
reproduced with permission of the authors.

ISBN: 978-0-262-53537-3

To the legions of students who have
inspired us to greater effort, and
awakened us to new perspectives.

CONTENTS

III. SYSTEMS

INTRODUCTION

Cybersecurity and Society

Howard Shrobe, David Shrier,
and Alex Pentland

Today's world is fraught with challenges. Rapid population growth and urban outreach have incurred enormous social and environmental problems. Cities are jammed with traffic; suffering from smog and pollution; pressured with demands for clean water, safe food; and energy; tortured by outbreaks of diseases and crimes; wary of financial and market crashes; and confronted with global warming and environmental deterioration that threatens cities in the long run and at colossal scale.

The traditional approach to managing these complex systems emphasizes provision of centralized services on health care, transportation, financing, public security, education, and governance. Unfortunately, this model has turned out less effective in coping with the problems given the reality of cities evolving more sophisticated and ever-changing for today.

The present-day society and cities are largely networked, inter-connected with modern information science and technology, where massive digital bits of information exchange and flow extraordinarily swiftly across web and mobile systems, penetrating every layer and corner of the human livings. Interconnected and networked, they provide an ample attack surface for cybercriminals, ranging from the mercenary to the state actor.

Running parallel to the continued urbanization of society, corporations have undergone globalization as well. Efforts to build scale have resulted in organizations that span every time zone on the planet, with distributed personnel grappling with centralized information technology systems and outmoded security systems. Efforts to address some of these deficiencies have opened even more security holes, such as the introduction of easily hacked fingerprint scanners and simplistic applications of cryptographic protection.

We have entered an epoch of big data. The de facto status calls for a new kind of digital infrastructure that takes on a dynamic, holistic approach that is able to integrate social, economic, political, behavioral, and mathematical measurements based upon big data analytics, to find a complete solution for achieving a more efficient, secure, inclusive, green, and sustainable future.

As our societies move from a world where interactions were physical and based on paper documents, toward a world that is primarily governed by digital data and digital transactions, our existing methods of managing identity and data security are proving inadequate. Large-scale fraud, identity theft, and data breaches are becoming common, and a large fraction of the population has only the most limited digital credentials. If we can create a web of trusted data that provides safe, secure access for everyone, then huge societal benefits can be unlocked, including better health, greater financial inclusion, and a population that is more engaged with and better supported by its government.

As a consequence, a central concern in building a rich data society is about data security and privacy protection. All activities of a rich data society that pertain to mining, filtering, storing, querying, using, analyzing, and aggregating the data and generating research reports and articles, must strictly comply with the relevant data security and privacy protection regulations.

Establishing a strict data security protection mechanism and complying relevant data security regulations is the key to moving forward the success of our future society.

We need new tools and technologies for fair and transparent analysis, for running queries over encrypted data, for auditing and tracking information, and for managing and sharing our own personal data in the future. Issues of data privacy will be relevant across so many aspects of our life, including banking, insurance, medical, public health, and government. We believe it is important to collectively address major challenges managing data privacy in a big data world.

We need systems that are intrinsically inimical to attack. We need self-healing networks and cyber-resilient hardware. We need executive leadership that has been trained to think about a new kind of enemy and fight with a new set of weapons. We need new levels of understanding about the dynamic, and often confusing, new world order that has emerged out of the digital revolution.

Resolving the tension between data sharing and privacy, to unlock the potential value of that data is a challenge, particularly for governments and regulated industries. Although centralized databases for processing may be conceptually simpler, distributed networks with privacy preserving algorithms can maximize security for data processing, in compliance with legal, regulatory, and ethical requirements without the limited scalability of current distributed, but independent processing platforms.

In this volume, we have assembled a team of cyber experts who provide a multi-dimensional view of the cybersecurity challenge—and the new solutions to face it. The leading minds from MIT's Computer Science & Artificial Intelligence Lab, the MIT Media Lab, and the MIT Sloan School of Management, are joined by colleagues from Lincoln Lab, Draper Lab, The University of Cambridge, and SRI for an ecumenical and holistic "systems view" of cybersecurity.

We posit approaches that range from the market-driven to the fundamental. We reveal new problems that arise in a fully decentralized, IoT world, and begin to reinvent the overall concept of what optimal systems architecture and management might look like. Join us, as we share with you a vision of the near future, which you can apply to your current context.

Howard Shrobe, David Shrier, and Alex Pentland

Cambridge, MA, July 2017

SECTION I
MANAGEMENT, ORGANIZATIONS & STRATEGY

CHAPTER 1

Institutions for Cybersecurity: International Responses and Data Sharing Initiatives

Nazli Choucri, Stuart Madnick,
and Priscilla Koepke

INTRODUCTION

The expansion of cyberspace has occurred at a dramatic pace over the past two decades. Almost every location on the globe now has some degree of cyber access, outpacing even the most optimistic expectations of the early architects of the Internet. Less anticipated, however, by the initial innovators or anyone else, was the subsequent introduction of cyber threats and the accompanying innovations in the disruption and distortion of cyber venues.

This chapter is positioned at the intersection of the long tradition of international institutions and the nascent area of theorizing about cyberpolitics in international relations. Its purpose is to provide an initial baseline, for representing and tracking institutional responses to a rapidly changing international landscape, real as well as virtual. In this chapter, we shall argue that the current institutional landscape managing security issues in the cyber domain has developed in major ways, but that it is still "under construction." We also anticipate that institutions for cybersecurity will support and reinforce the contributions of information technology to the development process.

For purposes of context and background, we (a) begin with highlights of international institutional theory and an empirical "census" of the institutions-in-place for cybersecurity, and then turn to (b) key imperatives of information technology–development linkages and the various cyber processes which enhance developmental processes, (c) major institutional responses to cyber threats and cyber crime as well as select international and national policy postures so critical for industrial countries and increasingly for developing states as well, and (d) the salience of new mechanisms designed specifically in response to cyber threats.

INTERNATIONAL INSTITUTIONS: THEORETICAL ANCHORS AND EMPIRICAL RECORD

Over the better part of a decade, the convergence of four distinct but interconnected trends in international relations created demands for formal interventions involving governments and international coordination. First, Internet usage continued to rise, coupled with an expansion in forms of use. Second, many governments recognized that cyber vulnerabilities continued to threaten not only the security of their own networks, but also those of their citizens involved in routine activities daily. Third, a noted absence of coordinated industry response or of efforts to develop cooperative threat reduction strategies, reinforced an unambiguous gap-in-governance. Finally, a growing set of cyber incidents, large and small, signaled to governments the potential impact of their failure to address the emerging threats. In response to these trends, governments, in various ways, mobilized significant national and international resources toward the creation of a broad cybersecurity framework.

Theoretical context

There is a long, respected, and distinguished tradition of institution-centric scholarship in modern international relations. The classical literature in this field focused on the United Nations (UN) and its institutions against a background of the failures of the League of Nations;[1] this literature was largely descriptive, highlighting structure and function.[2] With the evolution of European integration, institutionalism took a new turn, seeking to connect domestic and international politics and to signal potentials for diffusion of institutional development.[3] Subsequently, the conceptual frame of reference shifted to focus on the "demand" and the "supply" driving the development of international institutions.[4] Consequently, the concept of regime emerged as an important anchor in the field.

In this chapter, however, we focus on the formal aspects of regimes, namely the institutional manifestations, rather than on underlying norms and principles. In a review of institutionalism theory, Hall and Taylor (1996) argue that contemporary institutionalism, known as "new institutionalism," is actually an amalgam of three types of theoretical considerations rather than one single theory—namely historical institutionalism, rational choice institutionalism, and sociological institutionalism. The first focuses largely on constitutional issues, bureaucratic arrangements, and operating procedures of interaction. The second, rational choice institutionalism, centers on the value of reduced transaction costs, the relationship between principals and agents, and strategic interaction—all based on the underlying logic of rational choice. Sociological institutionalism, the third variant, concentrates largely on why organizations adopt particular sets of institutional forms, including procedures and symbols.

A somewhat different perspective on institutional issues in the context of the sovereign state, put forth by Reich (2000), argues that the relevant institutional features or theoretical perspectives should be viewed in the context of the specific case in question. This view is based on Lowi (1964), who argues that the policy domains, or subject matter, dictate the "best" institutional forms, thus placing the empirical context in the forefront and matters of theory in a derivative position. This pragmatic perspective fits well with the policy imperatives created by the cyber domain.

While the literature tends to argue that consensus on norms precedes the formation of institution, we suspect that in the cyber domain the reverse dynamics hold, namely that institutions may well be the precursors for formalizing norms and principles that, in turn, might consolidate and strengthen the institutions themselves. This contingency is especially likely in the development context.

Institutional "ecosystem": a baseline

Building a "baseline" for cybersecurity institutions in international relations is particularly daunting given the trajectory of evolution for the cyber domain.

To begin with, cyberspace was constructed by the private sector—albeit with the support and direction of the dominant power in world politics, the United States. The state system formally defined in cyberspace is a relatively recent development; the entire cyber domain is managed by non-state entities, an important aspect of scale and scope in international relations.

Second, the usual mechanisms for tracking activities in the physical world— statistics, standards, measurements, etc.—are not automatically conducive to "virtual" traces or counterparts.

Third, the very nature of the "virtual" contradicts that which is physical. Threats in the "virtual" domain are often identified after the fact, rather than tracked "in process." In the cyber domain, there is not only no early warning system; there are, as yet, few early signals of a cyberthreat, if any.

The broad institutional domain presented in table 1.1 provides a baseline view of the cybersecurity "institutional ecosystem"—a complex assortment of national, international and private organizations. Parallel to the organic fashion in which cyberspace itself developed, these organizations often have unclear mandates or possess overlapping spheres of influence. Our purpose here is only to highlight these major entities and, to the extent possible, to signal their relationships and interconnections, compiling something of a census of institutions. A secondary, but also important, objective is to explore data quality and the extent to which we may infer organizational performance from public metrics, creating a performance assessment of sorts.

While we catalogue many of the major institutional players in this aspect of cybersecurity, we do not claim to provide an exhaustive "census." We used two criteria for the selection of institutions, namely, (a) data provision of public qualitative or quantitative data in each of our areas of focus (international, intergovernmental, national, non-profit, and private sector) and (b) coordination responsibility based on formal mandates issued by recognized international or national bodies. For the national sphere, we focused on the United States as a representative model but also included several examples of non-US national entities; detailed analysis of other national efforts is beyond the scope of this chapter.

Table 1.1 International institutional ecosystem

Institution	Role	Data availability	Example variables (if applicable)
CERTs			
AP-CERT	Asian regional coordination	High	Collation of security metrics from member CERTs in Asia
CERT/CC	Coordination of global CERTs, especially national CERTs	Moderate	Vulnerabilities catalogued; hotline calls received; advisories and alerts published; incidents handled
FIRST	Forum and information sharing for CERTs	Low	Secondary data from conferences and presented papers
National CERTs (e.g., US- CERT)	National coordination; national defense and response	High	Varies—volume of malicious code and viruses; vulnerability alerts; botnets; incident reports

Institution	Role	Data availability	Example variables (if applicable)
TF-CSIRT: Computer Security Incident Response Teams	European regional coordination	N/A	N/A
ISACs			
Critical Infrastructure Sector-focused ISACs	Collect, analyze, and disseminate actionable threat information	Moderate	Operation Centers collect, catalog, and share threat information and vulnerabilities with members. Some industry best-practices presented; newsletters summarizing ongoing activities for members
National Council of ISACs	Collaborate and coordinate cyber and physical threats and mitigation strategies among ISACs	Low	Secondary data from conferences and testimonies
International Entities			
CCDCOE: Cooperative Cyber Defense Centre of Excellence	Enhancing NATO's cyber defense capability	Low	Secondary data from NATO member states on individual cybersecurity strategies and legislation
Council of Europe	International legislation	Moderate	Legislation and ratification statistics; secondary data from conferences and presented papers
EU: European Union	Sponsors working parties, action plans, guidelines	N/A	N/A

Institution	Role	Data availability	Example variables (if applicable)
ENISA: European Network and Information Security Agency	Awareness-raising, cooperation between the public and private sectors, advising the EU on cybersecurity issues, data collection	Low	Awareness-raising stats; spam surveys; regional surveys; country reports. Qualitative data assessing the EU cybersecurity sphere
G8: Subgroup on High-Tech Crime	Sponsored 24/7 INTERPOL hotline, various policy guidelines	N/A	N/A
IMPACT	Global threat response center, data analysis, real-time early warning system	N/A	N/A
INTERPOL	Manages 24/7 hotline, trains law-enforcement agencies, participates in investigation	N/A	N/A
ITU	Sponsors IMPACT. Global Cybersecurity index. Organizes conferences, releases guidelines and toolkits, facilitates information exchange and cooperation	Moderate	Internet usage and penetration statistics; publishes cyber wellness profiles of countries and a Global Cybersecurity Index to promote information exchange. Publishes secondary data from conferences and presented papers
NATO	Responding to military attacks on NATO member state	N/A	N/A: classified

Institution	Role	Data availability	Example variables (if applicable)
OECD	Develops policy options, organizes conferences, publishes guidelines and best practices	Low	Secondary data from conferences and presented papers
UNODC: United Nations Office on Drugs & Crime	Promotion of legislation, training programs, awareness, enforcement	N/A	N/A
UNODA: United Nations Office of Drugs & Crime	Issuance of information security reports	Low	Publishes country views of information technology and trends in cybersecurity
WSIS	Global summit on information security; publishes resolutions and monitors implementation through stock-taking efforts	Low	Stock-taking database and secondary data from conferences and presented papers
OAS: Organization of American States	Supports efforts to fight cyber crime; strengthen cybersecurity capacity of member states	Low	Publishes reports and methods to respond to incidents
US national entities			
NSA: National Security Agency	Shares Director, Admiral Michael Rogers, with US CYBERCOM; specializes in cryptology services and research	N/A	N/A: classified

Institution	Role	Data availability	Example variables (if applicable)
CIA: Central Intelligence Agency	Defense of intelligence networks, information gathering	N/A	N/A: classified
DHS	Protection of federal civil networks and critical infrastructure; information sharing and awareness; coordinating federal response and alerts	Moderate	Data released through US-CERT; National Vulnerability Database; Automated Indicator Sharing initiative through the National Cybersecurity and Communication Integration Center (NCCIC)
DoD: Department of Defense	Defense of military networks, counterattack capability	N/A	N/A: classified
DOJ: US Department of Justice	Federal prosecution	Moderate	Non-aggregated data: prosecuted cases; crime by industry
FBI	Federal investigation	Low	Total reported incidents, number of referrals to law enforcement agencies; Annual surveys on corporate computer crime including type and frequency of attacks; dollar loss; attack source
CTIIC: Cyber Threat Intelligence Integration Center	Investigating foreign cyber threats	N/A	N/A: classified

Institution	Role	Data availability	Example variables (if applicable)
DoS: Department of State	Promotion of an open, interoperable, secure, and reliable information and communications infrastructure	Low	Office of Coordinator for Cyber Issues publishes testimonies; speeches; and cyber policy strategy reports
FTC	Consumer protection	Low	Publishes best practices and other advisory guides
IC3	Cybercrime reporting and referral center	High	Total complaints; referred complaints; estimated dollar loss; complaints by industrial sector
NW3C: National White Collar Crime Center	Provides training and support to law enforcement agencies, helps administer the IC3 with the FBI	N/A	N/A: statistics released through IC3
FSSCC: Financial Services Sector Coordinating Council	By DHS mandate, identifies threats and promotes protection to protect financial sector critical infrastructure assets	N/A	N/A
Secret Service	Investigation of economic cybercrimes	N/A	N/A
US-CERT	Defense of federal civil networks (.gov), information sharing and collaboration with private sector	Moderate	Incidents and events by category; vulnerability reports

Institution	Role	Data availability	Example variables (if applicable)
DOE: Department of Energy	Assists energy sector asset owners by developing cybersecurity solutions for energy delivery systems	Moderate	Publishes models to help organizations enhance cybersecurity capabilities; issues guidance; reports; risk mitigation plans
ISAOs: Information Sharing and Analysis Centers	Information sharing organizations to facilitate public-private exchanges	N/A	N/A
Non-US national entities (frequent collaborative partner)			
GCHQ: Government Communications Headquarters (UK)	One of three of Britain's intelligence agencies responsible for information assurance and cryptology; Britain's leading authority on cybersecurity	N/A	N/A
National Cyberdefense Centre (Germany)	Agency for cybersecurity in Germany; responds to reports of cyberattacks on critical infrastructure	N/A	N/A
National Police Bureaus (e.g., Taiwan, South Korea, Japan, France)	Investigation, enforcement	Varies	Cases; arrests; prosecutions; demographics

Institution	Role	Data availability	Example variables (if applicable)
Center for the Protection of National Infrastructure (UK)	Provide advice on physical security, personnel security and cybersecurity/ information assurance to critical national infrastructure entities	Moderate	Publishes reports; case studies on attacks; best practices and research
Non-profits			
GICSR: Global Institute for Security and Research	Conducts R&D with industry leaders, public-private sector, and academia to develop policy and strategy for cyberspace	N/A	N/A
Internet Society	Non-technical branch of Internet Engineering Task Force; provides leadership in addressing policy issues that confront the future of the Internet	N/A	N/A
CyberWatch	Develops educational programs and curriculum to train next generation of cybersecurity experts	N/A	N/A
CAIDA: Cooperative Association for Internet Data Analysis	Gathers data that will increase situational awareness of Internet topology structure, behavior, and vulnerabilities	High	Graphs and visuals of Internet traffic patterns

Institution	Role	Data availability	Example variables (if applicable)
NERC: North American Electric Reliability Corporation	Assures the reliability of the bulk power system in North America.	Moderate	Publishes reliability standards; coordinates with Electricity ISAC; conducts GridEx security exercise
The Honeynet Project	Investigates attacks and develops open-source tools to improve Internet security	low	Publishes reports and holds annual security workshops
The SANS Institute	Develops, maintains, and makes available a collection of research documents about various aspects of information security; operates the Internet's early warning system - the Internet Storm Center.	Moderate	Publishes reports; trainings; enterprise solutions; and webcasts on threats; vulnerabilities; and tools to improve security
Center for Internet Security	Provides resources to enhance the cybersecurity readiness and response of public and private sector entities; fosters collaboration between communities	Low	Publishes annual reports; intelligence advisories; hosts MS-ISAC

Institution	Role	Data availability	Example variables (if applicable)
Internet Security Alliance	Multi-sector international trade association focused on advancing the development of a sustainable system of cybersecurity, and increased awareness	Moderate	Publishes policy reports; books; and blogs on APTs, cyber risk, mobile security, supply chains, and insider threats; promotes information sharing programs with government and private sector
International Association of Cryptologic Research	Researches cryptology	Low	Secondary data from conferences and workshops and presented papers
ISRA: Information Security Research Association	Security research and cybersecurity awareness activities	Low	Hosts forums for discussing and sharing information on vulnerabilities; forensics; malware; cryptography; information security management
CSA: Cloud Security Alliance	Researches and promotes awareness of best practices to ensure a secure cloud computing environment	Low	Educational opportunities an certifications; publishes research and secondary data from working groups
Cyber Threat Alliance	Share threat information to improve defenses against advanced cyber adversaries across member organizations	Moderate	Cryptowall Dashboard with detailed data on threats, IPs, URLs, SHA256s

Institution	Role	Data availability	Example variables (if applicable)
Private Sector			
McAfee	Industry leader in antivirus software; computer security services	Moderate	White papers
Raytheon	Cyber security solutions division offers a wide range of information assurance services	N/A	N/A
Lockheed Martin	Defense contractor that supplies consulting, training and solutions for many governmental cybersecurity G&S and for private institutions	N/A	N/A
Kaspersky Labs	World leading cybersecurity company, focused on endpoint protection	N/A	N/A
FireEye/Mandiant	Cyber security endpoint solutions and consulting leader	Low	Publishes threat intelligence reports
Ponemon Institute	Research on privacy, data protection and information security policy; strategic consulting	Moderate	Publishes research studies and white papers

Institution	Role	Data availability	Example variables (if applicable)
Arbor Networks	DDoS and advanced threat protection services	Moderate	Publishes threat briefings, data visualization attack map, data from ATLAS global threat monitoring system, annual security report, whitepapers, and data sheets; holds webinars and briefs
Facebook	Sponsors Threat Exchange, a platform for sending and receiving information about cyber threats for developers	Low	Educational videos and product documents; Threat Exchange platform
Microsoft	Security division provides annual reports and worldwide infection and encounter rate maps	Moderate	Publishes white papers
IBM Security	Division of IBM that offers security intelligence, integration, expertise, and R&D to protect against cybersecurity threats	Moderate	X-Force Exchange platform for community collaboration, information sharing on cyber threats and vulnerabilities; publishes annual threat intelligence report
Red Tiger Security	Investigates cyberattacks	N/A	N/A
International Computer Security Association	Specializes in antivirus, antispam, and firewall services among a wide array of other cybersecurity services	Moderate	Graphs of which countries sent the most spam per week

Institution	Role	Data availability	Example variables (if applicable)
Palo Alto Networks	Network and enterprise security with specialization in firewalls	N/A	N/A
Verizon	Enterprise security solutions, products, and services	High	Publishes annual data breach investigations and compliance reports, solutions briefs, and fact sheets

INFORMATION TECHNOLOGY AND DEVELOPMENT LINKAGES

The academic as well as the policy communities worldwide have long focused on challenges associated with economic, social, and political development, broadly defined. Throughout the entire immediate World War II period, the decolonization process created a whole new "generation" of governments whose vision of governance required adaptation to the new challenges, and whose limited capability required immediate enhancement if any possibility of effective performance was to be realized.

The development agenda of the international community recognized the complexity of the aforegoing, and over time the requisite institutional mechanisms were put in place. Some were appended to the organizations created to manage the aftermath of World War II, and others were created specifically for meeting the development challenges.

Sustainable development

By 1990, the entire development discourse had shifted away from growth per se (i.e., expansion of output) and toward sustainable development (a more comprehensive and nuanced process). "Sustainability" had become central to our daily concerns as well as to policy and decision in all contexts and in nearly all parts of the world.

Without undue simplification, it is fair to say that the traditional view of development focused on productivity and the expansion of economic output.

Later on, concepts of human development took hold, and the well-being of individuals and society were seen as essential features of development. Sustainable development, first formally introduced at the United Nations

Conference on Environment, 1990, recognized the sanctity of nature and its life-supporting services, thus placing the growth imperative in a broader context. Agenda 21 framed and reflected an international consensus and a plan of action articulated in Millennium Development Goals. The view of sustainable development at the time was that of meeting the needs of present and future generations without undermining the cohesion of the social system or the life-supporting properties of the natural system.

During the last decade of the 20th century, cyberspace was recognized almost universally as being of great importance. By an accident of chance, by design, or by the logic of technological development, this human-constructed environment had already assumed near-worldwide scale and scope. Many parts of the world were still unconnected, but everyone recognized it was just a matter of time until the world's population became interlinked. It was an unstated assumption that the Internet would simply proliferate.

With the benefit of hindsight, we now appreciate that the assumption, while correct, missed almost all of the underlying institutional dynamics, the emerging political contentions, the growing efforts of the state, and the state system to shape trajectories, rules, and norms of a cyber system—with the Internet as its core—that had been built as an open domain, shaped by only the minimal regulatory conventions necessary for effective operation.

Unless proven otherwise, all evidence suggests that never before in modern times has a major technological innovation exhibited such rapid diffusion throughout the world. Differences in infrastructure, skills, literacy, and capabilities aside, cyber access in developing countries has expanded rapidly over the past decades.

During the early days of the Internet, the open ethos dominated. With greater understanding of uses and growth in the diversity of users, networks were no longer secure. A wide range of malevolent intrusions with varying degrees of damaging effects demonstrated without doubt the vulnerability of the Internet. With this near-certain vulnerability and threat, the very sustainability of the human-constructed cyber domain was at stake. Cybersecurity had now become a matter of national and, to the extent possible, international priority as well.

Critical convergence of information and development

The process shaping and managing the World Summit on Information Society (WSIS) places cyberspace at the center of international policy discourse. As a UN-based initiative, decisions at the WSIS were made at the state level, and only sovereign states served as "decision makers." At the same time, all stakeholders wishing to participate in the overall process—from agenda setting to various forms and forums of deliberations—were encouraged to do so. This practice dated back to the United Nations Conference on Environment and Development (UNCED) in 1990, a major landmark in the history of international collaboration.

The WSIS intergovernmental initiative is a milestone in its own right as it sought to combine several distinct aspects of the UN's twentieth-century development agenda with emergent implications of information technology. WSIS was the first comprehensive response to the emergent "virtual" global society in a world increasingly concerned with the dilemmas of sustainable development. Although it was not conceived as a security-centric activity, the WSIS objectives that dealt with cybersecurity were broadly consistent with developmental concerns.

Operationally, WSIS was organized into two phases, each standing as a global conference in its own right. The first phase, held in Geneva in 2003, had representatives from over 175 countries committed to a wide-ranging action plan. Action Line C5 focused on "building confidence and security," and committed member countries to increasing security awareness, enacting legislation, and cooperating more extensively with the private sector (WSIS, 2003).

These goals were expanded upon in 2005 at the second phase in Tunis, when member organizations reaffirmed their Geneva commitments and agreed upon a collective stock-taking method to track action line implementation. The efforts by member states to implement Action Line C5 are viewable in a public database, and are also published in annual reports (WSIS, 2009a). The combined conclusions transformed the general consensus into a Plan of Action. The Plan centered around information society in the developing world. This is the point of convergence between information and development.

At the WSIS meeting in Paris, 2013, we put forth the proposition that the overarching conditions for sustainability, and for the process of sustainable development, broadly defined, rest not only on the sustainability of the social and the natural system, but also on the sustainability of the cyber system. In other words, sustainable development is contingent on the sustainability of all three systems: social, environmental, and cyber (Choucri, 2012). In other words, this proposition recognizes that humans are now embedded in three interconnected systems.

This concept was further explored at the 2015 WSIS meeting in Geneva, where it was recognized that access to secure and trustworthy information and communication technologies is an essential tool needed to achieve sustainable development. Member states agreed that building trust and collaboration in cyberspace through a simplified exchange network among CERTs and law enforcement agencies is important, and that enabling laws and regulatory frameworks are key for sustainable development in the cyber system.

In December 2015, the United Nations Member States met to review the WSIS goals progressed over the last 10 years and adopted the WSIS +10 outcome document to bridge the digital divide between nations, ensure freedom of speech, and address Internet governance to achieve the 2030 Agenda for Sustainable Development. This meeting highlighted the important role of information and communications technologies and noted the ambition to move beyond "information societies" to "knowledge societies," in which information is created, disseminated, and put to the benefit of human development. A review of the implementation of the WSIS outcomes will occur in 2025 (United Nations, 2015).

The new security calculus

Traditionally, national security focuses on security at the state borders and protection against military or other threatening intrusions. Over time this simple doctrine was refined into a more comprehensive view of security. In addition, the near universal expansion of government responsibility, the conception of a stable state, or alternatively, a failing one, became closely tied to the evolving developmental agenda.

To simplify, security and sustainability gradually converged into one general vision of imperatives for survival. It was a vision that included border protection, social viability, and government capability. In its execution, defense was clearly the responsibility of the military. Social viability included, by emergent definitions, meeting the needs of present and future generations and the protection of nature's life supporting properties.

The construction of cyberspace created a new set of imperatives and an entirely new set of threats to security for the state system and all non-state entities—for profit and not for profit. No one could foresee the scale, scope, and damage potentials. Most important of all, the anonymity of the perpetrator created an unprecedented threat to both the traditional view of security, (defense of borders) and the revised view (military security, security of society and environment, and security of governance). Thus, cybersecurity became a critical feature of overarching security, for industrial and developing states. It had to be managed at all levels of international relations—national, transnational, international, and global.

COMPUTER EMERGENCY RESPONSE TEAMS (CERTS)

New institutions were created specifically in response to cyber threats. These new institutions were created under national authority, with international scope, but not intergovernmental in form. Named *Computer Emergency Response Teams* (CERTs),[5] these are the only worldwide institutions created specifically in response to the new cyber threats. CERTS are an important addition to the dense network of international entities in the "real" or physical arena, and occupy a salient role in the cybersecurity landscape.

As defined by the CERT Coordination Center (CERT/CC)—addressed later on—these entities focus on security emergencies, promote the use of valid security technology, and ensure network continuity (CERT Program, 2009a). In principle, this means that CERTs concentrate on identifying vulnerabilities and fostering communication between security vendors, users, and private organizations. Although the majority of CERTs were founded as non-profit organizations, many have transitioned towards public-private partnerships in recent years.

This type of lateral institutional design anchored in national governments attempts to build upon the successes of non-profit CERTs by providing a level of structure and resources hitherto unavailable. However, while the CERT network is becoming increasingly formalized, individual CERTs may differ considerably in their ability to effectively perform their mandates. By 2016, there were over 351 recognized CERTs, with widely different levels of organization, funding, and expertise (Forum of Incident Response and Security Teams [FIRST], 2016).

At least three results are expected from CERT activities and interactions: a reduction in unaddressed security vulnerabilities, improved understanding of the nature and frequency of cyber threats, and enhanced communicating and reporting of incidents to other security teams and the general public. Although CERTS are not established to serve as information gathering institutions per se, their activities involve active threat monitoring and information exchange. As a result, many CERTs attempt to provide quantitative data for the cybersecurity community. To date, however, there is little effort to align or coordinate methods of data collection, and availability and reliability of reported information thus varies widely across the CERT landscape. This means that the focus on organization has not yet extended to matters of performance and coordination.

Organizational structure

In general, CERTs share a common structure and backbone. In principle, this should help coordination. The majority of CERT teams are organized according to guidelines originally published by CERT Coordination Center

(CERT/CC), and many use common toolkits to establish their organizations (Killcrece, 2004). As a result, CERTs tend to differ from each other mainly in their area of focus (academic, private, national, regional), or their respective area of expertise (phishing, viruses, information security). These roles are largely self-defined based on each team's level of funding (which can vary widely), technical expertise, and the presence of perceived gaps within the CERT collaborative network. This means that the principle of autonomy supersedes that of collaboration.

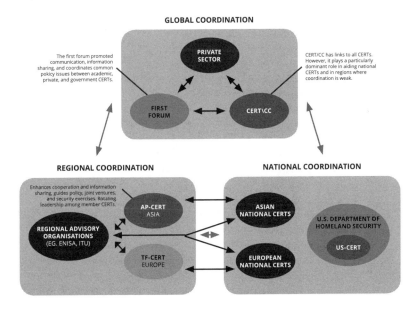

Figure 1.1 International CERTs

The flexibility of this system greatly improves the possibility of coordination between CERTs; however, the loose network structure reduces the locus of responsibility or accountability for individual performance. In traditional institutional theory, the underlying generic objectives are to facilitate collective action, reduce transaction costs, and enable the performance of functions or the provision of services. To illustrate the complexity of arrangements, table 1.1 presents a subset of these structured relationships at different levels of analysis and organization.

Coordinating organizations

A distinguishing feature of the CERT system is its coordinating mechanism, CERT/CC, established at Carnegie Mellon University in 1998—in response to a major Internet worm. CERT/CC was also the first operational CERT, and defined many functional parameters. The US Defense Advanced Research Projects Agency (DARPA) originally provided federal funding for the organization with the expectation that CERT/CC would serve as a center for direct threat assessment and response.

As cyberspace and cyber access expanded, a single organization proved insufficient to handle the increasing volume of security incidents. CERT/CC was forced to reframe its activities and priorities. Rather than responding directly to emerging incidents, CERT/CC's renewed mission utilized the lessons learned to provide guidelines, coordination, and standards for other CERTs. By relinquishing operational control in favor of a collaborative structure, CERT/CC laid the foundation for the establishment of regional, focused organizations. Today, the CERT network has expanded beyond the scope and control of CERT/CC, although CERT/CC continues to play an influential role in establishing national CERTs in developing countries and fostering inter-CERT communication.

In addition to CERT/CC, many CERTS also interact with parallel coordination networks, such as the *Forum of Incident Response and Security Teams* (FIRST). This body was established to enhance information sharing between disparate security groups (FIRST, 2009b). Now composed of more than 300 organizations, FIRST is notable for its influential annual conferences and its extensive integration of national, academic, and private CERT teams (FIRST, 2016). The establishment of these conferences in itself provides a basis for reinforcing communication and, as theory would suggest, enhances potentials for coordination.

Moreover within the US, the DHS's National Cybersecurity and Communication Integration Center (NCCIC) sits at the nexus of cyber and communications integration for the federal government, intelligence community, and law enforcement, providing a 24/7 cyber situational awareness, incident response, and management center. The NCCIC shares information with the public and private sectors, and industrial control systems users can subscribe to information products, feeds, and services. It comprises four branches: NCCIC Operations and Integration, US-CERT, Industrial Control Systems CERT, and the National Coordinating Center for Communications (See figure 1.2). The primary goal of the NCCIC is to reduce the likelihood and severity of incidents that could significantly compromise United States' critical information technology and communications network by synchronizing analysis, information sharing, and incident response efforts (DHS, 2016b).

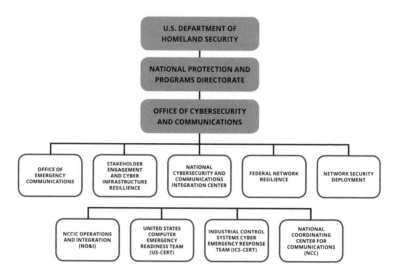

Figure 1.2 DHS Cybersecurity Structure

National CERTs

The collaborative structure maintained by coordinating agencies such as
FIRST and CERT/CC clearly facilitates information flow among security teams.
But there were limitations. If CERTs were only organized in this fashion,
it would be unclear which organizations possessed regional authority to
coordinate the actions of other CERTs, for instance, in the event of a national
attack on civilian networks. This problem was addressed by transitioning
the CERT structure to the national level. One valuable side effect of this shift
to national-level jurisdiction was the creation of public-private partnerships
between national CERTs and existing national agencies.

But a solution to one problem can often give rise to additional complications.
Given the diversity of national political systems and bureaucratic practices,
the transition to national CERTs exacerbated the realities of legal and

jurisdictional diversity. For example, while some national CERTs, such as US-CERT, were specifically tasked by their governments to defend civilian networks, other organizations operate in a legal vacuum and assume national responsibility via general consensus. Often, this legitimacy is granted by regional organizations such as Asia-Pacific CERT (AP-CERT) and Task Force Computer Security Incident Response Teams (TF-CIRTs) in Europe (see figure 1.1) that steer regional CERT policy. While this diversity is not necessarily a problem, it may impede information sharing, and suggests that national CERTs may or may not be held to international operating standards.

Although national CERTs are endowed with regional authority, they remain restricted in their capacity to respond to cyber criminals. National CERTs occupy a first-line responder role in the event of attacks on national civilian networks, but lack the jurisdictional authority to shut down criminal networks and prosecute perpetrators. As a result, national CERTs focus primarily on responding to and preventing *technical* cyber threats – a necessary requisite for coordination, but not a sufficient one.

To effectively deal with legal issues, clear lines of communication between national CERTs and government agencies are essential. This link has been formalized in some countries, such as the United States, but other nations are still developing the requisite connections between national CERTs and legal authority. At the same time, however, current CERT structure also includes vertical linkages—national, regional, and international connections—that are always difficult to forge, but facilitate resilience and robustness of institutional performance over time.

CERT data provision

At this writing, the level of CERT cooperation and standardization does not extend to the collection or assessment of quantitative data. As suggested earlier, data availability varies widely among CERTs, and organizations that publish statistics do not necessarily use similar reporting methods (Madnick, Li, & Choucri, 2009). Moreover, there are no efforts underway to formally align and standardize metrics.

Overall, the lack of robust data can be traced to three underlying factors. First, it is inherently difficult to quantify cyber data due to uncertainties surrounding the nature, geographical location, and target of attacks. The rapid pace of technological development, coupled with a lack of standards-providing organizations, has thus led to significant disparities in the diagnosis and classification of cyber events. Second, many CERTs lack a compelling business reason to gather or verify the accuracy of their quantitative data. CERTs typically possess limited funding capacity and many organizations choose to allocate their resources to cyber response in lieu of robust data collection. Lastly, there is no central authority or volunteer organization tasked with disseminating, collecting, or verifying CERT data. If there is an impediment to effective data use, it is to be found in the domain of motivation—the foundations and the data are in place, but there appears to be little incentive in taking the next steps to disseminate gathered data. An initial step in this direction is reported in Madnick, Choucri, et al. (2009).

Although quantitative data are fragmented, the collaborative nature of the CERT network means that a significant amount of information remains available on CERT activities. From a research standpoint, CERT/CC and FIRST provide a means to analyze global CERT policy. In addition, CERT/CC provides a variety of data sources that can be used to evaluate historical CERT activity.

These statistics include the number of security alerts, vulnerability notes, and advisories published per year. Although these figures are self-reported, and the threshold necessary to publish an alert may vary from year to year, they provide a baseline for estimating global CERT activity. This analysis can be complemented by CERT/CC statistics on the number of incident reports and hotline calls received from member organizations and national CERTs.[6]

Useful data can also be gleaned by viewing aggregate data at the regional level. In particular, AP-CERT and several other regional bodies publish statistics that cover the number of incidents handled and reported, attack vectors, counts of defaced websites, and other Web vulnerabilities. While these statistics are not as robust as those provided by the private sector, they are partitioned along national lines and provide country-specific statistics, which are valuable for analyzing divergent responses to cyber threats. By coupling this information with widely available metrics such as Internet connectivity or arrest rates, and controlling for data quality, it may be possible to develop a statistical model to analyze the overall effectiveness of cyber defense across nations, such as illustrated in Madnick, Choucri, Li, and Ferwerda. (2011).

CERTs occupy an important role in the international security ecosystem. But their core competencies or self-defined responsibilities do not extend to consensus building, legislation, or awareness-raising. This set of functions remained largely unclaimed in the early years of Internet development, but they have recently been embraced by a variety of intergovernmental organizations.

INFORMATION SHARING AND ANALYSIS CENTERS (ISACS)

On May 22, 1998, Presidential Decision Directive-63 created the concept of Information Sharing and Analysis Centers (ISACs) to help critical infrastructure industry players protect their facilities, personnel, and customers from cyber and physical security threats. The directive prescribed that each critical infrastructure sector establish sector-specific organizations to share information about threats and vulnerabilities. ISACs were developed as national in scope, and today are either federally directed or are non-profit organizations. Many have 24/7 threat-warning and incident reporting capabilities, with positive track records of responding to and sharing actionable information more quickly than government partners. Within the private sector space, ISACs have become important entities in risk mitigation, incident response, and information sharing, building critical trust and relationships between members through technical exchanges, annual meetings, workshops, and webinars (NCI, 2016a).

ISACs collaborate and coordinate with each other through the National Council of ISACs (NCI). As of 2016, the NCI is a voluntary organization comprising of 24 ISACs including the following sectors: automotive, aviation, communications, defense industrial base, defense security information, downstream natural gas, electricity, emergency management and response, financial services, healthcare, information technology, maritime, multi-state, national health, oil and natural gas, real estate, research and education, retail, supply chain, transportation, and water. A few critical infrastructure sectors also maintain a presence within DHS's NCCIC, including the Communications and Financial Services ISACs, to share information between the US government and industry. The Multi-State ISAC receives programmatic support from DHS and is designated as the cybersecurity ISAC for state, local, tribal, and territorial governments. Through the NCCIC, DHS maintains operational-level coordination with the MS-ISAC to provide state, local, tribal, and territorial governments information on cybersecurity threats and incidents (NCI, 2016b).

This type of industry-based information sharing group was designed to build trust between networked environments of similar or identical institutions, thus making sharing information more likely, while further facilitating sharing with the US government. However, while ISACs have become more formalized within the past decade, the effectiveness of individual ISACs differs greatly in their ability to deliver timely and relevant incident response and risk mitigation. The Financial Services ISAC is often labeled as the most effective due to its high membership and recognition of the financial services sector as one of the most cyberattacked sectors. In fact, its membership now extends beyond the financial services industry to affiliate members who want to support the mission and help protect the financial services industry. In 2013, the FS-ISAC also extended its charter to share information between financial services firms worldwide, and now includes members in South America, Europe, the Middle East, and Asia-Pacific (FSISAC, 2016).

Different from the vertical industry ISACs described above, the Industrial Control Systems ISAC (ICS-ISAC) is a horizontal ISAC, which captures and disseminates critical cybersecurity information between vertical ISACs and impacted parties. Ranging from building operations, healthcare, power generation, transportation, manufacturing, and agriculture, the ICS-ISAC crosses all 18 national critical infrastructure sectors, as determined by DHS. ICS-ISAC members consist of asset owners, vendors, integrators, industry associations, and other organizations that share knowledge through the Situational Awareness Reference Architecture (SARA), which is a compilation of industry standards, technical practices, and processes. (ICS-ISAC, 2016).

ISAC data provision

The primary functions of ISACs are to collect, assess, and distill threat information. Once a member submits threat information to an ISAC, typically industry experts analyze the threat and identify recommended solutions before alerting and anonymously disseminating the information to all ISAC members. Due to differences in size and formality between sector ISACs, the level of data collection, analysis, and distillation between different ISACs varies widely. This hub-and-spoke model facilitates the collaborative nature of the ISACs networks and transfers a significant amount of information, which is primarily available only to members, who often have to pay for subscription (NCI, 2016s).

As mentioned earlier, the NCI serves as the institution that helps facilitate collaboration and coordination between ISACs. It serves as a forum for sharing cyber and physical threats and mitigation strategies among ISACs and with government and private sector partners, when appropriate. This is done through daily and weekly calls between ISAC operations centers, and through reports, meetings, exercises, and requests-for-information. The NCI does not provide meaningful data sources for use by non-members to evaluate ISAC activity (NCI, 2016b).

Individual ISACs provide a disparate amount of information on ISAC activity, analyses of vulnerabilities, or best practices. As the most formalized, the Financial Services ISAC publishes monthly newsletters, which discuss upcoming webinars, events, workshops, trainings, and meetings. It also provides documents on industry best practices, such as guides to help firms improve operational continuity and reduce risks associated with a destructive cyberattack; however, it does not provide statistics on threats shared between members to non-FS-ISAC members. This is a common pattern that all ISACs follow, allowing ISACs to maintain their value-added services models and to maintain high levels of trust among members (FSISAC, 2016).

ISACs play an important role in confronting cyber and physical security threats among critical infrastructure industry players and within the security ecosystem. They are widely used tools for building trusted relationships and sharing information between private institutions, sectors, states, and regions around the world.

INFORMATION SHARING AND ANALYSIS ORGANIZATIONS (ISAOS)

To encourage private sector information sharing, which extends beyond industry sectors, the Obama administration issued Executive Order 13691 in February 2015 directing DHS to encourage the development of Information Sharing and Analysis Organizations (ISAOs). While ISACs have long been the essential drivers of effective cybersecurity collaboration, it became clear that some organizations do not fit neatly within an established sector or have unique needs, so the ISAO organizational term was created to assist organizations that have a need for cyber threat information. EO 13691 also set in motion an effort to develop more efficient means for granting clearances to private sector individuals who are members of an ISAO via a designated critical infrastructure protection program, and placed the NCCIC as the organization to engage in continuous, collaborative, and inclusive coordination with ISAOs (DHS, 2016a).

As part of the process of developing an ISAO ecosystem, an ISAO Standards Organization was established in October 2015, led by the University of Texas at San Antonio with support from the Logistics Management Institute (LMI) and the retail Cyber Intelligence Sharing Center. This organization works with existing information sharing organizations, owners, and operators of critical infrastructure, relevant agencies, and other public- and private-sector stakeholders to identify best practices and lessons learned from existing ISACs and other information sharing organizations, and then develop a common set of standards for the creation and functioning of ISAOs. Currently, the standards development process includes regular working group meetings with industry, government, and academic experts. The ISAO SO is also advising organizations on the creation and operation of ISAOs (ISAO Standards Organization, 2016).

While the ISAO SO has yet to publish any documents or information, it intends to post standards once they are developed. Along these lines, the goal is for standards to address contractual agreements, business processes, operating procedures, technical specifications, and privacy protections, among other issues. The standards are intended to be voluntary, transparent, inclusive, actionable, and flexible. The ISAO SO will also collect and publish metrics reflecting the effectiveness of cybersecurity information sharing (ISAO Standards Organization, 2016).

INTERGOVERNMENTAL RESPONSES

By definition, international organizations consist of sovereign states. All of the major international organizations and many minor ones were established long before the creation of cyberspace. They are all major users of cyber venues and often significant data providers as well. Unlike the CERTS, which are based on collaborative and hierarchical principles, intergovernmental organizations are composed of equal actors defined by their status as sovereign entities. All of these organizations are expected to be driven first and foremost by their own formal mandates and priorities. Thus, to the extent that any large international organization considers security in cyber venues as relevant to their concerns, it is mostly as a secondary priority. Given the pervasiveness of cyber venues, however, we expect that these organizations will devote increasing attention to cyber issues in the years to come.

If we focus on organizations that, in principle, have some clear interest or focus on cyberspace, we can identify the major actors and their zones of activity or interest. Unsurprisingly, this leads to a diffuse network of organizations and a wide array of cross-cutting linkages. By way of orientation, we show in figure 1.3 several well-known international organizations (such as the UN) and new cyber-focused entities that do not have the status of "organization" but are likely to retain a long standing institutional presence on the international arena (such as the WSIS).

Early moves

The involvement of international organizations in cybersecurity issues can be traced to early meetings of the G8 Subgroup on Hi-Tech Crime. In 1997, the G8, comprising of the world's most developed economies, established in cooperation with the International Criminal Police Organization (INTERPOL) a 24/7 "Network of Contacts" to help national governments "identify the source of terrorist communications, investigate threats and prevent future attacks" ("G8 24/7 High Tech Contact Points," 2009). As part of the program, countries were asked to cooperate with INTERPOL in international investigations by sharing information on electronic crimes, and by designating an official cybercrime point of contact. While the success rate of the program remains classified, a similar referral model was later mirrored by the Federal Bureau of Investigation (FBI) in the form of Internet Crime Complaint Center (IC3), which speaks to its relative success. As of 2007, 47 countries were actively involved within the network (Verdelho, 2008).

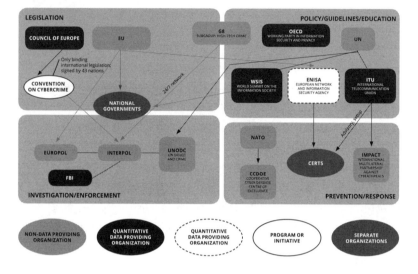

Figure 1.3 Key Intergovernmental Institutions

Organization for Economic Co-operation and Development-sponsored conferences

The Organization for Economic Co-operation and Development (OECD, 2009a) has been actively involved in the cybersecurity domain since 2002. Meeting twice a year in Paris, the *Working Party on Information Security and Privacy* (WPISP) has published several influential white papers, including "Guidelines for the Security of Information Systems and Networks" (2002) and "Promotion of a Culture of Security for Information Systems and Networks" (2005). These guidelines have been accompanied by stock-taking efforts that track the implementation of policy in member countries (OECD, 2009b). The WPISP has also released several surveys on information security policies in member countries, and has created a "Culture of Security" Web portal for member states. Since the WPISP is contained within the OECD framework, it represents a formalized extension of OECD's core mission and provides a common approach for all member states.

For the most part, the aforegoing efforts can be seen as "self-initiated," whereby private or public entities voluntarily take on a particular function in the emergent cybersecurity domain. However, more recently, the international community has issued operational mandates to specific organizations. Here we note some of the most dominant initiatives.

International Telecommunication Union

One of International Telecommunication Union's (ITU 2009b) core missions is to standardize telecommunication technology and release statistics that can be used to track the Internet connectivity of nations. Utilizing a group of high-level experts, ITU provides a variety of resources and toolkits addressing legislation, awareness, self-assessment, botnets, and CERTs (ITU, 2009a). Additionally, ITU publishes guides that educate developing nations on cybercrime and promote best practices and approaches.

Although the ITU core competencies are mission-specific, they have recently acted in a direct fashion by establishing an arm that will provide international threat response. The ITU was given the primary responsibility for coordinating the implementation of WSIS's Action Plan C5 (WSIS, 2009b). In response, the organization launched the "Global Cybersecurity Agenda" in 2007, working with the International Multilateral Partnership Against Cyber Threats (IMPACT), headquartered in Malaysia.

Envisioned as a global response center focused on combating cyber terrorism and protecting critical infrastructure networks, IMPACT is a public-private partnership that serves as a politically neutral global platform to bring together governments of the world, industry, academia, international organizations, and think tanks, to enhance cyber threat capabilities (IMPACT, 2015a). In addition to being the home of ITU's Global Cybersecurity Agenda, in 2011, IMPACT was given a pivotal role in also supporting the United Nations

Office on Drugs and Crime efforts to mitigate risks posed by cybercrime. Among other services, IMPACT facilitates a real-time warning network to 193 member countries, 24/7 response centers, and the development of software that allows security organizations across the globe to pool resources and coordinate their defense efforts (IMPACT, 2015b). Additionally, IMPACT maintains a research division, hosts educational workshops, and conducts high-level security briefings with representatives of member states. These efforts are intended to make IMPACT "the foremost cyberthreat resource center in the world" (ITU, 2009c).

Although IMPACT has only been operational since March 2009, it is likely that the organization will become a significant provider of technical security data in the near future. If this initiative is successful, an important precedent would be set for the proposition that an international organization can effectively perform a mission that lies beyond its initial cyber mandate, build upon its core competencies, and extend its regulatory domain in response to technological innovations. Its efforts to promote cybersecurity arose as a function of the increasing threat rather than as part of its original mission; thus, the international community chose to build upon existing organizational strengths rather than establishing a new institution.

North Atlantic Treaty Organization

A major adaptive initiative has been demonstrated by North Atlantic Treaty Organization (NATO) in a way roughly similar to IMPACT. Given the dramatic demonstration of cyberattacks against Estonia (a NATO member), this intergovernmental organization established a technical response arm in the aftermath of the coordinated attacks on Estonia in 2007. Designated the Cooperative Cyber Defense Centre of Excellence (CCDCOE, 2009), this entity is responsible for training NATO member states, conducting attack exercises, supporting NATO in the event of an international cyberattack, and enhancing the capability, cooperation and information sharing among NATO nations and partners. To this end, CCDCOE created an interactive database in 2014 called the International Cyber Developments Review (INCYDER) to aggregate legal and policy documents adopted by international organizations active in cybersecurity. This is part of the CCDCOE's goal of facilitating the work of researchers, lawyers, and policy-makers (INCYDER, 2016).

Interestingly, not all NATO states have joined the CCDCOE program, with many countries opting to rely on their own traditional military cyber defense networks. There is no strong evidence that all members of NATO are willing to engage in a common approach to a shared problem, presumably because many states are developing their own strategies for cyber warfare. At the same time, however, the CCDCOE fills an important void for several European states, notably those whose own cybersecurity capabilities are yet to be developed.

European Network and Information Security Agency

All things considered, it is fair to conclude that the overall European technical response to cyber threats and cybersecurity has been somewhat limited in scope. Although the European Union has published numerous resolutions on cybercrime, and the European Police Office (EUROPOL) is actively engaged in investigation, the European Union's only substantive action thus far has been the creation of the European Network and Information Security Agency (ENISA). Tasked with a broad mandate "to enhance the capability of the European Union to prevent, address, and respond to network and information security problems," ENISA largely focuses on awareness building, promoting Internet safety practices, and working with regional CERTs, and does not provide a comprehensive defense against regional cyber incidents (Europa, 2009).

Convention on Cybercrime

One area in which European organizations have taken the lead is within the legislative realm. In partnership with the United States, Japan, and others, the Council of Europe ratified the *Convention on Cybercrime* in 2004, which remains the only binding international legislation dealing with the cybercrime issue (Council of Europe, 2009a). As of April 2016, 48 countries have ratified the treaty, and an additional 18 countries have signed but not yet ratified (Council of Europe, 2016). The convention defines the criminality of cybercrime, enables law enforcement agencies to effectively investigate electronic crimes, and fosters international cooperation and data sharing (Council of Europe, 2001). In particular, it defines crimes committed via the Internet and computer networks as illegal access, illegal interception, data interference, system interference, misuse of devices, computer-related forgery, computer-related fraud, child pornography, offenses related to copyright, and neighboring rights, as well as threats and insults motivated by racism or xenophobia, which were added in 2006 (Council of Europe, 2001).

In support of the Convention, the Council of Europe implemented two distinct action plans aimed at training law enforcement agencies and improving national legislation; it has hosted global conferences on cybercrime issues annually (Council of Europe, 2009c). Additionally, the Council of Europe maintains an extensive database on the progress of national cybercrime legislation (Council of Europe, 2009d). This growth in function is important as it provides evidence of institutionalized response and a broad framework necessary to effectively combat international cybercrime. However, it remains unclear whether the provisions of the Convention will be able to keep pace with the rapid development of the domain; international legislation is often reactive and generally lags behind technological efforts. The true value of the Convention may thus lie in its capacity to "jump-start" national cybercrime legislation via its provision of an adaptive legal framework.

Data provision

In this vein, many organizations provide valuable qualitative data, but few provide the quantitative statistics required for robust analysis. As a result, it is difficult to objectively determine the overall performance of these organizations.

This analytical gap may gradually close as organizations move from a passive posture to an active and fully engaged role within the security landscape, as is evident with the establishment of IMPACT and CCDCOE. Until then, the data provided by inter-governmental organizations can be most effectively used to trace the enactment of legislation, standards, and policies across member states. Utilizing stock-taking databases and ratification systems, it should be possible to determine which countries or regions are on the leading edge of enacting the necessary institutional frameworks to properly combat cybercrime.

Finally, it is important to stress that institutionalized data collection activities are always undertaken within a mission-framework. In other words, collection of data is driven by the overall self-defined objectives and priorities of each organization. This is one of the major sources of non-comparability across data sets. So far, at least, we have not yet seen efforts to standardize definitions, collection procedures, or reporting mechanisms. In one sense, this is not an unexpected development, as information standardization usually takes place only after widespread data provision and demand.

NATIONAL RESPONSES TO SECURITY THREATS AND CYBER CRIME

Overall, theoretical approaches to institutions at the international level
(generally addressed by scholars in the field of international relations)
are based on historical and conceptual foundations different from those
of institutional analysis at the national level (generally addressed by scholars
in the field of comparative politics). While there are some common concerns
and shared presumptions, the overall motivations, assumptions, and
perspectives on the underlying problems differ considerably. Here, we do
not need to explore the different epistemologies in any detail; suffice to note
that in the most general terms, institutions in all contexts and at all levels
of analysis are considered fundamental mechanisms of collective actions
and that, at the very minimum, they reduce transaction costs, facilitate
the provision of pubic goods, and enable the pursuit of social goals.

These core theoretical features are relevant to all institutional activities
in response to cyber threats and cyberattacks; however, the theoretical
foundations for understanding institutional responses at the national
level are based on domestic imperatives with little attention, if any,
to international considerations (we shall return to this issue later on).

Leading role

The United States has been at the forefront of institutional response to the
new realities formed by cyberspace. It is the leading world power, the state
that originally encouraged and supported the creation of cyberspace, and the
country that remains renowned for its innovative spirit. By default, the United
States has been thrust into a leadership position and has acted as a model for
other governmental responses to cyber issues, notably in Europe and Asia.
But while the United States possesses arguably the strongest known national
safeguards against various cyber threats, these programs appear to be far

from sufficient. Indeed, according to a policy review, "it is doubtful that the United States can protect itself from the growing threat" by maintaining its current security structure (The White House, 2009a). The review continues:

> The Federal government is not organized to address this growing problem effectively now or in the future. Responsibilities for cybersecurity are distributed across a wide array of Federal departments and agencies, many with overlapping authorities, and none with sufficient decision authority to direct actions.

To trace the foundations of this institutional condition, we must turn to the early federal efforts to combat cyber vulnerabilities. The government initially delegated civilian network defense to the private sector or federally funded organizations such as CERT/CC. In parallel, the intelligence and military communities developed and maintained closeted defense systems. Although the relative technological advantage that these organizations possessed initially allowed them to maintain superiority over external threats, the lack of data sharing and cooperation among agencies, coupled with a rise in global technical competence, led to a growing security dilemma.

After the events of 2001, the United States began a substantial revision of its Internet security policy. Through a series of presidential directives, the nascent Department of Homeland Security (DHS) was granted responsibility for cyber Internet security efforts. These aims were codified in *The National Strategy to Secure Cyberspace* (2003), which led to a dual approach to cyber defense. With the cooperation of CERT/CC, a national CERT (US-CERT) was established within the National Cybersecurity Division of the DHS and was tasked with defending federal civil networks (.gov domains). To coordinate the actions of various federal agencies, DHS was asked to develop contingency plans and warning systems, and was granted the ability to coordinate the efforts of 19 federal agencies in the event of a cyberattack of national significance (The White House, 2003). Notably, however, the document stressed that "the private sector is best equipped and structured to respond to an evolving cyber threat," and clearly delineated a separate approach for the "national security community" (The White House, 2003).

As a result, DHS assumed responsibility for a previously neglected area of defense (federal civil networks), but the compartmentalization of Internet defense strategies continued unchecked. However, it is important to note that this compartmentalization may be a normal byproduct of organizational and bureaucratic politics. As any legal scholar would be quick to point out, this segmentation is not an arbitrary development; rather, it is supported by a legal framework delineated by the discrete assignment of responsibilities.

The critical issue here is not that barriers to communication and information sharing—resulting from legal segmentation—create added constraints on rapid response to cyber threats. This situation is well-appreciated by most, if not all, parts of the bureaucracy. Periodic restructuring initiatives have consolidated the security arena; however these changes remain marginal given the scale and scope of cyberspace and the associated threat potential. Nevertheless, the US government appeared committed to discovering valid alternatives, and there are several efforts underway that may result in an effective response structure.

Emergent efforts

US cyber policy was further refined in 2008, when President Bush signed a presidential directive establishing the CNCI, or the *Comprehensive National Cybersecurity Initiative*. The initiative includes several major policy revisions. First, in conjunction with the Office of Management and Budget (OMB), the DHS was tasked with reducing the number of network connections between federal agencies and external providers from 4,000 to 50 within four months (Samson, 2008). Second, an optional DHS program, which monitored traffic to and from federal websites, codenamed EINSTEIN, was transferred to the authority of the National Security Agency. The new version of the program purportedly captures content as well as traffic, and proactively monitors federal, and possibly private, networks (Samson, 2008). Lastly, the CNCI includes several provisions that are aimed at increasing R&D, coordinating cyber counterintelligence, and promoting information sharing among government organizations (The White House, 2009b).

Upon assuming office, President Obama endorsed the CNCI plan, albeit under conditions of increased transparency. Additionally, the White House authorized a sweeping review of cyber policy. Recognizing the increasing compartmentalization of national cyber defense, the final report recommended establishing a cybersecurity office within the White House. Leading this office, an official (referred to as the Cyber Czar by the press) would be a member of the National Security Council and would have frequent access to the president.[7] The office would not possess the authority to make policy unilaterally, but it would coordinate the responses of federal departments and attempt to bridge communication and policy gaps by:

recommend[ing] coherent unified policy guidance to clarify authorities, roles, and responsibilities for cybersecurity-related activities across the Federal government (The White House 2009a).

Recognizing that "federal responses to cyber incidents have not been unified," the review recommended eliminating overlapping responsibilities between agencies and defining specific roles for cyber defense across government networks (The White House, 2009b).

These recommendations are still in the process of being implemented. However, considerable strides have been made in providing a coherent logic and rationale for the overall organizational response system. The proposed structure is presented in figure 1.4.

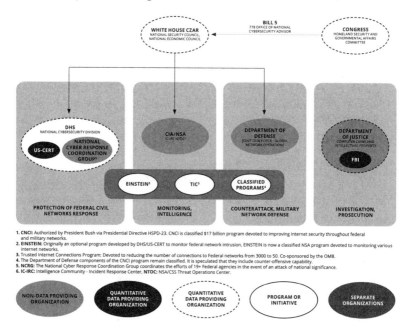

1. **CNCI:** Authorized by President Bush via Presidential Directive HSPD-23. CNCI is classified $17 billion program devoted to improving internet security throughout federal and military networks.
2. **EINSTEIN:** Originally an optional program developed by DHS/US-CERT to monitor federal network intrusion, EINSTEIN is now a classified NSA program devoted to monitoring various internet networks.
3. Trusted Internet Connections Program: Devoted to reducing the number of connections to Federal networks from 3000 to 50. Co-sponsored by the OMB.
4. The Department of Defense components of the CNCI program remain classified. It is speculated that they include counter-offensive capability.
5. **NCRG:** The National Cyber Response Coordination Group coordinates the efforts of 19+ Federal agencies in the event of an attack of national significance.
6. **IC-IRC:** Intelligence Community - Incident Response Center, **NTOC:** NSA/CSS Threat Operations Center.

Figure 1.4 Proposed US structure

The transition from an organic, overlapping defense network to organized hierarchies can best be observed as a recurring pattern within the cybersecurity landscape. However, while centralization and coordination are necessary to effectively respond to rapidly evolving threats, inefficient organizational structures may confound the problem by reinforcing barriers to bureaucratic adaptation. While few governments are as large and complex as that of the USA, the fact remains that US cyber policies and the mechanisms for their implementation provide important signals to other governments. Even if the US response does not serve as a formal model, its institutional responses will be closely scrutinized by others.

Since 2015, the Obama administration has taken an increasing number of steps through executive orders and presidential directives to enhance cybersecurity capabilities and coordination efforts. In February 2015, Executive Order 13691 was issued to encourage private-sector cybersecurity collaboration by establishing new "information sharing and analysis organizations (ISAOs) to serve as focal points for cybersecurity information sharing and collaboration within the private sector and between the private sector and government." In encouraging the creation of ISAOs, this EO expanded information sharing by encouraging the formation of communities that share information across a region or in response to a specific emerging cyber threat beyond the industry focus of ISACs. This EO also designated the NCCIC as a critical infrastructure protection program to promote security with respect to cybersecurity (The White House, 2015).

A presidential memorandum issued in February 2015 also established the Cyber Threat Intelligence Integration Center, or CTIIC, as a national intelligence center housed under the Office of the Director of National Intelligence focused on "connecting the dots" regarding malicious foreign cyber threats to the nation and cyber incidents affecting US national interests, and providing all-source analysis of threats to US policymakers.

Most recently in February 2016, President Obama announced a Cybersecurity National Action Plan as a capstone of his Administration's efforts to take a series of short- and long-term actions to improve the United States' cybersecurity posture, including the establishment of the Commission on Enhancing National Cybersecurity. This commission consists of 12 members appointed by the president, including "top strategic, business, and technical thinkers from outside of Government—including members to be designated by the bi-partisan Congressional leadership," who will make recommendations on how to use technical solutions and best practices to protect privacy and public safety. The Commission held its first of a series of public and private conferences to take place over the next eight months on April 15, 2016, to set the government's cybersecurity agenda for the coming decade (FederalTimes, 2016).

Cybercrime

The US is a signatory to the Convention on Cybercrime, with reservations. An important case of organizational restructuring in response to cyber threats is illustrated by its own responses to the threats of 2001, when the FBI collaborated with the National White Collar Crime Center to form the Internet Crime Complaint Center (IC3). Sharing some structural similarities with INTERPOL's 24/7 network, IC3 was created to provide a central contact point for reporting Internet crimes. The program is still active today, and by most accounts, has been a success. In 2008 alone, the IC3 processed over 275,000 complaints, 26% of which were deemed valid and referred to law enforcement agencies (National White Collar Crime Center, 2008). The number of complaints reported over the last five years has averaged around 300,000. However, while the organization serves as a successful model for a national reporting system, this model has been unable to constrain the growth of cybercrime. FBI surveys have shown that most Internet crime remains unreported, which the relatively unchanged processed reporting figures over the past seven years illustrate, and only a fraction of total cyber incidents are processed by the IC3. It is estimated that only 15% of Internet fraud victims in the United States report their crimes to law enforcement, primarily because detection is the most challenging piece of the puzzle (Internet Crime Complaint Center, 2015).

In some sense, the lack of dramatic success thus far is unsurprising. Efforts to halt the spread of cybercrime suffer from several inherent challenges. First, in contrast with traditional crime, the criminality of cyber activities remains ill-defined. Many individuals are not accustomed to reporting cybercrime to law enforcement organizations because issues may be deemed "minor" or purely technical in nature, or because events on the Internet are deemed outside the jurisdiction of a local police agency. This issue is present in the corporate sphere as well, as many companies view the public acknowledgement of security vulnerabilities as a corporate liability. Second, even when crimes are reported, investigation and prosecution remains difficult. Evidence is often ephemeral and transitory, and the global nature of cybercrime presents serious difficulties in pinpointing the location and identity of criminals. Lastly, it often proves difficult to assess the true monetary damage of cybercrime, for instance, in the case of information theft or security breach. Given that law enforcement agencies possess limited resources, this ambiguity surrounding the true impact of cybercrime creates difficulties in setting investigative priorities.

Although many of the efforts of the FBI and the Department of Justice (DOJ) have focused on combating cybercrime at the national level, some initiatives have attempted to ameliorate some of the aforementioned problems by embedding cybercrime experts in local institutions. For instance, since 2003 the FBI has established collaborative Computer Crime Task Forces, which assist police agencies in investigating local cybercrimes. As of 2006, there are over 92 task forces spread throughout the United States (Federal Bureau of Investigation, 2006). In a similar vein, the DOJ has established Computer Hacking & Intellectual Property units in local federal courts, which provide lawyers with the training to effectively understand and prosecute cybercrime.

In recent years, the Federal Trade Commission (FTC) has also played an active role in preventing the spread of cybercrime. This new area of focus was not specifically mandated, but rather arose as a byproduct of efforts to expand the FTC's role in consumer protection. Although the FTC is not tasked with prosecuting or investigating criminal networks, the commission acts by issuing formal complaints and restraining orders against Internet Service Providers (ISPs) that are suspected of hosting or promoting illegal activity. These actions prevent ongoing cybercrime activities while prosecution efforts are underway. The FTC thus occupies a critical role in cross-sector collaboration, as the organization possesses the legal authority to rapidly respond to time-sensitive security alerts from NGOs, CERTs, and local government agencies.[8]

In many ways, the US is simultaneously pursuing centralized and decentralized approaches to combating cybercrime (figure 1.4). Critical to the success of either approach is the establishment of a national culture that understands, recognizes, and reports cybercrime. Although statistics on the success of local efforts remain limited, it is important to recognize that initial investments in the sector may not display immediate dividends, due to the necessities of preliminary education and training (figure 1.5).

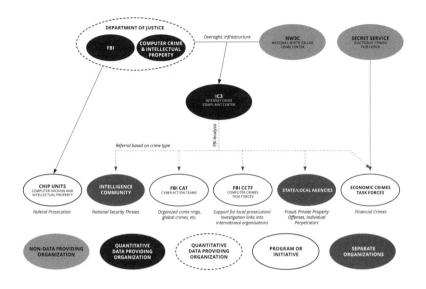

Figure 1.5 US investigation/prosecution organizations

The ITU comparison of cybersecurity initiatives worldwide revealed a wide range of approaches with different degrees of development (ITU, 2005). While the process of institutionalizing responses to cyber threats is at an early stage, one can discern possible emergent trajectories via the use of (highly incomplete) quantitative data provided by national governments. It is unlikely that governments will publically release data related to national security intrusions, and data relating to civilian criminal activities is only available for a select few countries.

For example, in the US, the DOJ maintains a partial database of high-profile cases and convictions, while the FBI regularly publishes IC3 and survey data on cybercrime trends.[9] Similarly, national governments in Korea, Japan, and Taiwan release comprehensive yearly statistics on cybercrime investigations, prosecutions, arrests, and demographic data. Although less directly available, statistics are also provided by countries such as the UK, Germany, and France.

Unfortunately, however, many countries lack robust legislation dealing with cybercrime; as a result, cybercrime is rarely reported as a distinct category within national police reports. Until such time that additional countries ratify the Convention on Cybercrime—and governments actively pursue its implementation—it is probable that cybercrime data will not become more widely available.

SOME BASELINE CONCLUSIONS

As presented above, the institutional cybersecurity landscape consists of a complex array of organizations that exhibit significant diversity with regard to missions, mandates, interests, opportunities, and constraints.

Characteristic Features

On these bases, we put forth the following observations:
a)   The information technology-sustainable development linkage has become an integral feature of the international community's policy priorities.
b)   The current institutional landscape resembles a security patchwork that covers critical areas rather than an umbrella that spans all of the known modes and sources of cyber threat.
c)   Given the multiple contexts and diverse institutional motivations, we expect that responses will be driven more by institutional imperatives and reactions to crisis than by coordinated assessment and proactive response.

d)   Due to the complex global agenda at all levels of development, states may not be willing to proceed until international norms are developed, rather they will "take matters in their own hands" and develop first-order responses.

e)   Cross-sector collaboration among public, private, and volunteer organizations may serve as a temporary measure to cover holes in the current defense network. However, at some point effective institutions will be necessary; they may develop in parallel with rising public awareness.

f)   So far, we have not yet seen large terrorist groups engaged in intense cyber malfeasance. This pattern cannot be expected to continue. Efforts to infiltrate critical US infrastructure and the devastating attacks on Estonia and Georgia in 2007 and 2008 underline the dangers of being lulled into a false sense of security. As the Internet becomes increasingly central to modern society, it is likely that criminals, terrorist groups, and other opponents to state authority will target this sector in the hopes of disrupting critical national functions. So far, the potential for significant threats is far greater than institutional capabilities to contain these threats. In other words, the "demand" for security far exceeds the provision of effective "supply."

Institutional anchors for cybersecurity

Such features notwithstanding, based on the evidence to date, we suggest that considerable strides have been made to establish foundations for collaborative responses. In the best of all possible worlds, we would expect to see the emergence of a collaborative framework—a large umbrella network—allowing autonomous organizations to flexibly adapt to emerging threats in a coordinated manner and increases the impetus for information sharing in the realm of cybersecurity. While the potential for such an umbrella network has yet to be realized, we can now point to some institutional anchors that could support, or even consolidate, such a development:

a)   The establishment of not-for-profit institutions designed to focus on cyber threats (CERT/CC, FIRST, private CERTs, and ISACs), however "disorganized," is a growing trend on the international landscape. In some instances, these institutions have transitioned to private-public partnerships.

b)   Several international institutions established to manage interactions among advanced states (notably supported by the OECD) reinforce rather than undermine this development.

c)   International conferences designed to communicate the potential for information technology to facilitate transitions towards sustainable development (WSIS), while not centered on security issues, nonetheless have the advantage of large-scale private and public participation, thus raising the political profile of cyber issues globally.

d)   The functional international organizations with core missions and competencies (notably the ITU) have adopted security as part of their missions.

e)   Despite these seemingly complex and uncoordinated responses at the national level, specific agencies are more and more tasked with responding to cybercrime (notably the FBI in the US).

f)   The development of binding international legislation (i.e., the Convention on Cybercrime) elevates the sense of vulnerability as well as the need to coordinate responses to a higher level of awareness than ever before.

g)   In the field of military security, framed more formally, we observe the salience of organizations and strategies focused on the defense of military and intelligence networks (i.e., CCDOE, CNCI).

h)   Sharing between public and private institutions is increasingly hampered by liability, reputational, and economic concerns, which the

US is increasingly addressing by establishing or promoting private-led information sharing institutions (notably ISACs and ISAOs) to further facilitate these exchanges.

Each of these institutional responses reflects mandates, rules, and responsibilities. None are accorded complete regulatory power. Indeed, there is little evidence of overarching institutional coordination or routinization. On one hand, this pattern represents a certain degree of disconnect. On the other, it can be seen as a dynamic and shifting response to dynamic set of cyber threats. In the latter context, one could argue that the increasingly dense landscape of institutional responses is an excellent indication that the international community is taking serious steps to control a cyber threat of epidemic proportions.

In this connection, we can expect that, over time, we will see more and more forms of lateral intergovernmental cooperation with the requisite institutional cross-border institutional collaboration. The theoretical foundations for such developments are accommodated by the structure of the process of transnational activities as framed by Nye and Koehane (1977) and the extensions in transnational governance outlined by Slaughter (2004) in the context of globalization processes.

Critical missing piece

Although the current system of institutional arrangements shows signs of weakness, it is also true that the level of organization and cooperation has been steadily increasing. Missing from these international institutional developments (and thus from the above analysis) is a critical piece of institutional architecture to support a fundamental function, namely systematic consideration for data issues and matters of data provision and alignment. To some degree, the effectiveness of this effort can be quantified through the use of statistics.

While a relatively small number of organizations produce reliable data, sufficient information exists to develop a model that maps degree of vulnerability versus the effectiveness of organizational response. For instance, international data on cybercrime legislation and awareness can be correlated with arrest rates in individual countries. When combined with stock-taking databases, this method allows one to determine the rate of progress in individual nations versus cybercrime issues. Similarly, quantitative data provided by national CERTs can be used to obtain insights about their performance in their respective national contexts and constituencies. An example of these kinds of analysis, along with a Data Dashboard tool, can be found in the report (Madnick, Li, et al., 2009b).

Over time, we anticipate the possibility of pairing international and national statistics with information from the private sector. Security and monitoring companies such as Symantec, Arbor Networks, Microsoft, and McAfee provide quantitative data that address the global spread of Internet vulnerabilities. In many cases, the volume and quality of data released by these organizations far outpaces the information released by international and national organizations; however, the true value of this information lies not in an isolated analysis, but in the intersection of private data with the national and international sphere. For instance, statistics concerning the originating country of cyberattacks or the absolute volume of attacks can potentially be paired with national CERT data to determine the degree of national vulnerabilities and traffic that each CERT is capable of handling.

These metrics, and others that can potentially be derived, may provide a powerful method of simultaneously evaluating data quality and organizational performance. An important next step in our inquiry is to examine additional data providers and explore ways of pairing this data with national and international organizations to form evaluative statistical models.

While doing so, it is important to remain cognizant of the institutional context that enables or constrains the provision of information.

ACKNOWLEDGMENT

The work reported herein was supported, in part, by the MIT Interdisciplinary Consortium for Improving Critical Infrastructure Cybersecurity and the Explorations in Cyber International Relations (ECIR) project funded by the Office of Naval Research (ONR) contract number N00014-09-1-0597. Any opinions, findings, and conclusions or recommendations expressed in this chapter are those of the authors and do not necessarily reflect the views of the Office of Naval Research. This work builds on previous research reported in (Choucri, Madnick, et al. 2014).

NOTES

1. See for example, Goodrich, (1947), Claude (1967) , and Hoffmann (1987).
2. See, for example, Mitrany (1948).
3. Hass (1961) is a good example.
4. See Keohane (1983) as an example. The concept of regime emerged as an important anchor in this field.
5. These organizations are also referred to as Computer Security Incident Response Teams (CSIRTs).
6. Unfortunately, CERT/CC has announced that no statistics will be published after Q3 2008. As a result, analysis is limited to historical applications (1988-2008).
7. Note that the position has been established, and is currently filled by Howard Schmidt.
8. These are all examples of institutional developments in response to cybersecurity threats.
9. Note, however, that the United States does not currently provide any comprehensive statistics on arrests or prosecutions.

REFERENCES

CERT Program. (2009a). *About CERT*. Retrieved September 17, 2009, from http://www.cert.org/meet_cert/

Charney, Scott. (2009). *Rethinking the Cyber Threat: A Framework and Path Forward*. Retrieved from http://www.microsoft.com/download/en/details. aspx?displaylang=en&id=747

Choucri, Nazli (2012), *Cyberpolitics in International Relations*, Cambridge, MA: MIT Press.

Claude, Inis L., Jr. (1967). Collective Legitimization as a Political Function of the United Nations, in Oran R. Young (Ed.), *The International Political Economy and International Institutions, Volume 1* (pp. 22-52). Cheltenham, UK: Edward Elgar Publishing Limited.

Council of Europe. (2001). *Convention on Cybercrime.* Retrieved May 21, 2016, from https://rm.coe.int/CoERMPublicCommonSearchServices/DisplayDCTMContent?documentId=09000 01680081561

Cooperative Cyber Defence Centre of Excellence. (2013). Retrieved January 11, 2009, from http://www.ccdcoe.org/

Council of Europe. (2001). *ETS No. 185 - convention on cybercrime.* Retrieved September 19, 2009, from http://conventions.coe.int/Treaty/en/Treaties/Html/185.htm

Council of Europe. (2009a). *Council of Europe action against economic crime.* Retrieved September 28, 2009, from http://www.coe.int/t/dghl/cooperation/economiccrime/cybercrime/Default_en.asp

Council of Europe. (2009b). *Convention on cybercrime.* Retrieved September 27, 2009, from http://conventions.coe.int/Treaty/Commun/ChercheSig.asp?NT=185&CM=1&DF=09/09/ 2009&CL=ENG

Council of Europe. (2009c). *Project on cybercrime (phase 1).* Retrieved September 26, 2009, from http://www.coe.int/t/dghl/cooperation/economiccrime/cybercrime%5Ccy%20Project/ projectcyber_en.asp

Council of Europe. (2009d). *Cybercrime legislation - country profiles.* Retrieved September 28, 2009, from http://www.coe.int/t/dg1/legalcooperation/economiccrime/ cybercrime/Documents/CountryProfiles/default_en.asp

Council of Europe. (2016). *Cybercrime@coe Update.* Retrieved April 24, 2016, from https://rm.coe.int/CoERMPublicCommonSearchServices/DisplayDCTMContent?documentId=09000 0168063ea01

Department of Homeland Security. (2016a). *Information Sharing and Analysis Organizations.* Retrieved June 19, 2016 from https://www.dhs.gov/isao

Department of Homeland Security. (2016b). *National Cybersecurity and Communication Integration Center.* Retrieved May 21, 2016, from https://www.dhs.gov/national-cybersecurity-and-communications- integration-center

Europa. (2009). *European Network and Information Security Agency (ENISA).* Retrieved September 21, 2009, from http://europa.eu/legislation_summaries/

justice_freedom_security/fight_against_ organised_crime/l24153_en.htm

Federal Bureau of Investigation. (2006). *Netting cyber criminals.* Retrieved February 20, 2010, from http://www.fbi.gov/page2/jan06/ccctf012506.htm

FederalTimes. (2016). Initial meeting lays out how commission with enhance cybersecurity. Retrieved May 21, 2016, from http://www.federaltimes.com/story/government/ cybersecurity/2016/04/15/cyber-commission-first-meeting/83080592/

Forum of Incident Response and Security Teams. (2009a). *Alphabetical list of FIRST members.* Retrieved September 20, 2009, from http://www.first.org/members/teams/

Forum of Incident Response and Security Teams. (2009b). *FIRST history.* Retrieved September 29, 2009, from http://www.first.org/about/history/

Forum of Incident Response and Security Teams. (2016). *Alphabetical list of FIRST members.* Retrieved May 19, 2016, from https://www.first.org/members/teams

Financial Services Information Sharing and Analysis Center. (2016). *About FS-ISAC.* Retrieved April 30, 2016, from https://www.fsisac.com/about

Goodrich, Leland M. (1947). From League of Nations to United Nations, in Oran R. Young (Ed.), *The International Political Economy and International Institutions, Volume 1* (pp. 22-52). Cheltenham, UK: Edward Elgar Publishing Limited.

G8 24/7 High Tech Contact Points. *Cybersecurity Co-Operation.* Retrieved October 28, 2009, from http://www.cybersecuritycooperation.org/moredocuments/24%20Hour%20Network/ 24%207%20invitation.pdf

Haas, Ernest B. (1961). International Integration: The European and the Universal Process, in Oran R. Young (Ed.), *The International Political Economy and International Institutions, Volume 1* (pp. 22-52). Cheltenham, UK: Edward Elgar Publishing Limited.

Hall, Peter A., and Rosemary C.R. Taylor. (1996). Political Science and the

Three New Institutionalisms. *Political Studies*, 44 (5), 936-957.

Hansen, Derek L., John Carlo Bertot, Paul T. Jaeger. (2011). Government Policies of the Use of Social Media: Legislating for Change. In *Proceedings of the 12th Annual International Conference on Digital Government*. (pp. 131-140). College Park, MD.

Hoffmann, Stanley. (1987). International Organization and the International System, in Oran R. Young (Ed.), *The International Political Economy and International Institutions, Volume 1* (pp. 22-52). Cheltenham, UK: Edward Elgar Publishing Limited.

INCYDER. (2014). Resources. Retrieved April 24, 2016, from https://ccdcoe. org/incyder.html

Industrial Control Systems Information Sharing Analysis Center. (2016). *About ICS-ISAC*. Retrieved May 21, 2016, from http://ics-isac.org/blog/home/about/

IMPACT. (2009). *Welcome to the coalition*. Retrieved October 23, 2009, from http://www.impact-alliance.org/

IMPACT. (2015a). *Mission and Vision*. Retrieved May 21, 2016, from http://www. impact-alliance.org/aboutus/mission-&-vision.html

IMPACT. (2015b). *ITU-IMPACT*. Retrieved May 21, 2016, from http://www. impact-alliance.org/aboutus/ITU-IMPACT.html

Information Sharing and Analysis Organizations Standards Organization. (2016). *About Us*. Retrieved June 19, 2016 from https://www.isao.org/about/

International Telecommunication Union. (2005). *A Comparative Analysis of Cybersecurity Initiatives Worldwide*. Retrieved December 16, 2011, from http:// www.itu.int/osg/spu/cybersecurity/docs/Background_Paper_Comparative_ Analysis_Cybersec urity_Initiatives_Worldwide.pdf

International Telecommunication Union. (2009a). *Global Cybersecurity Agenda (GCA)*. Retrieved September 25, 2009, from http://www.itu.int/osg/csd/ cybersecurity/gca/

International Telecommunication Union. (2009b). *Information and communication technology (ICT) statistics*. Retrieved September 25, 2009, from http://www.itu.int/ITU-D/ict/

International Telecommunication Union. (2009c). *Global Cybersecurity Agenda (GCA): Technical and security measures.* Retrieved September 25, 2009, from http://www.itu.int/osg/csd/cybersecurity/gca/tech-proced.html

Keohane, Robert O. (1983). The Demand for International Regimes, in Oran R. Young (Ed.), *The International Political Economy and International Institutions, Volume 1* (pp. 22-52). Cheltenham, UK: Edward Elgar Publishing Limited.

Killcrece, Georgia. (2004). *Steps for creating national CERTs.* Carnegie Mellon Software Engineering Institute. Retrieved September 13, 2009, from http://www.cert.org/archive/pdf/NationalCSIRTs.pdf

Lowi, Theodore J. (1964). American Business, Public Policy, Case Studies, and Political Theory. *World Politics, 16* (4) 677-715.

Madnick, Stuart, Choucri, Nazli, Camina, Steven, Fogg, Erik, Li, Xitong, Wei, Fan (2009, August), Explorations in Cyber International Relations (ECIR)—Data Dashboard Report #1: CERT Data *Sources and Prototype Dashboard System.* Cambridge, MA: Sloan School of Management, MIT (Sloan School of Management Working Paper SWP #4754-09).

Madnick, Stuart, Li Xitong, & Choucri, Nazli. (2009, December). Experiences and challenges with using CERT data to analyze international cybersecurity. In Merrill Warkentin & Rita Walczuch (Eds.) *Proceedings of the AIS SIGSEC Workshop on Information Security & Privacy,* (pp. 6-16).Phoenix, AZ: Association of Information Systems Special Interest Group on Information Security and Privacy.

Madnick, Stuart, Choucri, Nazli, Li, Xitong, Ferwerda, Jeremy (2011, December 3-4). Comparative Analysis of Cybersecurity Metrics to Develop New Hypotheses. In Karin Hedström, Fredrik Karlsson & Zhengchuan Xu (Eds.), *Proceedings of the Workshop on Information Security & Privacy, (Jointly hosted by AIS SIGSEC and IFIP TC11.1),* Shanghai: Association of Information Systems Special Interest Group on Information Security and Privacy.

Mitrany, David. (1948). The Functional Approach to World Organization, in Oran R. Young (Ed.), *The International Political Economy and International Institutions, Volume 1* (pp. 22-52). Cheltenham, UK: Edward Elgar Publishing Limited.

National Council of ISACs. (2016a). *About ISACs.* Retrieved April 30, 2016, from http://www.nationalisacs.org/#!about-isacs/vu5l7

National Council of ISACs. (2016b). *About NCI.* Retrieved April 30, 2016, from http://www.nationalisacs.org/#!about-nci/cee5

Internet Crime Complaint Center. (2015). *IC3 2015 Internet Crime Report.* Retrieved June 19, 2016, from https://pdf.ic3.gov/2015_IC3Report.pdf

Nye, Joseph S., and Robert O. Keohane. (1977). *Power and Interdependence: World Politics in Transition.* Boston, MA: Little, Brown and Company.

OECD. (2009a). *What is the Working Party on Information Security and Privacy (WPISP)?* Retrieved October 23, 2009, from http://www.oecd.org/document/46/0,3343,en_2649_34255_36862382_1_1_1_1,00.html

OECD. (2009b). *Initiatives by country.* Retrieved September 27, 2009, from http://www.oecd.org/document/63/0,3343,en_21571361_36139259_36306559_1_1_1_1,00.html

Reich, Simon. (2000). The Four Faces of Institutionalism: Public Policy and a Pluralistic Perspective. *Governance, 13* (4), 501-522.

Samson, Victoria. (2008, July 23). *The murky waters of the White House's cybersecurity plan.* Center for Defense Information. Retrieved September 26, 2009, from http://www.cdi.org/program/document.cfm?DocumentID=4345&from_page=../index.cfm

Slaughter, Anne-Marie. (2004). Disaggregated Sovereignty: Towards the Public Accountability of Global Government Networks. *Government and Opposition. 39* (2) pp. 159-190.

The White House. (2003). *The National Strategy to Secure Cyberspace.* Retrieved September 20, 2009, from http://www.dhs.gov/xlibrary/assets/National_Cyberspace_Strategy.pdf

The White House. (2009a). *Cyberspace policy review: assuring a trusted and resilient information and communications infrastructure.* Retrieved September 23, 2009, from http://www.whitehouse.gov/assets/documents/Cyberspace_ Policy_Review_final.pdf

The White House. (2009b). *The Comprehensive National Cybersecurity Initiative.* Retrieved March 20, 2010, from http://www.whitehouse.gov/cybersecurity/ comprehensive-national-cybersecurity-initiative

The White House. (2015). *Executive Order—Promoting Private Sector Cybersecurity Information* Sharing. Retrieved April 30, 2016, from https://www. whitehouse.gov/the-press-office/2015/02/13/executive-order-promoting-private-sector-cybersecurity-information-sharning

UNESCO. (2009, March 23). *UN-backed anti-cyber-threat coalition launches headquarters in Malaysia.*
Retrieved March 24, 2009, from http://portal.unesco.org/ci/en/ev.php- URL_ ID=28464&URL_DO=DO_TOPIC&URL_SECTION=201.html

United Nations. (2015, December 16). *Press Release: WSIS +10 Outcome.* Retrieved May 19, 2016, from http://www.un.org/pga/70/2015/12/16/press-release-wsis10-outcome/#lightbox/0/

Verdelho, Pedro. (2008). *The effectiveness of international co-operation against cybercrime.* Council of Europe. Retrieved September 27, 2009, from http:// www.coe.int/t/dghl/cooperation/economiccrime/cybercrime/ T-CY/DOC-567study4-Version7_en.PDF/

WPISP. (2002). *OECD Guidelines for the Security of Information Systems and Networks: Towards a Culture of Security.* Paris: OECD.

WPISP. (2005). *The Promotion of a Culture of Security for Information Systems and Networks in OECD Countries.* Paris: OECD.

WSIS. (2003). *Plan of action.* Retrieved October 17, 2009, from http://www.itu. int/wsis/docs/geneva/official/poa.html

WSIS. (2009a). *Stocktaking.* Retrieved October 17, 2009, from http://www.itu. int/wsis/stocktaking/index.html

WSIS. (2009b). *WSIS C5.* Retrieved October 17, 2009, from http://www.itu.int/

osg/csd/cybersecurity/WSIS/

Choucri, Nazli, Madnick, Stuart, Ferwerda, Jeremy (2014), "Institutions for Cyber Security: International Responses and Global Imperatives," *Information Technology for Development,* Vol. 20, Issue 2, 96-121.

CHAPTER 2

Cybersafety: A Systems Theory Approach to Managing Cybersecurity Risks— Applied to TJX Cyberattack

Hamid Salim and Stuart Madnick

INTRODUCTION

Cybercrime is impacting a broad cross section of our society. The cyber environment is continuously evolving as the world continues to become more connected, contributing to increasing complexity. This also introduces more opportunities for hackers to exploit new vulnerabilities.

The insight that motivated this research was that significant efforts and progress has been made in past decades in methods for reducing industrial accidents, such as System-Theoretic Accident Model and Processes (STAMP). Although there are definite differences between cyberattacks and accidents, e.g., deliberate action versus unintentional, there are also significant similarities that can be exploited.

The idea of using safety approaches to address cybersecurity concerns had been mentioned previously.[1, 2, 3, 4] In Young and Leveson, "An integrated approach to safety and security based on systems theory,"[5] the authors briefly suggest that the STAMP safety methodology can be used to prevent or mitigate cyber-attacks. To the best of our knowledge, this chapter summarizes the first STAMP-inspired detailed analysis, which we call Cybersafety, of a major cyberattack, TJX. We endeavor to explain reasons for the limited efficacy of traditional approaches, and to evaluate the effectiveness of Cybersafety.

To apply Cybersafety, cybersecurity needs to be viewed holistically from the lens of *systems thinking*; "Systems thinking is a discipline for seeing wholes. It is a framework for seeing interrelationships rather than things, for seeing patterns of change rather than static 'snapshots.'"[6] Furthermore, Cybersafety takes a top-down approach. That is, it focuses on what needs to be protected or prevented. As a simple example, imagine that your organization has 1,000 doors that should be locked at night. A bottom-up approach would expend considerable energy trying to have all doors locked. A top-down approach would focus most energy on the doors that pose a hazard that could impact that which is to be protected.

LITERATURE REVIEW

There have been various approaches proposed for addressing cybersecurity, such as Chain-of-Events Model and Fault Tree Analysis (FTA). In addition, we looked at other widely used frameworks for cybersecurity best practices. We found all these methods limited. Existing cybersecurity approaches mostly focus on technical aspects, with the goal of creating a secure fence around technology assets of an organization. This limits systemic thinking for three main reasons: First, it does not view cybersecurity holistically at an organizational level, which includes people and processes. Second, focus on security technology reinforces the perception that it is solely an Information Technology department problem. Third, within the context of the cyber ecosystem, focusing only on a technical solution ignores interactions with other systems/sub-systems operating beyond an organizational boundary.

We argue that technical approaches address only a subset of cybersecurity risks.

Savage and Schneider[7] summarize this point by highlighting that cybersecurity is a holistic property of a system (the whole) and not just of its components (parts). They further emphasize that even small changes to a part of system can lead to devastating implications for overall cybersecurity of a system.

The above discussion highlights that people and management are essential dimensions of any successful holistic cybersecurity strategy. That view is explicitly addressed in this chapter using Cybersafety analysis, which is based on STAMP.

SYSTEM-THEORETIC ACCIDENT MODEL AND PROCESSES (STAMP) FRAMEWORK

In STAMP, to understand causal factors leading to an accident requires understanding *why* a control was ineffective. The focus is not on preventing failure event(s) but on implementing effective controls for enforcing relevant constraints. This is the foundation of STAMP model, with (1) *safety constraints,* *(2) hierarchical safety control structures,* and *(3) process model* as core concepts.

Safety constraints are critical; missing or lack of enforcement of relevant constraints leads to elevated safety risks, which may cause loss event(s). In the hierarchical safety control structure, a higher level imposes constraints over the level immediately below it, as depicted in figure 2.1. If these control processes are ineffective in controlling lower level processes and safety constraints are violated, then a system can suffer an accident.

Four factors may contribute to inadequate control at each level of a hierarchical structure: missing constraints, inadequate safety control commands, commands incorrectly executed at a lower level, or inadequate communication or feedback with reference to constraint enforcement.[8] Each level in the control structure is connected by communication channels needed for enforcing constraints at lower level and receiving feedback about the effectiveness of constraints. As shown in figure 2.2, the downward channel is used for providing information to impose constraints and the upward channel is used to measure effectiveness of constraints at the lower level.

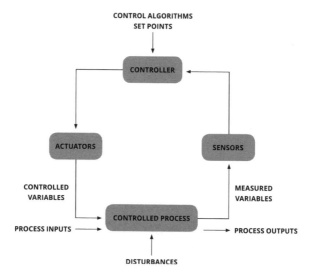

Figure 2.1 Standard control loop.[9]

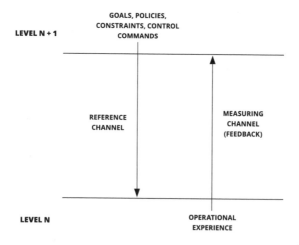

Figure 2.2 Communication channels in a hierarchical safety control structure.[8]

The third concept is the process model. There are four conditions necessary to control a process as shown in table 2.1.

Table 2.1 Conditions required for controlling a process and corresponding STAMP context.

Conditions for Controlling a Process	STAMP Context
Goal	Safety constraints to be enforced by each controller.
Action Condition	Implemented via downward control channel, in STAMP context communication between hierarchical control structures.
Observability Condition	Implemented via upward feedback channel, in STAMP context communication between hierarchical control structures.
Model Condition	To be effective in controlling lower level processes, a controller (human—mental model, or automated—embedded in control logic) needs to have a model of the process being controlled—STAMP context.

STAMP can be used both for hazard analysis (ex-ante) and accident analysis (ex-post). In hazard analysis, the goal is to understand scenarios and related causal factors that can lead to a loss, and to implement countermeasures to prevent losses. This method is called *System-Theoretic Process Analysis (STPA)*. The second STAMP-based method, called *Causal Analysis based on STAMP (CAST)*, is used to analyze accidents. The goal is to maximize learning and fully understand why a loss occurred. The focus of this chapter is CAST, though the ex-ante analysis is quite similar.

Causal Analysis Based on STAMP (CAST)

CAST allows us to go beyond a single failure event and analyze a broader sociotechnical system, to understand systemic and non-systemic casual factors[10] and helps understand *why* loss occurred, and to implement countermeasures to prevent future accidents or incidents. CAST emphasizes people's behaviors and what caused a certain behavior that led to an accident or incident.[10] CAST analysis is a nine-step process, listed in Table 3.2. Analysis can be performed in any order. In the following sections, we will perform CAST analysis applied to a cyberattack rather than an industrial accident. We will refer to this analysis method as Cybersafety.

Table 2.2 CAST steps for analyzing accidents.[10]

No.	Step	Brief comment(s)	
1	Identify the system(s) and hazard(s) associated with the accident or incident.	a.	Steps 1–3 form the core of STAMP-based techniques.
2	Identify system safety constraints and system requirements associated with that hazard.	b.	Regarding step 3, the control structure is composed of roles and responsibilities of each component,[1] controls for executing relevant responsibilities, and feedback channel.
3	Document safety control structure in place to control hazard and ensure compliance with the safety constraints.		
4	Ascertain proximate events leading to accident or incident.	To understand the physical process, events chain will be used to identify basic events leading to an accident or incident.	

No.	Step	Brief comment(s)
5	Analyze the accident or incident at a physical system level.	a. This step is the start of analysis, and helps to identify the role each of the following factors played in the events leading up to an accident or incident. b. Physical/operational controls. c. Physical failures. d. Dysfunctional interactions/ communications. e. Unhandled external disturbances.
6	Move up levels of the hierarchical safety control structure, establish how and why each successive higher level control allowed or contributed to inadequate control at the current level.	After deficiencies have been identified, next step is to investigate causes for those deficiencies. This requires understanding higher levels of hierarchical safety control structure, requiring consideration of the overall sociotechnical system focused on *why* controls were deficient. This contrasts with the Chain of Events Model where focus is on a failure event and analysis stops once a failure event is identified.

No.	Step	Brief comment(s)
7	Analyze overall coordination and communication contributors to the accident or incident.	This step examines coordination/communication between controllers in the hierarchical control structure.
8	Determine dynamics and changes in the system and the safety control structure relating to an accident or incident, and any weakening of safety control structure over time.	Most accidents/incidents occur when a system migrates towards a higher risk state *over time.* Understanding dynamics of this migration towards less safe and secure environment will help with implementing appropriate countermeasures.
9	Generate recommendations.	Many factors can drive which recommendation to implement depending on a particular situation. Decision factors can include cost, effectiveness, and/or practicality of a particular recommendation.

TJX CYBERATTACK

TJX cyberattack was one of a series of attacks, executed as part of operation *Get Rich or Die Tryin'* and continued for five years until 2008. The ring leader, Albert Gonzalez, was even the focus of an episode of the television show *American Greed.*[11]

As the 2006 holiday season was coming to a close, TJX was working to address a breach of its computer systems. On January 17, 2007, TJX announced that it was a victim of an unauthorized intrusion. The breach was discovered on December 18, 2006, and payment card transaction data of approximately 46 million customers had been potentially stolen. The cyberattack was, at the time, the largest in history, measured by a number of payment card numbers stolen.

The cyberattack highlighted operational and IT related weaknesses, which will be studied further using Cybersafety. The goal of the analysis is to understand *why* weaknesses existed and if/how they contributed to the cyberattack.

CYBERSAFETY ANALYSIS OF THE TJX CYBERATTACK

Step #1: System(s) and Hazard(s)

System(s)

Cyberattack resulted in a loss of payment card data, and TJX suffered financial losses of over $170 million. To understand why the hackers were able to steal so much of the information without detection, the system to be analyzed is *TJX payment card processing system.*

Hazard(s)

The hazard to be avoided is *TJX payment card processing system allowing unauthorized access.*

Step #2: System Safety Constraints and System Requirements

1. TJX must protect customer information from unauthorized access.
2. TJX must provide adequate training for managing technology infrastructure.
3. Measures must be in place to minimize losses from unauthorized access including:
4. TJX must communicate with payment card processors to minimize losses.
5. TJX must work with law enforcement and private cybersecurity experts.
6. TJX must provide support to customers whose information may have been stolen.

Step #3: TJX Hierarchical System Safety Control Structure

Hierarchical system safety control structure comprises two parts—system development and system operations. Safety control structure includes roles and responsibilities of each component, controls for executing those responsibilities, and feedback to gauge the effectiveness of controls.[10]

Figure 2.3 shows the hierarchical system safety control structure. Dotted arrows and boxes indicate development part of the control structure, and solid arrows and boxes indicate operational part. Each box (dotted or solid) represents a component. A dashed rectangle labeled as *System Boundary* indicates the need for the boundary of the system to be analyzed. Numbers represent control structures with control and feedback channels forming a loop. Physical processes (discussed in forthcoming sections) are identified by a dashed oval.

Solid bold arrows (loop #16, loop #17, and loop #18) indicate interactions between development and operation parts. The first interaction is between Project Management and Operations Management (loop #16). Second interaction is between Systems Management and Payment Card Processing System (loop #17), and third interaction is between Systems Management and TJX Retail Store System (loop #18).

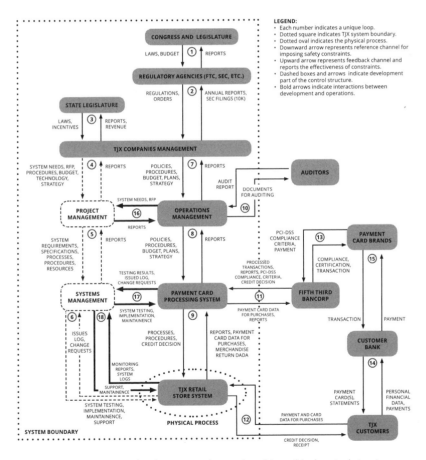

Figure 2.3 TJX system development and operations hierarchical control structure.

Step #4: Proximate Event Chain

Event chain analysis is not capable of providing critical information with reference to the causality of an accident, but basic events of the cyberattack are identified for understanding the physical process involved in the loss.[10]

Normally in CAST proximate implies a short time-horizon, generally ranging from hours to a few months. But in the context of cybersecurity, causal factors underlying a cyberattack may have been in place long before actual loss occurred. In the TJX case, the cyberattack started eighteen months before detection, and contributing causes were in place since 2000, five years before the cyberattack. Proximate events are summarized below.

1. In 2005, TJX decided against upgrading to a stronger encryption algorithm from deprecated WEP encryption.
2. In 2005, hackers used war-driving method to discover a misconfigured AP at a Marshalls store in Miami, FL.
3. Hackers join the store network and start monitoring data traffic.
4. Hackers exploited inherent encryption algorithm weaknesses, and decrypted keys to steal employee accounts and passwords.
5. Using stolen account information, hackers accessed corporate servers in Framingham, MA.
6. In late 2005 hackers downloaded *previously stored* customer payment card data from corporate servers using Marshalls store Wi-Fi connection in Florida.
7. In 2006, hackers discovered that TJX was processing and transmitting transactions without encryption.
8. In 2006, hackers installed a script on TJX corporate servers to capture unencrypted payment card data.
9. In 2006, hackers installed VPN connection between TJX server in Framingham, MA, and a server in Latvia controlled by hackers.

Then using TJX corporate servers as staging area, hackers created files containing *current* customer payment card data, and downloaded the files to the Latvian server.

Step #5: Analyzing the Physical Process

As shown in figure 2.3, the key process in hierarchical control structure is the TJX Retail Store System. The goal of this step is to determine *why* controls were ineffective in preventing the system from transitioning into a hazardous state leading to the cyberattack. Several factors will be considered, including.[10]

- How and why controls were ineffective in preventing system hazard and contributed to an accident.
- What physical failures (if any) were involved in the loss.
- Were there any communication and coordination flaws between the physical system and other interacting component(s).

TJX Retail Store System

TJX Retail Store System is the subject of analysis, and is a part of four control loops as shown in figure 2.3. It is the direct touch point of TJX with its customers, where Point of Sale (POS) transactions occur.

Inadequate control/feedback

Security Technology Management Capabilities

The TJX store was targeted because hackers used "war-driving," which specifically looks for Wi-Fi networks that accept connection(s) without authentication, because the store's Access Point (AP) was misconfigured and did not require authentication. This contributed to weakening of control by Systems Management over the process both via loop #6 and loop #18, and further, there was inadequate feedback from the process to Systems Management during support and maintenance phase (loop #18).

Monitoring

The hacker's presence was never detected, despite the fact that they were downloading large amounts of data from TJX corporate server, using Wi-Fi network in Miami, FL. Loop #18 in figure 2.3 will be analyzed further to understand causes underlying the weakened control.

Encryption technology

Software utilities for decrypting deprecated WEP key were freely and publically available. Hackers leveraged AP misconfiguration and inherent weaknesses of WEP encryption algorithm to steal employee account and password. To understand why Systems Management did not replace the deprecated algorithm at the physical process level, higher levels of the control structure would need to be analyzed. CAST analysis of the process is summarized in figure 2.4.

Safety Requirements and Constraints Violated:

- Prevent unauthorized access to customer information.

Emergency and Safety Equipment (Controls):

- Security technology at the store included following barriers to prevent unauthorized access.
    - AP authentication for devices requesting to join stores Wi-Fi network.
    - WEP encryption for in-store Wi-Fi communication network.
    - Use of account ID/password by store employees accessing corporate servers.

Failures and Inadequate Controls:

- Access Point (AP) misconfiguration
  - The AP was misconfigured with a default setting of open authentication that allowed connections to anyone without authentication.
- Inadequate monitoring of Wi-Fi network for unauthorized access and/or data traffic at the physical process level.
  - Hackers joined the store network without authentication and downloaded large amounts of data undetected.
- Inadequate implementation/maintenance of processes and/or procedures at the physical process level.
  - Stores were collecting customer information that was not required to make a purchase or a return (e.g., driver's license). Lack of process and/or procedures about data collection policy exposed more of customer information to hackers.
- Inadequate encryption technology used at the physical process level.
  - TJX stores were using deprecated encryption WEP.

Physical Contextual Factors:

- Wi-Fi technology became available in 1999.
- TJX was an early adopter of first generation Wi-Fi technology at over 1200 retail stores in 2000, requiring a significant learning curve, training, and new knowledge base in a short span of time.
- Vulnerability in the Wi-Fi technology was known since 2001, but an updated version was not available until 2003. Therefore, TJX and retail industry, in general, were using vulnerable technology though TJX did not suffer a cyberattack during this time.

Figure 2.4 CAST analysis of TJX Retail Store System (Physical Process Level).

Step #6: Analysis of Higher Levels of the Hierarchical Safety Control Structure

Step 5 highlighted three key control/feedback inadequacies at the physical process level: AP was incorrectly configured, Wi-Fi network monitoring was inadequate, and deprecated encryption was in use for processing payment card transactions. To understand why these inadequacies existed at the physical level, both development and operational components at higher levels of the hierarchical safety control structure need to be analyzed.[10]

Payment Card Processing System

Moving one level up from the physical process in the hierarchical control structure, note that TJX Retail Store System physical process is controlled by Payment Card Processing System, as shown in figure 2.3 (loop #9) Payment Card Processing System also interacts with Systems Management (loop #17). This link is to ensure that systems are subjected to rigorous testing, for the secure processing of payment card transactions by incorporating them during system design.

Inadequate control/feedback

Compliance with Payment Card Industry-Data Security Standard (PCI-DSS)

At the time of cyberattack in 2005, TJX was not PCI-DSS compliant, which is usually a requirement for accepting payment card(s). To be compliant a merchant must satisfy *all* twelve requirements of PCI-DSS and its sub-requirements comprising approximately eighty pages,[1] requiring a significant effort on the part of the merchant. As an example, TJX was in violation of the following requirements and sub-requirements:

- *Requirement 3:* Protect Stored Card Holder Data[12]

  - *Sub-requirement 3.1:* Keep cardholder data storage to a minimum by implementing data retention and disposal policies, procedures, and processes.

PCI-DSS does not allow for storing authentication data after a transaction has been approved, which was not the case at TJX. In 2005, hackers downloaded payment card data that was two years old from TJX corporate servers. Furthermore, TJX Operation did not have a formal data retention policy.

- *Requirement 4:* Encrypt transmission of cardholder data across open, public networks.[12] TJX was storing and transmitting customer payment card data to the Fifth Third Bancorp without encryption.[13]

To understand why TJX was not in compliance, it will help to gain an understanding of the role a bank plays in credit approval process as shown in figure 2.3 (loop #11). Payment card transactions flow through multiple entities and systems before a credit decision is made, VISA transaction flow is shown in figure 2.5.

In 2005, Fifth Third Bancorp was TJX's major acquirer bank and responsible party for ensuring PCI-DSS compliance by merchants. Based on our analysis, the following issues have come to light.

THE TRANSACTION JOURNEY

| CARDHOLDER | MERCHANT | AQUIRER | VISANET | ISSUER |

Figure 2.5 VISA transaction flow.[14]

- There is a conflict of interest/role between Fifth Third Bancorp and TJX when it comes to enforcement of PCI-DSS. Because TJX is a customer of Fifth Third Bancorp, and TJX could choose another processor and since PCI-DSS was not legally required, Fifth Third Bancorp leverage is limited in requiring it.
- It is difficult for Fifth Third Bancorp to gain deep insights into TJX systems to validate and verify the degree that PCI-DSS has been implemented, because it has no regulatory role.
- For these reasons implementing PCI-DSS is the responsibility of TJX, which submits voluntary yearly reports regarding compliance status.
- Per PCI-DSS, Fifth Third Bancorp is not responsible for auditing TJX with reference to PCI-DSS compliance.

Payment Card Processing System and Systems Management Interaction

The Payment Card Processing System was sending unencrypted information to the bank for possibly several reasons: PCI-DSS requirements were not effectively communicated to system development, there was systemic lack of awareness of PCI-DSS requirements, and there was lack of clarity on roles and responsibilities with reference to PCI-DSS implementation between development and operations. The analysis of Payment Card Processing System is summarized in compressed form in figure 2.6. Analysis of higher level components is needed to understand why these oversights occurred and for what reason.

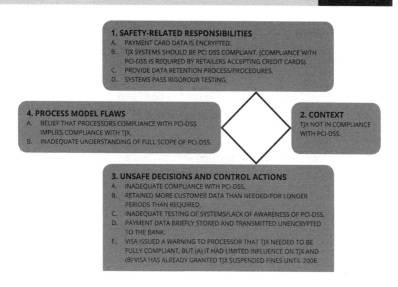

Figure 2.6 CAST analysis of Payment Card Processing System.

Operations Management and Other Upper Levels

Next level up in the control structure is Operations Management, which provides policies, processes, and procedures for the secure handling of customer information, customer data management guidelines (retention, disposal, archiving), compliance with PCI-DSS, and budget for resources needed to implement policies.

A similar analysis was conducted for this level and all the upper levels. A detailed description of these analyses can be found in Salim, "Cyber safety."[15] But, to give an example of the range of factors that can contribute to such a cyberattack, we will briefly mention one of the interesting upper levels of the control structure: the role of the State Legislature.

State Legislature

TJX is headquartered in Massachusetts. If its headquarters had been in Nevada, certain factors would have been different. That is because, in Nevada, all retail operations are required to be PCI-DSS compliant, which was not the case in Massachusetts at that time. Thus, the Massachusetts State Legislature also controls TJX Management by enacting laws. Although we have not investigated the reasons, we suspect that, much like VISA and Fifth Third Bancorp, Massachusetts wants to be "business-friendly" and impose as few regulations as possible. This is illustrated in the feedback shown in figure 2.3 (loop #3).

Step #7: Coordination and Communication

- The CAST analysis revealed key coordination and communication weaknesses discussed below.
- Payment Card Processing System is controlled by Operations Management (loop #8), and interacts with Fifth Third Bancorp (loop #11), which should be responsible for ensuring that TJX is compliant with PCI-DSS but was relying on TJX to satisfy all requirements of PCI-DSS. Also, at TJX the general view was that PCI-DSS compliance is a technology issue and that First Third Bancorp compliance implies TJX compliance.
- Cyber security risk posed by use of WEP was well understood within TJX,[16] but because PCI-DSS was not a priority, the risks were not effectively communicated to the executive level. Further, there was no dedicated role within TJX that was responsible for managing cybersecurity risks company-wide.
- Disconnect between system development and operations during system design.

Step #8: Dynamics and Migration to a High-Risk State

According to Leveson, most major accidents are a result of migration of a system to a high-risk state over time. Understanding the dynamics of migration will help in redesigning the system.[10] This step discusses some operational and behavioral aspects revealed that contributed to the TJX cyberattack.

A major change that contributed to the cyber-attack was TJX's early move from wired to wireless networking (Wi-Fi) in 2000, in a short span of one year. By 2003, the environment had changed because the inherent weaknesses of WEP became publically known, and hackers started to exploit it for launching cyberattacks. TJX decided against upgrading to a more secure encryption algorithm for cost reasons.

TJX's short implementation timeframe for a major technology leap introduced additional risk. It is plausible that technology team's inadequate experience led to misconfiguration of AP's that allowed hackers to launch an attack. The same reasoning may also explain lack of monitoring of Wi-Fi network for data traffic and unauthorized connections.

Lack of full compliance with PCI-DSS also contributed to the cyberattack, and TJX gradually moved towards a state of higher cybersecurity risk.

Overtime, from 2000 until the cyberattack in 2005, the cybercrime ecosystem became increasingly sophisticated. As the cybersecurity risks increased, TJX did not have a dedicated role for managing these risks, further contributing to an already high level of exposure to a cyberattack. This also led to an inaccurate assessment of cyberattack risks.

Recall Bias

Biases can contribute to flawed decisions by managers. One such bias is *ease of recall bias* that relates to decision-making process where recent experiences, or lack thereof, strongly influence the decision. Having no experience of a breach at TJX and oblivious to cyberattacks at other retailers, it is plausible that the *recall bias* heuristic played a role in management's decision to not upgrade to a stronger encryption in favor of cost savings.[16]

Confirmation Trap

Another behavioral aspect, called *confirmation trap*,[17] is a decision maker's tendency to favor/seek information that confirms his/her own beliefs and discount contradicting information. Table 2.3 depicts a message from the TJX CIO in November 2005 to his staff,[16] regarding security technology upgrades. In this memo, he is requesting agreement on his belief that cybersecurity risk is low. The majority of his staff agreed with his assessment. This confirmation trap led to postponing upgrades, therefore migrating security technology infrastructure to a higher risk of a cyberattack.

Table 2.3 TJX CIO memo regarding security technology upgrade.[16]

"My understanding [is that] we can be PCI-compliant without the planned FY07 upgrade to WPA technology for encryption because most of our stores do not have WPA capability without some changes," Butka wrote. "WPA is clearly best practice and may ultimately become a requirement for PCI compliance sometime in the future. I think we have an opportunity to defer some spending from FY07's budget by removing the money for the WPA upgrade, but would want us all to agree that the risks are small or negligible."

Step #9: Recommendations

Following are some key recommendations that can help TJX and other such organizations in managing cybersecurity risks more effectively in the future.

*   A dedicated executive role is needed with cybersecurity responsibilities and authority for executing cybersecurity risk management policies. Further, it will help with better coordination between System Development and System Operations, integration of compliance requirements during system design, and with communication and proper framing of security technology risks.
*   Per PCI Security Standards Council, compliance is a business issue requiring management attention and is an ongoing process of assessment, remediation, and reporting. TJX needs to understand and communicate effectively the risks of non-compliance and importance of integrating PCI-DSS early in the system lifecycle.
*   Building a Cybersafety culture can help reduce risks of a future cyberattack significantly.
*   Specific steps can include:

    *   Identifying critical systems, trends, processes, and procedures concerning cybersecurity.
    *   After critical entities are documented, implement a plan to manage these entities with periodic reviews to update the list.
*   Understand limitations standards and align them with cybersecurity and business needs of an organization. For example, PCI-DSS data standard states that "encrypt transmission of cardholder data across open, public networks".[12] PCI-DSS does not explicitly state that data must be encrypted when transmitted within TJX – that is over the *intranet or behind a firewall*. PPC-DDS did also not explicitly mandate using stronger encryption WPA until 2006.

With these recommendations, analysis of TJX cyberattack is complete. It can be observed that CAST highlighted system-level insights that otherwise could have been overlooked if another method of analysis was used.

COMPARING CYBERSAFETY FINDINGS WITH FEDERAL TRADE COMMISSION (FTC) AND CANADIAN PRIVACY COMMISSION (CPC) FINDINGS

This section presents comparisons between selected Cybersafety CAST recommendations, and actions proposed by the FTC and the CPC.

Both FTC and CAST generated recommendation #1 albeit with a difference. FTC proposed designating an *employee or employees* to be accountable for information security program. CAST specifically recommends an executive level role for managing cybersecurity risks. With reference to recommendations #2, #3, #4, and #5 in all of these were generated by CAST and have been discussed in either this report, or in the more complete analysis,[15] but importantly, omitted by CPC and FTC.

Recommendations #6 and #7, regarding a lack of encryption and monitoring of systems, were explicitly proposed by the CPC. CAST analysis identified causal factors and revealed non-linear issues at TJX which led to weakening or lack of these controls. Although, our CAST analysis did not explicitly provide recommendations #6 and #7, the insights were addressed by way of recommendations #1, #2, and #3.

Recommendation #8 provided by FTC is an important point, but vague. FTC states that TJX "establish and implement, and thereafter maintain, a comprehensive information security program that is reasonably designed to protect the security, confidentiality, and integrity of personal information collected from or about consumers."[18] TJX already had in place security measures to protect customer information, but the controls were inadequate, missing, or failed due to systemic issues revealed by our analysis.

The Cybersafety analysis covers the FTC proposal in all five of its recommendations and provides specifics; for example, with reference to PCI-DSS, we provide actionable steps. Importantly, our analysis, provided insights that other investigations either did not reveal or revealed in incomplete form; therefore, it can be a valuable supplement for understanding cyberattacks and, specifically, systemic and non-linear causes leading to increased cybersecurity risks.

Table 2.4 Comparison of Cybersafety CAST recommendations with FTC and Canadian Privacy Commission.

No.	Recommendation	CPC	FTC	STAMP/CAST
1	Create an executive level role for managing cybersecurity risks.	No	*	Yes
2	PCI-DSS integration with TJX processes.	No	No	Yes
3	Develop a safety culture.	No	No	Yes
4	Understand limitations of PCI-DSS and standards in general.	No	No	Yes
5	Review system architecture.	No	No	Yes
6	Upgrade encryption technology.	Yes	No	*
7	Implement vigorous monitoring of systems.	Yes	No	*
8	Implement information security program.	No	Yes	*

CONTRIBUTIONS

Our research proposed a new method, Cybersafety, of analyzing cybersecurity risks drawing on prior research and experience in preventing accidents, based on Systems Thinking and Systems Theory and the STAMP methodology. The analysis revealed insights, which may otherwise be difficult or impossible to gain using traditional technology focused approaches.

Main contributions of this chapter include:
- Highlighting the value for a System Thinking and Systems Theory based approach for managing cybersecurity risks.
- Introducing Cybersafety as a new approach for managing cybersecurity risks
- Applying our analysis to the TJX cyberattack case providing new insights including:

  - General limitations of standards, specifically PCI-DSS.
  - Systemic causes that contributed to the TJX cyberattack.
  - Behavioral aspects that contributed to the TJX cyberattack.

NOTES

1. I. N. Fovino, M. Masera, and A. De Cian, "Integrating cyberattacks within fault trees," Rel. Eng. Syst. Safety, vol. 94, no. 9, pp. 1394–1402, 2009.

2. C.-W. Ten, C.-C. Liu, and G. Manimaran, "Vulnerability assessment of cybersecurity for SCADA systems using attack trees," in IEEE Power Eng. Soc. General Meeting, 2007.

3. Christopher Schmittner, Thomas Gruber, Peter Puschner, and Erwin Schoitsch, "Security application of failure mode and effect analysis (FMEA)," in 33rd Int. Conf. Comput. Safety, Rel. Security, Florence, Italy, 2014.

4. S. Kriaa, M. Bouissou, F. Colin, Y. Halgand, and L. Pietre-Cambacedes, "Safety and security interactions modeling using the bdmp formalism: Case study of a pipeline," in 33rd Int. Conf. Comput. Safety, Rel. Security, 2014.

5. W. Young and N. G. Leveson, "An integrated approach to safety and security based on systems theory," ACM, vol. 57, no. 2, p. 31–35, 2014.

6. P. M. Senge, The Fifth Discipline, 1st ed., New York: Doubleday/Currency, 1990, pp. 68-69.

7. S. Savage and F. B. Schneider, Feburary 2009. [Online]. Available: http://www.cra.org/ccc/files/docs/init/Cybersecurity.pdf. [Accessed 18 September 2013].

8. N. G. Leveson, "A Systems-Theoretic View of Causality," in Engineering a Safer World: Systems Thinking Applied to Safety, Cambridge, The MIT Press, 2011, pp. 73-102.

9. N. G. Leveson, "Systems Theory and Its Relationship to Safety," in Engineering a Safer World: Systems Thinking Applied to Safety, Cambridge, MA: MIT Press, 2011, pp. 61-72.

10. N. G. Leveson, "Analyzing Accidents and Incidents (CAST)," in Engineering a Safer World: Systems Thinking Applied to Safety, Cambridge, The MIT Press, 2011, pp. 350-390.

11.   American Greed Episode 40: Hackers, Operation Get Rich or Die Tryin'. [Film]. USA: CNBC, 2011.

12.   PCI Security Standards Council, "Payment Card Industry (PCI) Data Security Standard, Requirements and Security Assessment Procedures," PCI Security Standards Council, Wakefield, MA USA, 2013, Version 3.0.

13.   THE TJX COMPANIES, INC., "FORM 10-K," THE TJX COMPANIES, INC., Framingham, 2007.

14.   VISA, "How a Visa Transaction Works," VISA, 2014. [Online]. Available: http://usa.visa.com/merchants/become-a-merchant/how-a-visa-transaction-works.jsp. [Accessed 26 March 2014].

15.   H. M. Salim, "Cyber safety : a systems thinking and systems theory approach to managing cybersecurity risks," MIT, Cambridge, MA, 2014.

16.   Ericka Chickowski, "TJX: Anatomy of a Massive Breach," Baseline, pp. Issue 81, p28, 30 January 2008.

17.   M. H. Bazerman and D. Moore, Judgement in Managerial Decision Making, Hoboken, NJ: John Wiley & Sons, Inc., 2009.

18.   Federal Trade Commission (FTC), "Cases and Proceedings (TJX DECISION AND ORDER, DOCKET NO. C-4227)," 1 August 2008. [Online]. Available: http://www.ftc.gov/enforcement/cases-proceedings/072-3055/tjx-companies-inc-matter.[Accessed 16 April 2014].

19.   N. G. Leveson, "Questioning the Foundations of Traditional Safety Engineering," in Engineering a Safer World: Systems Thinking Applied to Safety, Cambridge, MA: MIT Press, 2011, pp. 7-60.

CHAPTER 3

Measuring Stakeholders' Perceptions of Cybersecurity for Renewable Energy Systems

Stuart Madnick, Mohammad S. Jalali,
Michael Siegel, Yang Lee, Diane Strong,
and Richard Wang

INTRODUCTION

Rising demand for renewable energy resources has led to a noticeable focus on undertaking technological innovations to expand the green energy industry and respond to demand. As a result, cybersecurity has emerged as a critical issue as the green energy sector faces growing cyber risks. For example, smart grids—which are meant to provide reliable and efficient power network systems to distribute renewable energy resources— open up more direct and indirect connections to the Internet and more connections among the nodes in the networks. Smart grids also require advanced computing and communication technologies.[1] Adding new sources of renewable energy to grids also requires an increase in the frequency and speed of technological adjustments. Consequently, while enhanced features and functionalities are introduced, the networked systems become increasingly vulnerable.[2,3] Other complications and vulnerabilities are also added with the Internet of Things (IoT), where intelligent devices are getting connected, as sensors and/or controllers, within energy networks. In fact, not only are vulnerabilities on the rise, but they also have the potential of becoming very sophisticated, given the unknown characteristics of new technologies. Because a great deal of attention is being focused on technological innovations in renewable energy systems, the cybersecurity research community has also focused mostly on the technical aspects. Overall, a similar trend is observed in energy companies as they face the challenges of the high cost of developing new technologies in a context of limitation of available resources. As a result, it is not surprising that the organizational aspects of cybersecurity have become a blind spot for both industry and academia.

Cybersecurity is an increasingly crucial and complex management issue. Many organizations have developed cybersecurity policies to protect their business information and operational systems. Although these policies are important, they are often not fully adopted, the reasons being that organizations are limited by the resources they can devote to cybersecurity, and they often misunderstand the status of their cybersecurity.

An organization's goal should be to develop the best possible, most cost-effective approach to cybersecurity, which is further complicated by the different priorities of organizational stakeholders. Stakeholders' perceptions of cybersecurity play a critical role in achieving this goal, since they are the main source of decision-making. Moreover, as organizations evolve into extended enterprises, which includes ties with suppliers, customers, and other partners, there is a significant increase in the number of stakeholders, and a wider range of security complications and requirements.

The current cybersecurity literature does not adequately address these issues. Many professionals and scholars have approached the study of cybersecurity by focusing specifically on the technical (e.g., hardware and software) and detailed elements of the security systems themselves, such as encryption,[4,5,6] firewall technologies[7,8,9] and antiviruses,[10,11] or have measured specific events, such as mean-time-to-failure. Although these efforts are necessary, they often do not look at cybersecurity holistically and commonly neglect to consider its organizational aspects. They especially neglect to consider the perceived needs and security views of organizational stakeholders.

In this chapter, we introduce the MIT House of Security (HoS) framework and present a survey instrument to measure stakeholders' perceptions of cybersecurity. We seek to identify similarities and differences, both within and between different organizations. This research has three major objectives:

- To identify how perceptions both shape and should potentially shape, decisions about investments in security systems, with a particular focus on identifying the areas most in need of cybersecurity, as perceived by the individuals in the organization.

- To identify perceived differences between importance and assessment of the HoS constructs among stakeholders. These differences are further compared among individuals with different organizational roles and functional areas; e.g., comparing the views of mid-level managers to those of senior management, or the views of information technology (IT) or operational technology (OT) workers with those of other members in the organization.

- To identify differences between the importance and assessment of the HoS constructs among different organizations (e.g., comparing two different organizations).

MIT'S HOUSE OF SECURITY

Through a comprehensive literature review and several surveys, researchers at MIT have divided cybersecurity issues primarily into eight meta-groupings (i.e., constructs). Good security protects the "confidentiality" and "integrity" of data while providing "availability" of the data, networks, and systems to appropriate and authorized users. Confidentiality, integrity, and availability, also known as CIA, are often used as the only critical information characteristics.[12] Good security practices also go beyond just technical solutions and are driven by a "business strategy," with associated "policies and procedures" for security, and are implemented in a "culture of security." Moreover, these practices are supported by "technology resources" and "financial resources" dedicated to security. These eight constructs form the proposed House of Security and are shown in figure 3.1.

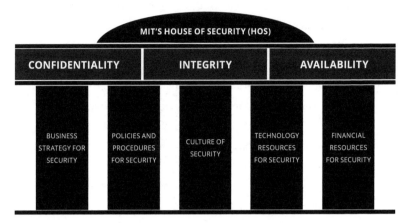

Figure 3.1 The eight constructs of the House of Security.[1]

SURVEY INSTRUMENT

The survey includes three questions related to each construct of HoS (a total of 24 questions). In each question, respondents are asked to specify their perception of both the level of "assessment" and "importance." For example, they first respond to their perception of a question (e.g., "Are people in the organization aware of good security practices?"), then identify the importance of that aspect. All questions are on a seven-point scale; "1" represents the smallest extent and "7" the largest extent.

The survey questions do not explicitly identify the construct being measured, but relate to aspects of the construct. Furthermore, there are multiple questions for each construct that are ordered randomly. The individuals are not aware of the categorization of the questions across the eight constructs.

A key part of this study involves gap analysis: How much does the perception of the current state of a cybersecurity aspect differ from the perception of its importance? Such gaps help identify potential opportunities for improvement within and across the extended enterprise. Differences in gaps among organizational stakeholders may represent different levels of understanding of security and help identify differences in local knowledge and needs.

We evaluated the quality of the survey instrument by measuring the statistical significance of the questions and the constructs and the reliability of the constructs by computing Cronbach's alpha.[13] While a key goal of our survey is to measure perceptions of the different constructs of security, we also plan to study the causes of these perception variations in our future research.

PRELIMINARY RESULTS OF THE PILOT STUDY

For this pilot study, we distributed the survey broadly to members of two energy and ICS organizations, which we will refer to as organizations A and B. Respondents ranged from employees to top-level managers and across all major functional areas. This diversity was important to identify variations in perceptions of cybersecurity. Here we briefly discuss some examples of the results based on: individual questions; constructs (i.e., a group of questions about a HoS construct); and construct gaps (i.e., the gap between assessment and importance of a construct).

Individual questions

An example of the results of a question for organizations A and B are shown in figure 3.2. The figure presents the assessment of a user (my perceived assessment, marked as MA), the importance (my perceived level of importance, marked as MI), and the gap between MA and MI. This illustrates that people in different organizations can have very different perceptions regarding their organization's cybersecurity. For example, for a question about well-defined and communicated cybersecurity strategy, there was a large gap (particularly in organization B), which implies that aspect falls far short of what is perceived to be needed among the respondents. Moreover, this example shows that organization A not only has a higher assessment about this question, but they also have a higher expectation.

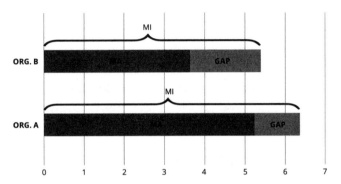

Figure 3.2 Responses to a question on a seven-point scale: "The organization has a well-defined and communicated cybersecurity strategy." MA: my perceived assessment, MI: my perceived level of importance, Gap=MI-MA

Constructs

Beyond the individual questions, the results of the constructs present a more holistic overview. Each HoS construct contains three related questions, and the results of the questions are aggregated to present the construct. We have found, so far, that for a given organization, the assessment levels are likely to differ across the eight constructs, while the importance levels are often similarly high. Comparing organizations, one can observe and study both similarities and differences between the organizations.

The aggregated results of the eight constructs for organizations A and B are presented in figure 3.3. The two organizations are relatively similar in their perceptions of availability, but differ noticeably in their perceptions of the state of policies and procedures for security—see figure 3.3.[1] At this point, we are not focusing on the specifications of organizations A and B. Obviously, there are other factors that might be at work, such as private vs. public company, or large vs. small company. Although these other factors may make it challenging to compare the organizations, these diagrams do provide important insights into the differences in perceptions. We will pursue these issues further in our next stage of research with a larger number of organizations.

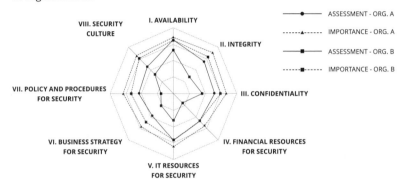

Figure 3.3 Assessment vs. importance in organizations A and B.[1]

Construct gaps

Although viewing the values of each of the constructs provides some quick insights, it is often more intuitive to examine the gaps between assessment and importance levels. The construct gaps in organizations A and B are presented in figure 3.4. As can be seen, in this case, organization B has significantly larger gaps than organization A, with Policy and Procedures for Security construct having the largest gap.

Gap analysis might show that one organization had an overall assessment of 5 in a construct, and if it viewed that construct as only having an importance value of 5, the gap would be 0 and the organization might be content. If another organization had the same overall assessment of 5, but viewed that construct's importance as being 6, the gap of 1 might indicate an area for improvement.

Figure 3.4 Gap analysis in organizations A and B (gap = importance – assessment).[2]

For the rest of this chapter, we discuss the results of stratified construct analysis along other dimensions, such as level within the organization or functional area within the organization.

CONSTRUCT ANALYSIS

Figure 3.5-A shows the distribution of cybersecurity perceptions (i.e., construct assessment levels) based on the organizational level of the respondents: from executive level, to line managers, to professionals. Significant differences can be seen: Executives giving generally lower assessments, professions and middle managers in the middle, and "Others" with highest assessments.

Although ratings of assessment and importance are individually important, the size of the gaps can provide more insights (see figure 3.5-B). The results show that top-level executives tend to have much higher gaps, across almost all constructs, than middle management and non-management personnel. This disparity in perceptions may imply that executives are more dissatisfied with the security situation in their organizations. Perhaps executives think situations are worse than they really are because they do not understand how and whether security measures are being correctly implemented.

Or alternatively, executives might see problems that people in other roles do not see and, as a result, their perceptions of a security gap are higher.

Overall, the sample sizes in this pilot study are small; hence, we use these findings to illustrate some of the issues that we expect will be significant in our larger study. We are currently conducting a large-scale study to better compare the results across various organizational levels. Follow-up studies and case studies would also help further clarify the underlying causes of differences in perceptions.

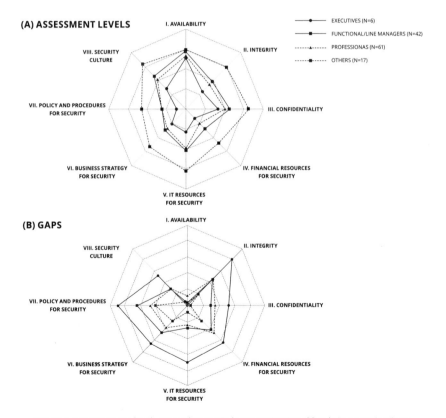

Figure 3.5 Assessment levels (A) and gaps (B) by organizational levels in organizations.

Figure 3.6 presents the gaps among IT, OT, and other areas in organization (such as Marketing or Finance). Interestingly, OT staff generally have higher gaps across the eight constructs. This is consistent with the frequent mention of IT/OT cultural gaps.

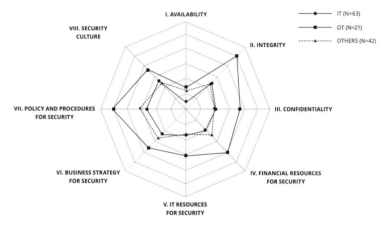

Figure 3.6 Gaps based on functional areas: information technology (IT), operational technology (OT), and other areas.

CONCLUSION

To identify security strategies and cross-organizational trends, we analyzed perceptions of importance and assessment of the eight security constructs of the House of Security. In addition to being a unique way to study organizational aspects of cybersecurity, this study sheds some light on perceptions, which are important, since they are the foundations of decision-making in an organization. We believe that the results of this pilot study and our follow-up large-scale study will have important implications in several areas, including assessment of an organization's cybersecurity needs, marketing of cybersecurity products, and development of an organization's cybersecurity technologies and policies, which is increasingly important in the renewable energy industry.

Opportunity to participate in our large-scale research

Using respondents from these two organizations, this research allowed us to conduct a pilot study using the survey instrument and analyze the constructs and gaps. To improve the comparisons, increase the generalizability of the findings, and study other dimensions, such as differences among industries, we are developing a larger dataset. We invite you and your organization to participate in our confidential organization benchmarking exercise, similar to organizations A and B in this chapter. If you would like more information about this opportunity, please contact the corresponding author.

ACKNOWLEDGMENT

This research was conducted by the MIT Interdisciplinary Consortium for Improving Critical Infrastructure Cybersecurity, also known as MIT-(IC)3. We would like to thank those who participated for taking the time to complete the survey. Early research was supported, in part, by Cisco Systems, Inc. through the MIT Center for Digital Business.

NOTES

1. Since assessment and importance values usually average above 4, we show the range 3 to 7 on the graph.
2. Since construct gaps are usually less than 2.0, we display gap values in multiples of 0.5 from 0 to 2.5.

REFERENCES

Gharavi, H., Ghafurian, R.: Smart grid: The electric energy system of the future. IEEE (2011)

Liu, J., Xiao, Y., Li, S., Liang, W., Chen, C.P.: Cyber security and privacy issues in smart grids. IEEE Communications Surveys & Tutorials 14, 981-997 (2012)

Pearson, I.L.: Smart grid cybersecurity for Europe. Energy Policy 39, 5211-5218 (2011)

Boneh, D., Franklin, M.: Identity Based Encryption From the Weil Pairing. Siam Journal of Computing 32, 586-615 (2003)

Dolev, D., Yao, A.: On the Security of Public Key Protocols. IEEE Transactions on Information Theory 29, 198-208 (1983)

Needham, R.M., Schroeder, M.D.: Using Encryption for Authentication in Large Networks for Computers. Communications 21, 993-999 (1978)

Cheswick, W.R., Bellovin, S.M., Rubin, A.D.: Firewalls and Internet Security: Repelling the Wily Hacker. Addison-Wesley (2003)

Oppliger, R.: Internet Security: Firewalls and Beyond. Association for Computing Machinery 40, 92-103 (1977)

Zwicky, E., Cooper, S., Chapman, D., Ru, D.: Building Internet Firewalls. O'Reilly & Associates (2000)

Furnell, S.: Cyber Threats: What Are the Issues and Who Sets the Agenda? In: SGIR Conference. (2004)

Kephart, J., Sorkin, G., Chess, D.W., S.: Fighting Computer Viruses. Scientific American November, (1997)

McCumber, J.: Assessing and Managing Security Risk in IT Systems. Auerbach Publications (2005)

Cronbach, L.J.: Coefficient alpha and the internal structure of tests. Psychometrika 16, 297-334 (1951)

CHAPTER 4

Fixing a Hole: The Labor Market for Bugs[1]

Ryan Ellis, Keman Huang, Michael Siegel, Katie Moussouris, and James Houghton

Over the past several years, "bug bounty" programs have grown in popularity. Bounty programs offer independent researchers rewards for valid bug submissions. This chapter analyzes the composition of the labor market for bounty programs. It analyzes data collected from 62 different bug bounty programs, including over 650 different participating researchers ("sellers"), 4,145 individual sales, and over $4.7 million in rewards. We note that the labor market is highly stratified, featuring a highly productive (and comparatively well-compensated) core set of workers and a large pool of modestly productive workers. It also uncovers that the majority of sellers demonstrate a low degree of flexibility—the overwhelming majority of participants only sell to a very small number of customers, while a small flexible core trade with several different customers. We consider the implications of the findings for firms experimenting with different bounty models. Importantly, we consider what, if anything, these insights can tell us about the utility of different approaches designed to disrupt the offensive acquisition, stockpile, and use of zero-day vulnerabilities.

THE ORIGINS OF BUG BOUNTIES

In 1995, Netscape launched a then-novel idea: A bug bounty program.[2] They agreed to offer cash rewards to anyone that reported a flaw in their new web browser, Netscape Navigator 2.0. The program was decidedly modest. They offered a range of prizes, including Netscape merchandise and cash payments capped at $1,000. In an announcement touting the new program, Mike Homer, Netscape VP for Marketing, offered a succinct rationale for the effort: "We're trying to find out about as many bugs as we can as fast as we can."[3] Homer noted that the program would provide a way to capitalize on the knowledge of the larger community of users and researchers and improve security: "There are a whole bunch of people out there with a lot of great computer science knowledge. We thought it was time to proactively harness all that energy to give them a reward."[4]

Twenty years later, bug bounty programs are now becoming commonplace. Companies routinely offer researchers payments for discovered flaws. Major tech companies—including Google, Facebook, and Microsoft—operate bounty programs. Non-tech companies are also joining the fray. Recently, United Airlines announced a new bug bounty program covering their web-facing properties.[5] Now, researchers that discover flaws in United's website will earn a windfall of frequent flyer miles. Currently, over 100 different companies offer programs that compensate independent security researchers for discovered flaws.[6] Thousands of researchers participate in these programs, earning anywhere from a few dollars to over $30,000 for a single reported flaw. Individual researchers have netted over $180,000 through multiple submissions.[7]

THE LABOR MARKET FOR BUGS: OVERVIEW AND KEY QUESTIONS

We provide a window into the labor dynamics of the market for bugs. The labor market consists of researchers or "sellers" submitting newly identified bugs to bug bounty programs for a price. We consider the composition of the labor market: It focuses on the degree of diversity in the market and worker mobility. It examines labor stratification both horizontally across different programs and vertically within individual programs. In this manner, we explore a range of related questions: Is the supply of bugs dominated by a few key suppliers or is it fed by a relatively diverse slate of sellers? Does the organization of labor look similar across different bug bounty programs? Are similar degrees of stratification found in different programs?

Additionally, with respect to programs characterized by high levels of stratification—that is, programs where a small number of sellers account for a disproportionate share of total sales, measured either in terms of volume of sales or earned revenue—another set of useful questions can be engaged. In particular, in programs dominated by a core of either high-volume or high-earning suppliers, what, if any value, do sellers operating at the margins offer? Are infrequent, low-volume sellers offering bugs that are high quality? Or are they providing, at best, low-quality commodities?

Finally, we examine what might be termed labor *mobility* or *flexibility*: The degree to which researchers sell to different bug bounty programs. Are researchers generalists that divide their time and talents across an eclectic set of targets? Or are workers specialists that focus narrowly on one customer—only working on one piece of software or web application? That is, are sellers catholic in their interests and activity, or rigid and narrow?

Exploring these questions is useful. Bug bounty programs currently evidence a significant amount of design diversity: Different firms are experimenting with different program configurations. Programs vary in several ways, including how they define market access (who can participate as a seller), program duration (when will sales be accepted), and compensation (what is offered as a reward). Indeed, while some programs are open to all participants, others have high barriers to entry and only allow invited sellers to participate.[8] Likewise, while many programs have standing offers to purchase bugs year-round, whenever they may be offered by a seller, other programs are experimenting with limited-purchase windows, offering to buy bugs only during a specified time period.[9] At the moment, different program designs are flourishing and other approaches are possible. An analysis of the labor market can help highlight the trade-offs associated with different program configurations.

Although the analyzed dataset—discussed below—focuses explicitly on what can be categorized as the "defensive market" for vulnerabilities—defined as programs that identify and disclose bugs to the impacted vendor—the analysis offers some limited insight into the viability of different strategies designed to counter the acquisition, stockpile, and exploitation of previously unknown and undisclosed vulnerabilities (what are known as "zero-days" or "0-days") by malicious actors.

DATA COLLECTION: EXAMINING PUBLIC AND PRIVATE DATASETS

We analyze two large datasets: Publicly available data on 61 different bug bounty programs hosted by HackerOne, a third-party coordination platform that supports a range of different individual programs; and comprehensive private data supplied by Facebook covering their vulnerability rewards program (see table 4.1). The HackerOne data includes 61 different bug bounty programs, 650 different participating sellers (individual researchers that successfully submitted a valid bug and received a monetary reward), and 2,177 different payments. Included within the HackerOne dataset are a range of different bug bounty programs, including programs offered by Yahoo!, Twitter, and Slack. Across these different programs, researchers earned $1,180,018 in sales. The data includes unique pseudonyms chosen by participating researchers; these identifies are consistently used across the 61 programs hosted by HackerOne (that is researchers selling to more than one of the bounty programs hosted by HackerOne are identifiable across each of these programs). Collected HackerOne data stretches from November 29, 2013, to October 28, 2015.

Table 4.1 Data Overview.

	HackerOne Dataset	Facebook Dataset
Included programs	61	1
Participating individual sellers	650	725
Total transactions (total volume of sales)	2177	1968
Total payments	$1,180,018	$3,562,684
Average payment per transaction	$542,04	$1810,31

The Facebook data was privately shared with the authors as part of a collaborative research project. The collected data stretches from June 14, 2011 (the start date of Facebook's vulnerability rewards program), to March 30, 2015. The data includes 725 different researchers and 1,968 different payments. In total, researchers participating in Facebook's program earned $3,562,684. The Facebook researcher data is anonymized: Individual researchers are not identified by name or by a self-selected pseudonym—preventing matching with the HackerOne dataset. However, anonymized researchers in the data are given consistent randomized identifiers, allowing for longitudinal analysis within the dataset (e.g., tracing careers of researchers within the Facebook data).

The HackerOne dataset makes possible an overview of the general stratification of the labor market. Additionally, a closer examination of select individual programs, including Facebook's programs (by total payments) included within the HackerOne dataset (Twitter, Square, Slack, Coinbase, and Flash), is valuable (see table 4.2). Here, analysis focusing on researcher behavior within—rather than across—programs provides a more fine-grained view into labor market stratification; it allows for a consideration of the ways in which sales and earned income are distributed within individual programs. Importantly, the aggregated HackerOne data allows for an analysis of labor mobility or flexibility. The data highlights the ways in which individual researchers move between different programs.

Table 4.2 Select Programs at a Glance

Program	Facebook	Twitter	Square	Slack	Coinbase	Flash
Participating individual sellers	725	120	94	128	101	10
Total transactions (total volume of sales)	1968	274	247	302	174	21
Total payments	$3,562,684	$191,120	$131,900	$102,554.50	$97,201	$96,000
Average number of sales per seller (within program)	2.71	2.28	2.63	2.36	1.72	2.1
Average total earnings per seller (within program)	$4,914.05	$1,592.67	$1,403.19	$801.21	$962.39	$9,600
Average price per transaction	$1,810.31	$697.52	$534.01	$339.58	$558.63	$4,571.45

BLENDING THEORETICAL INVESTIGATION AND EMPIRICAL STUDY: LITERATURE REVIEW

Academic investigations into questions related to the market for software vulnerabilities stretch back over a decade. Important early work bridged information economics and computer science. Initial research coincided with several high-profile, experimental, entries into the market, including the launch of iDefense's "Vulnerability Commercial Contributor Program" (2002), the Mozilla Foundation's bug bounty program (2004), and TippingPoint's "Zero Day Initiative" (2005).[11] Early research focused on the development of stylized market models and considered questions related to the possible effectiveness of markets as a means for improving software securit.[12] Additionally, early work wrestled with new ethical questions associated with the commercialization of flaws.[13] These initial research efforts were, to varying degrees, in conversation with a larger body of research focusing on related topics in software security. This includes work related to models of vulnerability disclosure, the likelihood of vulnerability rediscovery, and depletion.[14]

More recently, efforts have focused on empirical investigations into the growing market for vulnerabilities. The launch of bug bounty programs by Google (2010), Facebook (2011), and several other well-known vendors has been accompanied by research efforts that attempt to marry early theoretical work with newly available data.[15] Empirical inquiries have, in the main, considered a set of similar questions, questioning the utility and cost-effectiveness of vulnerability markets as a mechanism for improving security.

Our work usefully contributes to the existing literature. In line with both early foundational research and more recent empirical efforts, we employ collected data to consider the utility of different market approaches. The analyzed mix of publicly available and private data, offers an expanded window into the market for vulnerabilities and fleshes out how these markets are ordered and operating in practice. At the same time, our work importantly departs from the existing literature by taking the labor market as our main object of focus. Here, a new range of questions related to stratification and diversity are foregrounded. Focusing on the labor market opens new productive avenues for conversation and future research: It suggests linkages between research on vulnerability markets and a larger body of work rooted in the tradition of economic sociology.[16] These efforts consider markets not only—or, at times, not even primarily—as engines of efficient resource allocation, but move to address pressing descriptive questions related to the contingent and historical specificity of the construction of markets.

A STRATIFIED LABOR MARKET: ANALYSIS

The labor market for vulnerabilities is highly stratified. The market is characterized by a small set of high-volume, high-earning, and mobile sellers. These top-tier sellers stand out: They are the "core" of the labor market. They sell to several different programs, make frequent sales, and garner prices that are well above average. While small in number, this core accounts for a significant share of total sales and total revenue. In contrast, the larger pool of workers is characterized by a large number of sellers that make a very small number of sales at (comparatively) very low prices. The overwhelming majority of sellers demonstrate very little mobility: They sell to only one or two different programs during their career.

In contrast to the small core, most sellers comprise a large pool of infrequent, low-earning, and immobile workers.

The labor market largely comprises infrequent sellers. The HackerOne dataset is illustrative: A small sub-set of the labor pool are high-volume sellers. The majority of sellers engage in only a very small number of sales. 52% of all sellers (339 different researchers) in the HackerOne data set have only one sale to their name; while a significant majority—78% of all sellers (507 different researchers)—have 3 or fewer total sales (see table 4.2 and table 4.3). At the margins, only 7% of sellers have made 10 or more sales.

Table 4.3 Number of Sellers with (N) Sales: Aggregate HackerOne Data.

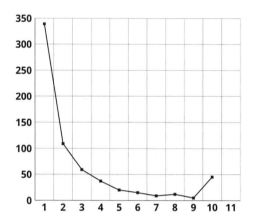

Table 4.4 Percentage of Sellers with (N) Sales: Aggregate HackerOne Dataset.

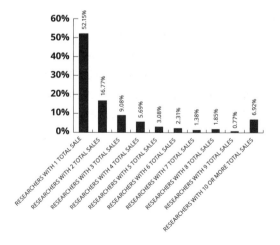

This pattern is consistent both across and within programs. Similar findings appear within Facebook's vulnerability rewards program and the five largest programs (defined by total payments) included within the HackerOne dataset (see Tables 5-10).

Table 4.5 Percentage of Sellers with N Sales: Twitter.

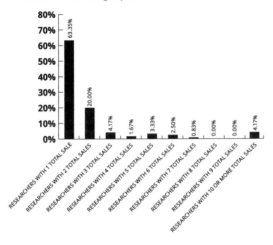

Table 4.6 Percentage of Sellers with N Sales: Square.

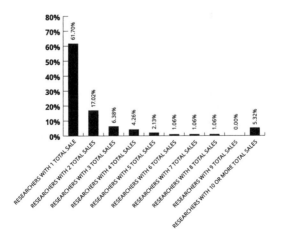

Table 4.7 Percentage of Sellers with N Sales: Slack.

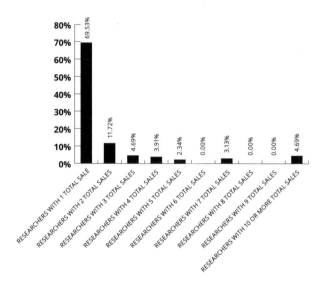

Table 4.8 Percentage of Sellers with N Sales: Coinbase.

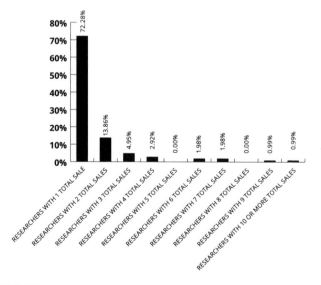

Table 4.9 Percentage of Sellers with N Sales: Flash.

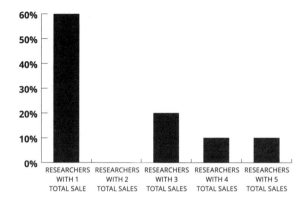

Table 4.10 Percentage of Sellers with N Sales: Facebook.

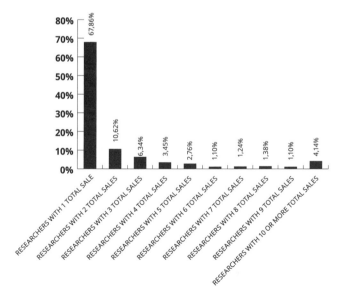

At the same time, a small number of key sellers are finding the overwhelming majority of all bugs. The top 5% of all sellers in the HackerOne dataset (defined by their total career earnings) account for 23% of all bugs sold within the 61 different sampled programs (see table 4.11). Just 32 individuals account for nearly one-fourth of all bugs sold. Moving out, the figures remain stark. The top 10% of all sellers account for 36% of all bugs that are sold; the top 30% account for 66% of total sales. Individual programs—like the broader ecosystem—are dependent on the labor of a small number of key sellers. Key suppliers also dominate the Facebook bounty program (see table 4.12). Here, the top 1% of sellers (7 individuals) account for nearly 14% of all bounties paid; the top 10% of sellers participating in Facebook's program account for 44% of all bugs sold; the top 30% account for 67.89% of bugs.

Table 4.11 Top-Tier Sellers at a Glance: HackerOne Dataset.

HackerOne Dataset	Top 1%	Top 5%	Top 10%	Top 20%	Top 30%
Number of sellers	6	32	65	130	195
Number of sales (percentage of total sales)	161 (7.4%)	508 (23.33%)	777 (35.69%)	1181 (54.25%)	1435 (65.92%)
Earnings (percentage of total payments)	$190,267 (16.12%)	$1507,515 (43.01%)	$695,744 (58.96%)	$907,714.25 (76.92%)	$1,003,954.25 (85.08%)
Average number of sales per seller (HackerOne average: 3.34)	26.83	15.88	11.95	9.08	7.36
Average career earnings per seller (HackerOne average: $1,815.41)	$31,711.17	$15,859.84	$10,703.75	$6,982.42	$5,148.48
Average number of customers	4.83	4.09	3.68	3.36	3.05
Average value per sale (HackerOne average: $542.04)	$1,181.78	$999.05	$895.42	$768.60	$699.62

Table 4.12 Top-Tier Sellers at a Glance: Facebook Dataset.

Facebook Dataset	Top 1%	Top 5%	Top 10%	Top 20%	Top 30%
Number of sellers	7	36	72	145	217
Number of sales (percentage of total sales)	274 (13.9%)	715 (36.33%)	873 (44.36%)	1158 (58.84%)	1136 (67.89%)
Earnings (percentage of total payments)	$899,184 (25.2%)	$11,784,984 (50.10%)	$2,248,384 (63.11%)	$2,731,884 (76.96%)	$3,014,034 (84,6%)
Average number of sales per seller (Facebook average: 2.71)	39.14	19.86	12.13	7.99	6.15
Average career earnings per seller (Facebook average: $4,914.04)	$128,455	$49,583	$31,228	$19,104	$13,890
Average value per sale (Facebook average: $1,810.31)	$3,281.69	$2,496.48	$2,575.47	$2,359.14	$2,2256.01

A small number of sellers earn most money paid by bug bounty programs (see table 4.11). The top 1% of sellers in the HackerOne dataset earn 16.12% of all money paid (six sellers earning $190,267 between them); the top 5% earn 43% of all payments; and the top 30% earn the overwhelming majority of payments offered—accounting for 85% of all money paid by the 61 different programs in the dataset. Facebook's figures follow a similar trajectory. Here again, a small collection of sellers are earning a very large share of the pie: The top 1% of sellers participating in Facebook's bounty program have earned 25% of all money paid (seven sellers netting $899,184). The top 5% of sellers participating in Facebook's program earn half of all money paid for bounties ($1,784,984); the top 30% earn 84.6% of the total Facebook payments.

The small core of sellers sell much more often than most sellers (see table 4.11). The top 1% of sellers in the HackerOne dataset average 26.83 sales in a career, while the average for the dataset is just over three sales total. Facebook shows an even greater divergence, the top 1% average 39.14 sales, while the program average is just over 2.5 sales. The 1% are not just frequent sellers, however. They are also earning substantially greater returns per-bug: The top 1% of sellers in the HackerOne dataset net $1,181.78 per-sale (better than the average of $542.04 per-transaction); the top 1% in the Facebook data earn $3,281.69 per-sale (against an average of $1,810.31).

Finally, while a small group of sellers appear to be catholic in their sales—selling to different outlets—most sellers demonstrate little mobility of flexibility. The majority of sellers only sell or one outlet or program (See Table 13). Drawing from the HackerOne data set, 65% of all sellers (423 different sellers) only sell to one particular program; while 89% of all sellers (576 total sellers) only sell to three or fewer different programs. At the margins, sellers participating in a large number of programs are exceedingly rare.

Table 4.13 Percentage of Sellers Participating in N Different Programs: HackerOne Dataset.

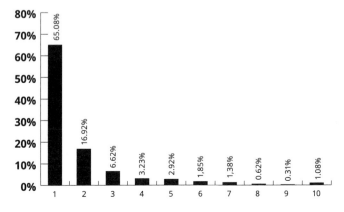

The picture that emerges is clear and unambiguous: The labor market is highly stratified. The labor pool is characterized by a minority of high-volume, flexible, and lucrative workers and a majority of low-volume, immobile, and low-earning workers. The core accounts for a disproportionate share of all bugs that are sold and, at the same time, a large share of total revenue generated through bug sales. The cleavage between high-volume and lucrative workers and low-volume workers returning low-value bugs is consistent both horizontally across the market, as represented by the aggregated collection of 61 different bug bounty programs included within the HackerOne dataset, and more narrowly, within the highlighted six individual programs (identified in table 4.4).

The market for vulnerabilities is interesting. It is at odds with a simplified model of mass production. Productive workers do not appear to be churning out low-cost goods at a high volume. At the same time, the market for vulnerabilities is at odds with a simplified "boutique" or artisanal market. Markets for luxury goods and highly specialized goods, for example, are often defined by a small number of sellers providing quite expensive goods in low volume. Here, however, we see that high-volume sellers are also returning the largest average price per-bug. Several possible explanations might account for this, including learning effects (as particular workers devote increasing time to discovering vulnerabilities, their skills might likewise improve and lead to the discovery of more high-value vulnerabilities), different levels of skills (some sellers are simply more talented than others) and, most significantly, different levels of effort (the high-volume core might be, in effect, professionals, while the rest are hobbyists working in spare moments).

IMPLICATIONS: REVISITING BUG BOUNTY PROGRAM DESIGN

Different firms are experimenting with different ways of configuring bug bounty programs. As noted above, bounty programs can—and often do—take different forms. Currently, bounty programs are not yet institutionalized: They have not coalesced around a normalized and accepted model of operation.[17] How, then, can the observation of significant stratification inform the operation and design of bug bounty programs?

The stratification of labor suggests that bug bounty programs should work to attract and engage the small number of high-volume, high-earning, and mobile sellers. Indeed, firms are already experimenting with efforts to entice key talent. Recently, Google launched a new "Vulnerability Research Grants" program to complement its various more straightforward bug bounty programs. The program offers small grants—the maximum amount offered is $3,133.70—to support the most frequent and most successful researchers participating in Google's reward programs, as well as other invited experts. These grants are given upfront as an encouragement to examine Google owned properties: The grant is paid regardless if the researcher uncovers a new flaw or not.[18] Offering these sort of open-ended grants is one way in which firms can hope to attract top-tier researchers/sellers to consider their program. Other possible ways of catering to key segments of the labor market are possible. For example, offering escalating prices, where prices increase with successive valid submissions, could encourage desired workers to focus their efforts on a particular program, rather than "straying" to identify and sell flaws within a different program. Here, a premium paid based on past performance can seek to encourage sellers to commit to one particular program. These, and other approaches to ensnaring core workers, appear to be justified: If the most productive sellers are also the most mobile, investing in ways to attract and retain key talent is wise. The wisdom of the crowd might be trumped by expertise.

Stratification also suggests that creating programs containing some barriers to entry may be beneficial and carry little downside. Infrequent sellers contribute a small fraction of total sales and small amount of total revenue. Programs that cater exclusively to frequent sellers, then, risk losing proportionally very little value. Closed and invitation-only programs, where only trusted or vetted sellers can participate, are understandably attractive. Open programs that accept submissions from anyone are plagued by high transaction costs. Vetting and responding to the flood of submissions that accompany an open program is costly. Sorting the few new valid issues from the deafening noise of submitted trivial bugs, non-issues, and duplicates is time consuming and can drain resources. Published figures suggest that invalid and duplicate submissions greatly outnumber valid submissions for open programs. For example, Google, Facebook, and GitHub wind up being eligible for a payment between 4-5% of all submissions.[19] That is a lot of noise.

A cyclical approach that has recurring periods of open participation, followed by a transition into periods where sales are only accepted from invited sellers (essentially rotating between operating "open" and "closed" programs), can allow firms to periodically spot new talent and refresh its pool of trusted sellers, while also limiting transaction costs associated with open programs.

Our observations are not only useful to program designers thinking about how best to tinker with their bounty programs. Indeed, recognizing the significant contributions made by a small subset of the labor market is also important for labor. A small number of workers are, more or less, indispensable to the ongoing success of bug bounty programs. These workers hold significant power—their exit from the marketplace would significantly reduce the volume and quality of bugs disclosed. Markets are, of course, not only a particular way of organizing economic activity; they are also most certainly sites where power is alive. The small productive core is a significant player in the market for bugs; they potentially have the power to help shape the outlines of the market (deciding on terms and acceptable practices). How, or if, they may wield this power, is currently an open question.

IMPLICATIONS: DISRUPTING THE OFFENSIVE MARKET

The stratification of the labor market can also help assess different approaches designed to disrupt the offensive acquisition, stockpile, and use of zero-day vulnerabilities. Previously unknown and undisclosed vulnerabilities, what are known as zero-days or 0-days, are a "dual use" good: They can be used to craft new malicious attacks and exploits (offense), or they can be fixed through patches and updates (defense). Limiting the use of zero-days by malicious actors is a significant challenge: For intelligence agencies, militaries interested in developing cyber capabilities, and criminals, zero-days are a valuable resource. Attacks and exploits that take advantage of a previously unknown and undisclosed flaw can be very difficult to detect or prevent.

Bug bounty programs are not the only outlets purchasing vulnerabilities. In effect, competing "offensive" and "defensive" markets have been created. The offensive market is defined by nation states looking to develop sophisticated exploits and attacks in the service of espionage and sabotage, criminals looking to develop intrusions for profit, and brokers that serve as middle-men between relevant parties.[20] The key difference between these two markets relates to how—or *if*—the newly discovered vulnerability is disclosed to the impacted vendor and patched. In the defensive market, bug bounty programs work to patch and fix discovered flaws. In contrast, the "offensive market" is characterized by non-disclosure. Here, purchased flaws are not disclosed to the relevant vendor, but rather are kept secret for later use as part of an exploit or attack.

Although the analyzed datasets focus explicitly on what can be categorized as the "defensive market" for vulnerabilities, the analysis offers limited, though useful, insights into the viability of different strategies designed to counter or control the acquisition, stockpile, and exploitation of previously unknown and undisclosed vulnerabilities by malicious actors. To be clear: Bug bounty programs differ significantly from the offensive market. Bug bounty programs are dealing with different actors (with different resources and different motivations), and often different sorts of flaws. It is unwise to directly compare the two markets. Several different strategies for countering the proliferation of the offensive market in zero-days have been suggested: Dan Geer, during his keynote at BlackHat, suggested that the U.S. government, in effect, corner the market for zero-days by offering to out-bid all other offers for newly discovered flaws.[21] Elsewhere, the viability of using export controls under the Wassenaar Arrangement to limit the sale of "intrusion software" and "intrusion software technology", which may or may not contain new zero-day bugs, has also been debated (and continues to be debated at length).[22]

The composition of the labor market suggests that cultivating and focusing on to the small core subset of researchers that are highly productive and mobile is a useful approach. Vulnerabilities, as Geer concedes, may not be sparse, but dense.[23] Creating what is, in effect, a fixed market for software in which the vulnerability count is dense, would not lead to improved security. Rather, it would lead to spiraling prices for new flaws and an ever-increasing supply of newly discovered flaws (without appreciable improvements in security or the declining availability of yet-to-be discovered flaws). So long as the question of relative sparseness or density of vulnerabilities remains open, and is often dependent upon the complexity of the software itself and the diligence by which the vendor has worked to eliminate bugs themselves, looking to find ways to accommodate core researchers is a prudent alternative approach. Talented researchers with the skills to identify flaws across a range of different targets are a scarce resource; while the available stock of flaws may be quite large—the number of individuals available to discover significant flaws in complex, well-secured software is somewhat small. To be clear, labor is a key driver of the supply of vulnerability. Although it is reasonable to assume that there is a very large pool of researchers available to discover flaws, the pool that can regularly discover serious flaws appears to be significantly smaller. Ensuring, then, that those with the resources to identify new, serious, flaws with some regularity are encouraged to disclose these flaws in a manner that ensures that they will be fixed, rather than sell or disclose them to offensive actors that are devoted to non-disclosure, is vital. A course of embracing these sorts of researchers makes sense and can take many forms, from offering interesting work with organizations devoted to improving security to providing significant awards (grants and payments) for open-ended research.

Export controls touching on zero-days are problematic for several reasons. However, simply viewed through the lens of the labor market, export controls appear ill-suited to the problem at hand. Export controls, if not narrowly tailored, can create significant liability for many software companies and others engaged in legitimate and beneficial activity. As they engage in the day-to-day practice of basic testing and review, these companies could, depending on how the controls were defined, find themselves at odds with an export control regime. Yet, this same regime would likely do little to stop the ad hoc sale of zero-days by a small number of talented individuals. Sales conducted outside the regular channels of commerce—black-market sales—are already informal and below the radar. They would likely continue to remain so even if strong export controls were to be introduced. Here, working to create incentives to encourage researchers to disclose to vendors, rather than creating administrative sanctions that are likely to be evaded by those that are in fact targeted (while imposing significant counter-productive burdens elsewhere) has obvious appeal.

CONCLUSION: FUTURE RESEARCH QUESTIONS

We open several possible additional avenues for inquiry. The examination of the labor market provides a useful elaboration of how the market for bugs is developing in practice. Yet, it is important to note that the market is very much still developing. The collected data in many ways extends beyond the scope of prior research efforts (gathering public and private data over a large set of programs), but the programs studied are still in their relatively early stages of life. In this regard, this chapter is a snapshot in time. Some of the observations regarding stratification could possibly be transitory features. As programs mature, perhaps the composition of the labor market will likewise continue to evolve. To this end, adding additional datasets, both public and private, can help refine our observations to a degree. But most importantly, collecting data on an ongoing basis as programs continue to evolve is key. Doing so can help to sort out whether or not stratification is an early growing pain associated with the birth of a relatively new market or a consistent feature of the market for bugs.

Additionally, while we provide a useful overview of the composition of the labor market, much about how and why workers go about discovering and selling vulnerabilities remains unknown. A qualitative study focusing on how researchers understand their labor, and how they decide to sell their findings rather than releasing the information through full disclosure or other means, is needed. One of the most striking things about the market for bugs is its novelty: For years, researchers identified and reported bugs with little expectation of receiving a reward. The movement to view this activity as work and seek (and receive) compensation as such is a complicated and important story. Markets are not inevitable: They are always actively created. A historical investigation into the creation of the market for flaws would usefully contextualize our findings: It would provide a detailed explanation of how we arrived at the contingent present.

Another important research thread that could extend this work relates to the *offensive* market. Looking to see if labor in the offensive market— defined as sales where the discovered vulnerability will not be disclosed but will be used (or kept available for use) to craft a malicious exploit or attack—mimics or departs from the observed trends captured here would be exceedingly helpful. A comparable study of the offensive market is most likely not possible: Most offensive sales are under the radar and large-scale data collection, as a result, is all but impossible. Understanding more clearly how the offensive and defensive markets are similar and different would greatly assist in refining thoughts about how to disrupt or otherwise control the offensive market. A complementary study of the offensive marker could help aid the creation of a model of the vulnerability ecosystem. Using system dynamics to understand points of control can assist in both refining the design of bug bounty programs and considering how to target and disrupt the offensive market.[24]

For decades, a small collection of scholars explored first the possibility of designing and creating a market for flaws and, later, began to examine the reality of such a market. While we are beginning to have a better sense of the contours of this market, as always, significant work remains.

NOTES

1. Research partially funded by a research grant from Facebook.

2. Joan E. Rigdon "Netscape Is Putting a Price on the Head Of Any Big Bug Found in Web Browser ". The Wall St. Journal. Oct. 11, 1995.

3. Ibid.

4. Ibid.

5. United Airlines. "United Airlines Bug Bounty Program." Available Online: <https://www.united.com/web/en- US/content/Contact/bugbounty. aspx>.

6. For a partial listing of programs, see: HackerOne. Available Online: <https://hackerone.com/>; BugCrowd. "Reward Programs." Available Online: <https://bugcrowd.com/programs/reward>; Bugsheet. "Bug Bounties & Disclosure Programs." Available Online: <http://bugsheet. com/directory>.

7. Two different researchers (Sergey Glazunov and "PinkiePie") participating in Google's Chromium Rewards Program earned $60,000 for a submission. A single researcher (anonymized id# 655637267804787) participating in Facebook's program earned $183,000 across 24 different payouts between May. 2013 and February. 2015.

8. See, Cory Scott. "Our Private Bug Bounty Program: Reducing Vulnerabilities by Leveraging Expert Crowds." LinkedIn Engineering. June 17, 2015. Available Online: <https://engineering.linkedin.com/security/ our-private-bug- bounty-program-reducing-vulnerabilities-leveraging- expert-crowds>.

9. See, Microsoft. "Internet Explorer 11 Preview Program Guidelines." Microsoft Security TechCenter. Sept. 2013. Available Online: <https:// technet.microsoft.com/en-us/security/dn425054.aspx>.

10. However, included individual programs rarely operated during the entirety of the sampled period; rather, individual programs operated for some shorter period of time, joining after July, 2013 or, in some cases,

ceasing operation before October, 2015.

11. Mirko Zorz. "Interview with Sunil James, Manager of iDEFENSE's Vulnerability Contributor Program." HelpNetSecurity. April 1, 2003. Available Online: <https://www.helpnetsecurity.com/2003/04/01/ interview-with- sunil-james-manager-of-idefenses-vulnerability-contributor-program/>; Mozilla. "Mozilla Foundation Announces Security Bug Bounty Program." Mozilla Press Center. Aug. 2, 2004. Available Online: <https://blog.mozilla.org/press/2004/08/mozilla-foundation-announces-security-bug-bounty-program/>; David Endler. "Remembering Five Years of Vulnerability Markets." DVLabs. July 26, 2007. Available Online: <http://dvlabs.tippingpoint.com/blog/2007/07/26/ remembering-five-years-of-vulnerability-markets>.

12. See, Stuart Schechter. "How to Buy Better Testing: Using Competition to Get the Most Security and Robustness for Your Dollar." Infrastructure Security Conference. 2002. Available Online:

13. <http://research.microsoft.com/pubs/192265/isc2002.pdf>; Andy Ozmet. "Bug Auctions: Vulnerability Markets Reconsidered." Workshop on Economics and Information Security. 2004. Available Online: <https:// www.dtc.umn.edu/weis2004/ozment.pdf>; Karthik Kannan and Rahul Telang. "An Economic Analysis of Market for Software Vulnerabilities." Workshop on Economics and Information Security. 2004. Available Online: < https://www.dtc.umn.edu/weis2004/kannan-telang.pdf>; Michael Sutton and Frank Nagle. "Emerging Economic Models for Vulnerability Research." Workshop on Economics and Information Security. 2006. Available Online: <http://www.econinfosec.org/archive/ weis2006/docs/ 17.pdf>. For example, see: David McKinney. "Vulnerability Bazaar." IEEE Security and Privacy. 5.6 (2007): 69-73.

14. See, Ashish Arora and Rahul Telang. "Economics of Software Vulnerability Disclosure." IEEE Security and Privacy. 3.1 (2005): 20-25; Eric Rescorla. "Is Finding Secuirty Holes a Good Idea?" IEEE Security and

Privacy. 3.1 (2005) 14-19; Andy Ozmet "The Likelihood of Vulnerability Rediscovery and the Social Utility of Vulnerability Hunting." Workshop on Economics and Information Security. 2005. Available Online: <http://infosecon.net/workshop/pdf/10.pdf>; Andy Ozmet and Stuart Schechter. "Milk or Wine: Does Software Security Improve with Age?" Proceedings of the 15th conference on USENIX Security (2006) Hasan Cavusoglu, Huseyin Cavusoglu, and Srinivasan Raghunathan. "Efficiency of Vulnerability Disclosure Mechanisms to Disseminate Vulnerability Knowledge." IEEE Transactions on Software Engineering. 33.3 (March 2007): 171-185; Andy Ozmet. "Improving Vulnerability Discovery Models." Proceedings of the 2007 ACM Workshop on Quality of Protection (2007): 6-11.

15. See, Google. "Encouraging More Chromium Security Research." Google Online Security Blog. Jan. 28, 2010. Available Online: <http://blog. chromium.org/2010/01/encouraging-more-chromium-security.html>; Joe Sullivan. "Updates to the Bug Bounty Program." Facebook. Aug. 29, 2011. Available Online: <https://www.facebook.com/notes/facebook-security/updates-to-the-bug-bounty-program/10150270651335766/>; 1.Stefan Frei. The Known Unknowns: Empirical Analysis of the Publicly Unknown Security Vulnerabilities. Analyst Brief. NSS Labs. 2013 Available Online: <https://library.nsslabs.com/sites/default/files/public- report/ files/The%20Known%20Unknowns_1.pdf>; Matthew Finifter, Devdatta Akhawe, and David Wagner. "An Empirical Study of Vulnerability Reward Programs." 22nd USENIX Security Symposium. 2013. Available Online: <https://www.eecs.berkeley.edu/~daw/papers/vrp-use13.pdf>; Mingyi Zhao, Jens Grossklags, and Peng Liu. "An Empirical Study of Web Vulnerability Discovery Ecosystems." Proceedings of the 22nd ACM SIGSAC Conference on Computer and Communications Security (2015): 1105-117.

16. See, Mark Granovetter and Richard Swedberg (eds.) The Sociology

of Economic Life. 2nd Edition. Boulder, CO: Westview, 2001; Richard Swedberg. Principles of Economic Sociology. 2001 Princeton: Princeton UP, 2003.

17. the heterogeneity of approaches may reflect not only the still relative novelty of paying for discovered flaws, but also the different purposes that motivate programs.

18. Google. "Vulnerability Research Grants." Available Online: <https://www.google.com/about/appsecurity/research-grants/>.

19. See, HackerOne. "Improving Signal Over 10,000 Bugs." HackerOne Blog. June 6, 2015. Available Online: <https://hackerone.com/blog/improving-signal-over-10000-bugs>.

20. See, Andy Greenberg, "Meet the Hackers Who Sell Spies the Tools to Crack your PC (And Get Paid Six-Figure Fees)," Forbes, March 21, 2012; Bruce Schneier, "The Vulnerabilities Market and the Future of Security." Forbes. May 30, 2012; Ryan Gallagher, "The Secretive Hacker Market for Software Flaws," Slate, January 16, 2013; Tom Simonite, "Welcome to the Malware-Industrial Complex," MIT Technology Review, February 13, 2013.

21. Dan Geer. "Cybersecurity as Realpolitik." BlackHat. Delivery Draft. Aug. 6, 2014. Available Online: <http://geer.tinho.net/geer.blackhat.6viii14.txt>.

22. See, Mailyn Fidler. "Proposed U.S. Export Controls: Implications for Zero-Day Vulnerabilities and Exploits." Lawfre. June 10, 2015. Available Online: <https://www.lawfareblog.com/proposed-us-export-controls-implications- zero-day-vulnerabilities-and-exploits>.

23. Geer. "Cybersecurity as Realpolitik."

24. Co-authors Moussouris and Siegel have worked on a preliminary version of such an approach. Katie Moussouris and Michael Siegel. "The Wolves of Vuln Street: The First System Dynamic Model of the 0Day Market." RSA. April 2015. Available Online: < https://www.rsaconference.com/writable/presentations/file_upload/ht-t08-the- wolves-of-vuln-street-the-1st-dynamic-systems-model-of-the-0day-market_final.pdf>

SECTION II

ARCHITECTURE

CHAPTER 5

Balancing Disruption and Deployability in the CHERI Instruction-Set Architecture (ISA)

Robert N. M. Watson, Peter G. Neumann, and Simon W. Moore

INTRODUCTION

For over two and a half decades, dating to the first widespread commercial deployment of the Internet, commodity processor architectures have failed to provide robust and secure foundations for communication and commerce. This is largely part due to the omission of architectural features allowing efficient implementation of the *Principle of Least Privilege*, which dictates that software runs only with the rights it requires to operate.[1,2] Without this support, the impact of inevitable vulnerabilities is multiplied as successful attackers gain easy access to unnecessary rights—and often, *all* rights— in software systems.

This omission is most visible at two levels of software abstraction: low-level code execution occurs with an excess of rights facilitating easy attacker manipulation, and higher-level encapsulation goals are poorly supported due to inefficiency.

First, virtual addresses and C-language pointers (the references through which code and data are accessed) are implemented using unprotected and unconstrained integers, and so are frequently exploited in attacks that escalate to arbitrary code execution. Second, compartmentalized software designs that constrain higher-level aspects of program behavior, mitigating lower-level vulnerabilities, scale poorly with current Memory Management Units (MMUs)—imposing a high penalty on use. Together, these gaps cause our most security-critical C-language software (e.g., operating systems, web browsers, and language runtimes) to offer an asymmetric advantage to attackers in which the defender must make no mistakes, and the attacker can exploit a single mistake to gain total control. This is a dangerous status quo for contemporary network-connected ecosystems, whether mobile devices, embedded systems, or servers.

Supported by DARPA's CRASH research program, the CTSRD Project has sought to address this concern through a clean-slate re-design project to create the *Capability Hardware Enhanced RISC Instructions (CHERI)* Instruction-Set Architecture (ISA), processor prototype, and software stack. Our goal has been to address these two omissions from the ground up, providing strong architectural support for the principle of least privilege, offering new innate protections that naturally mitigate inevitable software bugs. We have drawn on over four decades of computer-security research dating to early systems and security projects,[3,4,5,6,7,8] hardware-software co-design methodology, principled system design[9] and recent insights into techniques for hybridizing capability-system approaches with OS and programming-language design.[10,11] The surprising result has been a hardware-software approach that disrupts key tools used by attackers while continuing to support current software structures, and can be adopted within contemporary system designs.

Through CHERI, we seek to insert secure computer-architecture foundations beneath today's system software stacks with a minimum of disruption, while bringing fundamental improvements in robustness and security made efficient only through new hardware primitives. Key technical contributions include; the hybridization of a strong capability-system approach with a conventional MMU-based RISC design, permitting highly compatible integration with current OS and application designs; convergence of the C-language pointer semantics with capabilities; new programming models supporting fine-grained compartmentalization within conventional processes; and highly efficient architectural and micro-architectural approaches to memory protection. Each of these has been validated through full-stack hardware and software prototypes required to evaluate security, compatibility, and performance impact. In this chapter, we consider CHERI from four perspectives:

- **Methodology and philosophy of approach:** We describe the problem
  we seek to address, our motivating use cases, our key technical
  objectives, and our methodology and philosophy of approach grounded
  in hardware-software co-design.

- **CHERI architecture and software:** We present the key technical aspects
  of the work, including our goals of hybridizing a *capability-system model*
  with MMU-based operating systems (OSes) and the C programming
  language, and introduce our approach to fine-grained memory protection
  and scalable compartmentalization.

- **Research and development cycle:** We review the development of the
  key technical elements in CHERI, and the iterative cycle through six major
  instruction-set revisions over a (thus far) 7-year timeline.

- **Potential for impact:** We conclude by considering lessons learned,
  as well as the potential opportunities for impact within the current
  system designs. We believe that these lessons apply broadly to other
  work on architectural security. We also consider next directions for
  the CTSRD project as we enter a further two years of research and
  development on CHERI.

PROBLEM, OPPORTUNITY, GOALS, AND APPROACH

Despite half a century of research into computer systems and software
design, it is clear that security remains a challenging problem—and an
increasingly critical problem as computer-based technologies find ever
expanding deployment in all aspects of contemporary life, from mobile
communications devices to self-driving cars and medical equipment. There
are many contributing factors to this problem, including the asymmetric
advantage held by attackers over defenders (which causes minor engineering
mistakes to lead to undue vulnerability), the difficulties in assessing—
and comparing—the security of systems, and market pressures to deliver
products sooner rather than in a well-engineered state. Perhaps most

influential is the pressure for backward compatibility, required to allow current software stacks to run undisturbed on new generations of systems, as well as to move seamlessly across devices (and vendors), locking in least-common-denominator design choices, and preventing the deployment of more disruptive improvements that serve security.

Both the current state and, worse, the current direction supports a view that today's computer architectures (which underlie phenomenal growth of computer-based systems) are fundamentally "unfit for purpose": Rather than providing a firm foundation on which higher-level technologies can rest, they undermine attempts to build secure systems that depend on them. To address this problem, we require designs that mitigate, rather than emphasize, inevitable bugs, and offer strong and well-understood protections on which larger-scale systems can be built. Such technologies can be successful only if transparently adoptable by end users—and, ideally, many software developers. On the other hand, the resulting improvement must be dramatic to justify adopting substantive architectural change, and while catering to short-term problems, must also offer a longer-term architectural vision to support further benefit as greater investment is made.

Opportunity

Despite the challenge this problem represents, there are also reasons for hope:

- Improvements in physical fabrication technologies have allowed more complex computer architectures to be supported, while sustaining performance growth and reducing energy use. This creates the opportunity to invest greater computational resources in security at lower incremental cost.

- The desire to bring the benefits of electronic commerce to devices ranging from computer servers to phones and watches has created a strong financial incentive for computer vendors to improve security. This creates not just compliance obligations, but also the significant exposure to potential direct (and sometimes existential) financial loss for companies.

- There is increasing appetite for mitigation techniques on existing hardware from stack canaries and Address Space Layout Randomization (ASLR) that are transparent to software, but impact memory usage[12] through to process-based compartmentalization that is disruptive software:[13,14,15,16] Function calls become Inter-Process Communication (IPC) and additional virtual address spaces impact MMU efficiency. These techniques increasingly impact on performance on current architectures, but, due to a reliance on randomization, also increase in-field non-determinism, which affects maintainability. Recovering lost performance, reducing complexity, and restoring software determinism are all potential benefits to better architectural protection.

- Recent modest changes in architecture, such as adopting the dual-ISA world of Intel x86 on the desktop and ARM on mobile devices (motivated by diverse energy and performance requirements), and similarly the transition from 32-bit to 64-bit, have acclimated software developers and product vendors to the need for minor disruption, maintaining multi-architecture software stacks. They have accepted and benefited from minor changes required to better abstract pointers (by reducing confusion with integers to span 32-bit and 64-bit ISAs), and supporting legacy environments (such as 32-bit compatibility 64-bit operating systems). Where further disruption can be aligned with these existing patterns, it may be similarly tolerated as an accepted and well-understood set of costs.

- Multiple decades of system design evolution have led to a strong consensus on how to integrate current architectural security features (such as MMUs) into software stacks, and similarly on software structures, such as operating systems, programming languages/compilers, and applications. While that baseline omits many critical security functions, its existence means that new security technologies could be consistently applied (and incrementally composed) across multiple architectures and software structures.

- While security principles (such as the Principle of Least Privilege) have been known for decades, there is recent new understanding arising out of the security-research community about how to deploy those principles incrementally by hybridizing those approaches with the current system and language designs. This creates the opportunity to consistently introduce disruptive new security features incrementally within current designs, as well as to deploy use of these principles at multiple levels of abstraction, offering strong mitigation potential against as-yet undiscovered classes of vulnerabilities and exploit techniques.

- Developments in formal methodology relating to automation and large-scale application of theorem-proving tools give us the confidence to approach more tightly integrated security designs—but also dramatically improve the efficiency of a small team working in the complex arena of hardware-software co-design.

Technical Objectives and Implementation

From a purely technical perspective, the aim of the CHERI project is to introduce architectural support for the principle of least privilege to encourage its direct utilization at all levels of the software stack. Current computer architectures make this extremely difficult as they impose substantial performance, robustness, compatibility, and complexity penalties in doing so—strongly disincentivizing adoption of such approaches in off-the-shelf system designs despite the potential to mitigate broad classes of known (and also as-yet unknown) vulnerability classes.

Low-level Trusted Computing Bases (TCBs) are typically written in memory—unsafe languages such as C and C++, which do not offer compatible or performant protection against pointer corruption, buffer overflows, or other vulnerabilities arising from that lack of safety not offered directly by the architecture. Similarly, software compartmentalization, which mitigates both low-level vulnerabilities grounded in program representation and high-level application vulnerabilities grounded in logical bugs, is poorly supported by current MMUs, leading to substantial (crippling) loss of programmability and performance as the technique is deployed.

CHERI also seeks to minimize disruption of current designs, to support incremental adoption with significant transparency. Ideally, CHERI could be "slid under" current software stacks (such as Apple's iOS ecosystem, or Google's Android ecosystem) allowing non-disruptive introduction, yet providing an immediate reward for adoption. This requires supporting current low-level languages such as C and C++ more safely, but also cleanly supplementing MMU-based programming models required to support current operating systems and virtualization techniques. These goals have directed many key design choices in the CHERI-MIPS ISA.

Hardware-Software Co-Design Methodology

Changes to the hardware-software interface are necessarily disruptive. The ISA is a "narrow waist" abstraction that allows hardware designers to pursue sophisticated optimization strategies (e.g., to exploit parallelism), while software developers can simultaneously depend on a (largely unchanging) interface to build successively larger and more complex artifacts. Stable ISAs have allowed the development of operating systems and application suites that can operate successfully on a range of systems, and that outlast the specific platforms on which they were developed. This structure is inherently predisposed to non-disruption, as platforms that incur lower adoption costs will be preferred to those that have higher costs. However, substantive changes in underlying program representation, such as to support greater memory safety or fine-grained compartmentalization required to dramatically improve security, require changes to the ISA. Therefore, we aimed to:

- Iteratively explore disruptions to the ISA, projecting changes both up into the software stack including operating systems, compilers, and applications (to assess the impact on compatibility and security), as well as down into micro-architecture (assessing the impact on performance and viability).

- Start with a conventional and well-established 64-bit RISC ISA, rather than re-invent the wheel for general-purpose computation, to benefit from existing mature software stacks that could then be used for validation.

- Employ realistic open-source software artifacts, including the FreeBSD operating system, Clang/LLVM compiler suite, and an open-source application corpus, to ensure that experiments were run with suitable scale, complexity, performance footprint, and idiomatic use.

- Employ realistic hardware artifacts, developing multiple FPGA soft-core based processor prototypes able to validate key questions about integration with components such as the pipeline and memory hierarchy, as well as support performance validation for the full stack including software.

- Employ formal models of the ISA, to provide an executable gold model for testing, from which tests can be automatically generated, and against which theorem proving can be deployed to ensure that key properties relied on for software security actually hold.

- Pursue the hypothesis that historic capability-system models, designed to support implementation of the principle of least privilege, can be hybridized with current software approaches to support compatible and efficient fine-grained memory protection and compartmentalization.
- Take an initially purist capability-system view, incrementally adapting that model towards one able to efficiently yet safely support the majority of current software use. This approach allowed us to retain well-understood monotonicity and encapsulation properties, as well as pursue capturing notions of explicit valid provenance enforcement and intentional use not well characterized in prior capability-system work. Appropriately but uncompromisingly represented, these properties have proven to align remarkably well with current OS and language designs.
- Aim specifically to cleanly compose with conventional MMUs and MMU-based software designs by providing an in-address-space protection model, as well as be able to represent C-language pointers as capabilities.
- Support incremental adoption, allowing significant benefit to be gained through modest efforts (such as re-compiling) for selected software, while not disrupting binary-compatible execution of legacy applications. Likewise, support incremental deployment of more disruptive compartmentalization into key software through greater, but selective, investment.
- Provide primitives that offer an immediate short-term benefit (e.g., invulnerability to common pointer-based exploit techniques, scalable sandboxing of libraries in key software packages), while also offering a longer-term vision for future software structure grounded in strong memory safety and fine-grained compartmentalization.

CHERI ARCHITECTURE AND SOFTWARE

In this section, we briefly describe the CHERI-MIPS ISA and its use in protecting pointers in generated code, as well as software compartmentalization. Several software models can be layered over CHERI, including hybrid operating systems that employ the MMU for address-space separation, and CHERI for compiler-managed, capability-based in-address-space memory protection (see figure 5.1). This description is roughly synchronized to CHERI ISAv6 as published in late 2017.[17] While we have prototyped CHERI with respect to 64-bit MIPS, the approach described in this section implements a more general protection model potentially applicable to a range of ISAs including Intel x86, RISC-V, and ARM.

The CHERI-MIPS Instruction-Set Architecture (ISA)

In CHERI-MIPS, pointers may be represented as either integer virtual addresses or *tagged capabilities* that atomically combine virtual addresses with additional protection metadata. CHERI-MIPS supplements the general-purpose 64-bit MIPS register file with a *capability register file* that holds a set of 256-bit *capability registers* (see figure 5.2). A later 128-bit in-memory representation employs bounds-compression techniques to reduce the memory overhead, trading off reduced bounds precision on large allocations against pointer size. *Capability instructions* allow 256-bit capabilities to be loaded and stored from memory, inspected and manipulated (e.g., to get or set the bounds), dereferenced via load and store instructions, and to be the target of jump and branch instructions. *Capability permissions* control what operations can be performed via a capability—for example, restricting the use of a pointer for load, store, or execution. Access via a capability is subject to *tag* validity, relocation relative to its *base* and *offset*, and bounds checking relative to its base and *length*.

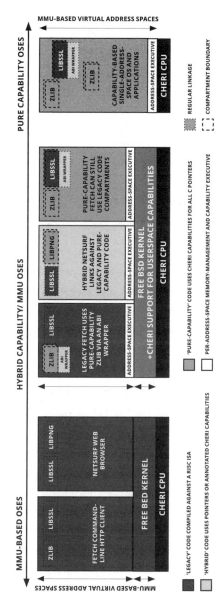

Figure 5.1 CHERI supports a spectrum of hardware-software architectures.

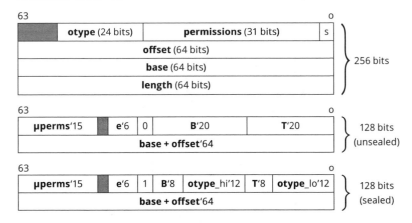

Figure 5.2 CHERI-256 and CHERI-128 memory representations for capabilities.

Most capability registers are available to compiler and Application Binary Interfaces (ABIs), but certain registers are reserved in the ISA. The program-counter capability (PCC) extends the MIPS program counter (PC) to constrain code execution, and the exception program counter (EPC) is extended to be the exception program-counter capability (EPCC). For compatibility, the default data capability (DDC) interposes on (or blocks) conventional MIPS loads and stores. Two special capabilities are available to exception handlers: the kernel code capability (KCC) and kernel data capability (KDC).

Capability instructions employ *guarded manipulation* to implement *monotonicity*: instructions cannot increase the rights associated with a capability. *Tagged memory* associates a 1-bit tag with each physical memory location that can hold a capability, indicating the presence of a valid capability. Stores to, and loads from, capabilities in memory are atomic with their tags, allowing safe concurrent access from multiple cores. Tags enforce the *integrity* and valid *provenance* of a pointer by ensuring that only values derived from a valid pointer, via valid transformations, can be dereferenced. The memory accessible to executing code is the transitive closure of capabilities in its capability register file, and any capabilities reachable through those capabilities. At reset, full capabilities are granted to the boot environment, from which point they may be *delegated* and *refined* from firmware to OS kernel, OS kernel to userspace, and then within user compartments. Capability-based compartmentalization is provided by the encapsulation instructions that operate on *sealed* capabilities.

Several architectural features are added to support software compartmentalization. *Sealed capabilities* allow capabilities to be made immutable and non-dereferenceable, allowing them to support software-defined object implementations while retaining strong integrity and provenance properties. *Object types* in capabilities allow sets of capabilities to be linked in a non-forgeable manner, supporting more complex structures such as linked code and data capabilities implementing objects. A *hardware-accelerated object invocation* exception combines a set of fast-path checks with a software-defined exception handler to implement domain switching. *Fast register clearing instructions* allow the register file to be quickly cleared when transitioning domains, further improving domain-crossing performance.

The CHERI FPGA soft-core processor implements a capability register file, capability instructions, and tagged physical memory. Detailed descriptions of the prototype may be found in our published papers and technical reports.[18,19,20,21,22]

Protecting Pointers with CHERI

Simply by recompiling C-code, all data pointers and code pointers are represented as capabilities. Despite the promiscuous use of pointers in C-code, the vast majority of pointers have a provenance that is summarized as a tree in figure 5.3. The following key properties emerge that allow important abstractions to be preserved:

- **Integrity and provenance** of the capability are guaranteed by the validity tag, cleanly separating pointers from data. Attackers can no longer inject pointers via the network, as data writes will be tag-free, preventing later dereference. The compiler represents all return addresses as capabilities, thereby making return-oriented programming (ROP) attacks much harder because the attacker not only has to overwrite the return address, but also has to ensure it is a code capability with integrity and provenance.

- **Bounds** (and the tag) prevent a capability referring to one object being used to access another. Bounds prevent buffer overflow and over-read attacks: for example, preventing bugs such as Heartbleed.

- **Monotonicity** guarantees that bounds and permissions can never be increased, preventing privilege escalation.

- **Permissions** prevent several attacks including code modification, or in the case of a JIT compiler, providing fine-grained control over what can generate code and where it can place that code.

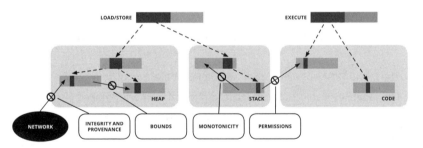

Figure 5.3 CHERI pointer provenance tree.

Capabilities also allow the *Principle of Intentional Use* to be expressed: where multiple rights are available to a program, the selection of rights used to authorize work on behalf of the program is explicit.[23] The effect of preserving this principle during the compilation process is to avoid the accidental or unintended exercise of rights that could lead to a violation of the intended policy. For example, memory loads and stores are with respect to an explicitly named capability register, and instruction fetches are via the program-counter capability, rather the register used for load, store, or fetch being selected implicitly from a table via an associative lookup. The effect of this principle is to counter what are classically known as "confused deputy" problems, in which a program will unintentionally exercise a privilege that it holds legitimately, but on behalf of another party who does not (and should not) hold that privilege. This principle, common to many capability systems, has been applied throughout the CHERI design, from architectural privilege management (e.g., operations via explicit capability registers) through to privilege management by software abstractions such as the CheriBSD object-capability systems, which are enabled in this by sealed capabilities.

Software Compartmentalization

Software compartmentalization is a fundamental abstraction that limits privileges and further attack surfaces available to attackers.[24,13,10] In compartmentalization, applications are decomposed into isolated ("sandboxed") components that are granted only selected access to system and application resources. For example, in conventional process-based compartmentalization, gunzip decompression can be executed in a sandbox that has been delegated only capabilities for the files being read from and written to. A successful exploit in the decompression code will yield only those limited rights, requiring the attacker to find and exploit further vulnerabilities.

Unlike more specific exploit mitigation techniques (which targets attack-vector characteristics such as remote code injection), compartmentalization does not depend on knowledge of specific attack vectors, and is resistant to an arms race as attack and defense co-evolve. Fine-grained compartmentalization improves mitigation by virtue of the principle of least privilege: attackers must exploit more vulnerabilities to gain rights in the target system. This means that improving the performance and scalability of compartmentalization can directly support improvements to software security.

Compartmentalization relies on two underlying trustworthy primitives, typically provided through a blend of hardware and software: *strong isolation*, often implemented using operating system (OS) process models grounded in virtual memory, and *controlled communication*, implemented as Inter-Process Communication (IPC) between processes. These primitives were designed for coarse-grained isolation—e.g., whole applications or even virtual machines; they limit *compartmentalization scalability* in the number of domains, rate of domain switches, and degree of memory sharing. This prevents use of more granular decompositions in larger, security-sensitive applications such as OpenSSH[13] and Chromium.[15]

Capability models prove particularly useful in implementing compartmentalization, as they allow programs to easily control what rights are delegated to compartments, and to configure sets of compartments with diverse trust relationships.[25,3,5,10] *Object-capability systems* blend object-oriented OS or programming-language facilities with capabilities to protect application-defined objects. Object encapsulation and interposition then allow programmers to express a range of security policies.

We have used CHERI's ISA facilities as a foundation to build a software *object-capability model* supporting orders of magnitude greater compartmentalization performance, and hence appropriate granularity, than current designs. We use sealed capabilities to build a *hardware-software domain-transition mechanism* and *programming model* suitable for safe communication between mutually distrusting software.

As with MMU-based memory protection, CHERI capabilities can be used to construct a software-defined (but hardware-supported) object-capability model based on isolation and controlled communication. The clean separation of policy and mechanism in object-capability systems aligns elegantly with the RISC (Reduced Instruction Set Computer) philosophy: with protection "fast paths" in hardware, policy definition is left to the OS, compiler, and application. The resulting hardware-software security model can efficiently implement diverse security policies including hierarchical models (e.g., sandboxing) and non-hierarchical models (e.g., mutually distrusting components).

In contrast to MMU-based approaches, CHERI-based compartmentalization optimizes sharing by allowing cheap delegation and avoiding aliasing problems experienced by TLBs as memory sharing increases.[26] This allows domain crossing to be performed at a low constant cost regardless of the amount of data sharing. These properties are critical to scaling up intra-application compartmentalization that is characterized by frequent domain crossings and extensive memory sharing. CHERI also eases programming for compartmentalized software by virtue of restoring a single address-space model, where MMUs imposed a multi-address-space model that programmers find difficult to reason about.

In addition to developing a high-performance compartmentalization mode, we have also explored how software static analysis can assist programmers in reasoning about decomposing software to accomplish mitigation objectives.[27]

RESEARCH AND DEVELOPMENT

Between 2010 and 2017, six major versions of the CHERI-MIPS ISA developed a mature hybridization of conventional RISC architecture with a strong (but software-compatible) capability-system model. Key research and development milestones can be found in figure 5.4 including major publications. The major ISA versions, with their development focuses, are described in table 5.1. This work occurred in several major overlapping phases as aspects of the approach were proposed, refined, and stabilized through a blend of ISA design, integrated hardware and software prototyping, and validation of the combined stack.

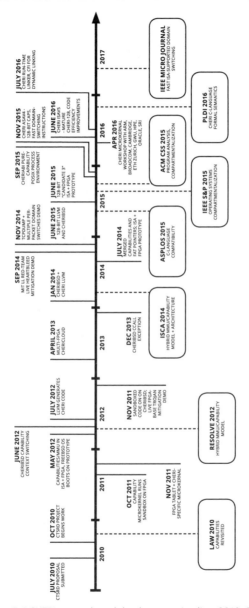

Figure 5.4 CHERI research and development timeline, 2010–2017.

Table 5.1 CHERI ISA revisions and major development phases.

Year(s)	Version	Description
2010- 2012	ISAv1	ISAv1 & RISC capability-system model w/64-bit MIPS Capability registers and tagged memory Guarded manipulation of registers
2012	ISAv2	ISAv2 & Extended tagging to capability registers Capability-aware exception handling MMU-based OS with CHERI support Fat pointers + capabilities, compiler
2014	ISAv3[33]	Instructions to optimize hybrid code Sealed capabilities, CCall/CReturn
2015	ISAv4[34]	MMU-CHERI integration (TLB permissions) ISA support for compressed capabilities Hardware-accelerated domain switching Multicore instructions: LL/SC variants
2016	ISAv5[23]	CHERI-128 compressed capability model Improved generated code efficiency Initial in-kernel privilege limitations
2017	ISAv6[17]	Mature kernel privilege limitations Further generated code efficiency CHERI-x86 and CHERI-RISC-V sketches Jump-based protection-domain transition

2010–2015: Composing the MMU with a Capability-System Model

A key early design choice was that the capability-system model would be largely orthogonal to the current MMU-based virtual-memory model, yet also compose with it cleanly.[18] We chose to place the capability-system model "before" the MMU, causing capabilities to be interpreted with respect to the virtual, rather than physical, address space. This reflected the goal of providing fine-grained memory protection and compartmentalization within address spaces—i.e., with respect to the application-programmer model of memory.

Capabilities therefore protect and implement virtual addresses dereferenced in much the same way that integer pointers are interpreted in conventional architectures. Exceptions allow controlled escape from the capability model by providing access to privileged capability registers, and execution in privileged rings grants the ability to manipulate the virtual address space, controlling the interpretation of virtual addresses embedded in capabilities.

This approach tightly integrates the capability-system model with the pipeline and register file, requiring that capabilities be first-class primitives managed by the compiler, held in registers, and so on. To protect capabilities in the virtual address space, we chose to physically tag them, distinguishing strongly protected pointers from ordinary data, in turn extending the implementation of physical memory, but also making that protection entirely independent from—and non-bypassable by—the MMU mechanism.

2012–2014: Composing C Pointers with the Capability-System Mode

Another key early design choice was the goal of using capabilities to implement C-language pointers—initially discretionarily (i.e., as annotated in the language), and later ubiquitously (i.e., for all virtual addresses in a more secure program). This required an inevitable negotiation between C-language semantics and the capability-system model, to ensure strong compatibility with current software.[19,28]

For example, C embeds a strong notion that pointers point within buffers. This requires that CHERI capabilities distinguish the notion of current virtual address from the bounds of the containing buffer—while also still providing strong integrity protection to the virtual address. This led us to compose fat-pointer[29,30,31] and capability semantics as the capability-system model evolved.

Similarly, we wished to allow all pointers to be represented as capabilities—including those embedded within other data structures—leading naturally to a choice to mandatorily tag pointers in memory. A less obvious implication of this approach is that operations such as memory copying must be capability-oblivious, maintaining the tag across pointer-propagating memory operations, requiring that data and capabilities not only be intermingled in memory, but also in register representation. Capability registers are, therefore, also tagged, allowing them to hold data or capabilities, preserving provenance transparently.

As part of this work, we also assisted with the development of new formal semantics for the C programming language, ensuring that we met the practical requirements of C programs, but also assisting in formalizing the protection properties we offer (e.g., strong protection of provenance validity grounded in an implied pointer provenance model in C).

CHERI should be viewed as providing primitives to support strong C-language pointer protection, rather than as directly implementing that protection: it is the responsibility of the compiler (and operating system and runtime) to employ capabilities to enforce protections where desired—whether by specific memory type, based on language annotations, or more universally. The compiler can also perform analyses to trade off source-code and binary compatibility, enforcing protection opportunistically in responding to various potential policies on tolerance to disruption.

2014–2015: Fine-Grained Compartmentalization

A key goal of our approach was to differentiate virtualization (requiring table-based lookups, and already implemented by the MMU) from protection (now implemented as a constant-time extension to the pointer primitive), which would avoid table-oriented overheads being imposed on protection.

This applies to C-language protection, but also to the implementation of higher-level security constructs such as compartmentalization.[20,26]

Compartmentalization depends on two underlying elements: strong isolation and controlled communication bridging that isolation. Underlying monotonicity in capabilities—i.e., that a delegated reference to a set of rights cannot be broadened to include additional rights—directly supports the construction of confined components within address spaces. Using this approach, we can place code in execution with only limited access to virtual memory, constructing "sandboxes" (and other more complex structures) within conventional processes. The CHERI exception model permits transition to a more privileged component—e.g., the operating system kernel or language runtime—allowing the second foundation, controlled communication, to be implemented.

Compartmentalization is facilitated by further extensions to the capability model, including a notion of "sealed" (or encapsulated capabilities). In CHERI, this is implemented as a software-defined capability: one that has no hardware interpretation (i.e., cannot be dereferenced), and strong encapsulation (i.e., whose fields are immutable). Other aspects of the model include a type mechanism allowing sealed code and data capabilities to be inextricably linked; pairs of sealed code capabilities and data capabilities can then be used to efficiently describe protection domains via an object-capability model. We provide some hardware assistance for protection-domain switching, providing straightforward parallel implementation of key checks, but leave the implementation of higher-level aspects of switching to the software implementation.

Here, as with C-language integration, it is critical that CHERI provide a general-purpose mechanism rather than enforce a specific policy. The sealed capability primitive can be used in a broad variety of ways to implement various compartmentalization models, with a range of implied communication and event models for software. We have experimented with several such models, including a protection-domain crossing primitive modeled on a simple (but now strongly protected) function call, and on asynchronous message passing. Our key performance goal was fixed (low) overhead similar to a function call, avoiding overheads that scale with quantity of memory shared (e.g., as is the case with table-oriented memory sharing configured using the MMU).

2015–2017: Architectural and Micro-Architectural Efficiency

Side-by-side with development of a mature capability-based architectural model, we also explored the implications on performance. This led to iterative refinement of the ISA to improve generated code, but also substantive efforts to ensure that there was an efficient in-memory representation of capabilities, as well as micro-architectural implementations of key instructions.

A key goal was to maintain the principle of a load-store architecture by avoiding combining computations with memory accesses—already embodied by both historic and contemporary RISC architectures. While pointers are no longer conflated with integer values, a natural composition of the capability model and ISA maintains that structural goal without difficulty.

One important effort lay in the reduction from a 256-bit capability (capturing the requirements of software for 64-bit pointer, 64-bit upper bound, and 64-bit lower bound, as well as additional metadata, such as permissions) to a 128-bit compressed representation. We took substantial inspiration from published work in pointer compression,[32] but found that our C-language compatibility requirements imposed quite a different underlying model and representation. For example, it is strictly necessary to support the common C-language idiom of permitting out-of-bounds pointers (but not dereference), which had been precluded by many proposed schemes.[19,28] Similarly, the need to support sealed capabilities led to efforts to characterize the trade-off between the type space (the number of unique classes that can be in execution in a CHERI address space) and bounds precision (the alignment requirements imposed on sealed references).

Another significant effort lay in providing in-memory tags, which are not directly supported by current DRAM layouts. In our initial implementation, we relied on a flat tag table (supported by a dedicated tag cache). This imposed a uniform (and quite high) overhead in additional DRAM accesses across all memory of roughly 10%. We have developed new micro-architectural techniques to improve emulated tag performance, based on a hierarchical table exploiting sparse use of pointers in memory, to reduce this overhead to <2% even with very high pointer density (e.g., in language runtimes).

2016–2017: Kernel Compartmentalization

Our initial design focus was on supporting fine-grained memory protection within the user virtual address space, and implicitly, also compartmentalization. Beyond an initial micro-kernel brought up to validate early capability model variants, kernel prototypes through much of our project have eschewed use of capability-aware code in the kernel due to limitations of the compiler, but also because of a focus on large userspace TCBs such as compression libraries, language runtimes, web browsers, and so on, which are key attack surfaces.

We have more recently returned to in-kernel memory protection and compartmentalization, where the CHERI model, in general, carries through without change—code executing in the kernel is not fundamentally different from code executing in userspace. The key exception is a set of management instructions available to the kernel, able to manipulate the MMU (and hence the interpretation of capabilities), as well as control features such as interrupt delivery and exception handling. We are now extending CHERI to allow the capability mechanism to control access to these features so that code can be compartmentalized within the kernel. We are also pursuing changes to the exception-based domain-transition mechanism used in earlier ISA revisions that shift towards a jump-based model, which will avoid exception-related overheads in the micro-architecture.

CHERI ISAv6: Looking Beyond MIPS

As we wrap up work on CHERI ISAv6, we are looking beyond the 64-bit MIPS ISA on which we based our hardware-software co-design effort towards further ISAs. These range from the still-developing open-source RISC-V ISA (which strongly resembles the MIPS ISA—hence to which most CHERI ideas will apply with minor translation) to the widely-used Intel x86-64 instruction set (which is quite far from the RISC foundations in which we have developed CHERI). This exploration has allowed us to derive a more general CHERI protection model from our work, rather than seeing CHERI as simply an extension to MIPS. We have focused on developing portable software-facing primitives and abstractions potentially supported by a variety of architectural expressions. We take some inspiration from the diverse range of MMU semantics and interfaces providing a common virtual-memory abstraction, and process model, across a broad range of architectures. New versions of the ISA specification also explore in much greater detail how architecture protection can be exploited by operating systems and compilers to reinforce program structure and mitigate vulnerabilities.

CONCLUSION

Over the last seven years, the CTSRD project has performed intensive and iterative hardware-software co-design to develop the CHERI-MIPS ISA, focusing on introducing architectural support for the principle of least privilege. The resulting approach (a hybridization of architectural and software techniques building on capability systems, C-language memory safety, virtual memory, and operating systems) is surprisingly adoptable in large realworld software stacks. Many security benefits can be achieved simply by recompiling current C-language TCBs with little or no source-code-level change, thus achieving fine-grained referential integrity and protection that mitigates many known classes of pointer-related exploit. With further investment in refactoring software described earlier, scalable support for fine-grained software compartmentalization opens the door to vulnerability and exploit-class non-specific mitigation, both accelerating current software compartmentalization and supporting the introduction of much great compartmentalization.

By starting with a conventional RISC architecture, a C-language operating system, and application corpus, we have been able to demonstrate and validate our approach against large, extant software stacks (e.g., the FreeBSD operating system), as well as provide an easier path to potential transition. Using FPGA-based prototypes, which allow a far tighter design cycle between hardware and software, we have also been able to support detailed resource and performance analyses, validating micro-architectural aspects of the approach. This hardware-software co-design approach has paid enormous dividends in forcing a vital iterative design and refinement process over several years. It is increasingly clear that the CHERI protection model is applicable to a broad range of architectures and micro-architectures, rather than being specific to the 64-bit MIPS architecture on which we have prototyped.

As the project enters its next two years (now seven years into a 4-year project), we continue our focus on building larger demonstrations of the approach, maturing our software stack—including demonstrating how CHERI converges with OS design choices and the compiler stack), as well as improving performance through research into architectural and micro-architectural features, such as capability compression and efficient hierarchical tag tables. We are also turning our attention from formal modeling (which has allowed us to precisely specify behaviors of the ISA for the purposes of informal reasoning and automated testing) to formal reasoning—yielding early proofs of key underlying security properties in the ISA, such as strong capability monotonicity, capability unforgeability, and protection-domain isolation.

More information about the CHERI architecture and our ongoing work, along with open-source hardware and software artifacts, may be found on the CTSRD project website: https://www.cl.cam.ac.uk/research/security/ctsrd/

ACKNOWLEDGMENTS

The work described in this chapter would not have been possible without numerous contributors to the CTSRD project over an extended period. This includes our co-authors on our published papers and technical reports: Jonathan Anderson, Ross Anderson, David Brazdil, Ruslan Bukin, David Chisnall, Brooks Davis, Nirav Dave, Khilan Gudka, Alexandre Joannou, Wojciech Koszek, Ben Laurie, James Lingard, A. Theodore Markettos, Ilias Marinos, J. Edward Maste, Justus Matthiesen, Kayvan Memarian, Steven J. Murdoch, Kyndylan Nienhuis, Robert Norton-Wright, Philip Paeps, Alex Richardson, Michael Roe, Colin Rothwell, Hassen Saidi, Peter Sewell, Stacey D. Son, Munraj Vadera, Jonathan Woodruff, and Hongyan Xia.

We also gratefully acknowledge the contributions of our colleagues at SRI International and the University of Cambridge, including John Baldwin, Hadrien Barral, Gregory Chadwick, Lawrence Esswood, Steven Hand, Stephen Kell, Patrick Lincoln, Anil Madhavapeddy, Alfredo Mazzinghi, Andrew W. Moore, Will Moreland, Alan Mujumdar, Prashanth Mundkur, Jeunese Payne, John Rushby, Hans Petter Selasky, Philip Withnall, and Bjoern Zeeb. Finally, the larger DARPA CRASH and MRC program communities, in which the CHERI project took place and who provided critical support for our work; we are indebted to Howie Shrobe, Bob Laddaga, John Launchbury, Stu Wagner, Dan Adams, and Laurisa Goergen for their support throughout.

This work is part of the CTSRD and MRC2 projects sponsored by the Defense Advanced Research Projects Agency (DARPA) and the Air Force Research Laboratory (AFRL), under contracts FA8750-10-C-0237 and FA8750-11-C-0249. The views, opinions, and/or findings contained in this chapter are those of the authors and should not be interpreted as representing the official views or policies, either expressed or implied, of the Department of Defense or the U.S. Government. We also acknowledge the EPSRC REMS Programme Grant [EP/K008528/1], the EPSRC Impact Acceleration Account [EP/K503757/1], Isaac Newton Trust, UK Higher Education Innovation Fund (HEIF), Thales E-Security, and Google, Inc.

NOTES

1. J. Woodruff, R. N. M. Watson, D. Chisnall, S. W. Moore, J. Anderson, B. Davis, B. Laurie, P. G. Neumann, R. Norton, and M. Roe, The CHERI Capability Model: Revisiting RISC in an Age of Risk, in Proceedings of the 41st International Symposium on Computer Architecture, June 2014.

2. R. N. Watson, P. G. Neumann, J. Woodruff, J. Anderson, D. Chisnall, B. Davis, B. Laurie, S. W. Moore, S. J. Murdoch, and M. Roe, Capability Hardware Enhanced RISC Instructions: CHERI Instruction-Set Architecture, Version 1.14, tech. rep., SRI International and the University of Cambridge, September 2015.

3. R. N. M. Watson, J. Woodruff, P. G. Neumann, S. W. Moore, J. Anderson, D. Chisnall, N. Dave, B. Davis, K. Gudka, B. Laurie, S. J. Murdoch, R. Norton, M. Roe, S. Son, and M. Vadera, CHERI: A Hybrid Capability-System Architecture for Scalable Software Compartmentalization, in Proceedings of the 2015 IEEE Symposium on Security and Privacy, (San Jose, California), IEEE Computer Society, May 2015.

4. Robert N. M. Watson, Robert Norton, Jonathan Woodruff, Alexandre Joannou, Simon W. Moore, Peter G. Neumann, Jonathan Anderson, David Chisnall, Nirav Dave, Brooks Davis, Khilan Gudka, Ben Laurie, A. Theodore Markettos, Ed Maste, Steven J. Murdoch, Michael Roe, Colin Rothwell, Stacey Son, and Munraj Vadera, Fast Protection-Domain Crossing in the CHERI Capability-System Architecture, special issue of IEEE Micro journal, vol. 36, no. 5, pp. 38--49, Sept/Oct 2016, This paper is an extension and refinement of R2. http://www.qmags.com/R/?i=3355a1 2&e=771639&doi=63528695&uk=2FE1161B16B0D7E013144E421115BC63 82FF14E57D.htm

5. Robert N. M. Watson, David Brazdil, Jonathan Woodruff, A. Theodore Markettos, J. Edward Maste, Robert Norton, Stacey Son, Michael Roe, Simon W. Moore, Peter G. Neumann, and Ben Laurie. Sinking the Java Security Model into the C. Proceedings of the 22nd ACM International

Conference on Architectural Support for Programming Languages and Operating systems (ASPLOS 2017). Xi'an, China, April 8--12, 2017.

6. P. G. Neumann, Principled assuredly trustworthy composable architectures, tech. rep., SRI Int'l, Menlo Park, CA, December 2004. http://www.csl.sri.com/neumann/chats4.html and pdf.

7. B. Beurdouche, K. Bhargavan, A. Delignat-Lavaud, C. Fournet, M. Kohlweiss, A. Pironti, P.-Y. Strub, and J. K. Zinzindohoue, ``{A Messy State of the Union: Taming the Composite State Machines of TLS,'' in Proceedings of the 2015 IEEE Symposium on Security and Privacy, San Jose, California, IEEE Computer Society, May 2015. https://www.smacktls.com/smack.pdf.

8. J. H. Saltzer and M. D. Schroeder, The protection of information in computer systems, Proceedings of the IEEE, vol. 63, pp. 1278--1308, September 1975.

9. J. H. Saltzer and F. Kaashoek, Principles of Computer System Design. Morgan Kaufmann, 2009. Chapters 1-6 only. Chapters 7-11 are online: http://ocw.mit.edu/Saltzer-Kaashoek

10. P. G. Neumann, Practical architectures for survivable systems and networks, tech. rep., Final Report, Project 1688, SRI Int., Menlo Park, California, June 2000. http://www.csl.sri.com/neumann/survivability.html.

11. E. I. Organick, The Multics System: An Examination of Its Structure. MIT Press, Cambridge, Massachusetts, 1972.

12. M. Bishop, Computer Security: Art and Science. Addison-Wesley, Reading, Massachusetts, 2002.

13. M. Bishop, Introduction to Computer Security. Addison-Wesley, Reading, Massachusetts, 2004.

14. M. Curtin, Developing Trust: Online Security and Privacy. Apress, Berkeley, California, and Springer-Verlag, Berlin, 2002.

15. F. J. Corbató, J. Saltzer, and C. T. Clingen, ``Multics: The first seven

years,'' in Proceedings of the Spring Joint Computer Conference, vol. 40, Montvale, New Jersey, AFIPS Press, 1972.

16. F. J. Corbató, On building systems that will fail, 1990 Turing Award Lecture, with a following interview by Karen Frenkel), Communications of the ACM, vol. 34, pp. 72--90, September 1991.

17. P. G. Neumann, The role of motherhood in the pop art of system programming, in Proceedings of the ACM Second Symposium on Operating systems Principles, Princeton, New Jersey, pp. 13--18, ACM, October 1969. http://www.multicians.org/pgn-motherhood.html.

18. D. L. Parnas, On a ``buzzword'': Hierarchical structure, in Information Processing 74 (Proceedings of the IFIP Congress 1974), vol. Software, pp. 336--339, North-Holland, Amsterdam, 1974.

19. K. Biba, Integrity considerations for secure computer systems,'' Tech. Rep. MTR 3153, The Mitre Corporation, Bedford, Massachusetts, June 1975. Also available from USAF Electronic Systems Division, Bedford, Massachusetts, as ESD-TR-76-372, April 1977.

20. D. Denning, P. G. Neumann, and D. B. Parker, Social aspects of computer security, in Proceedings of the 10th National Computer Security Conference, September 1987.

21. P. G. Neumann, Rainbows and arrows: How the security criteria address computer misuse, in Proceedings of the Thirteenth National Computer Security Conference, (Washington, D.C.), pp. 414--422, NIST/NCSC, 1--4 October 1990.

22. W. H. Ware, A retrospective of the criteria movement, in Proceedings of the Eighteenth National Information Systems Security Conference, (Baltimore, Maryland), pp. 582--588, NIST/NCSC, 10--13 October 1995.

23. C. Hunt, TCP/IP Network Administration, 3rd Edition. O'Reilly \& Associates, Sebastopol, California, 2002.

24. R. J. Feiertag and P. G. Neumann, The foundations of a Provably Secure Operating system (PSOS), in Proceedings of the National Computer

Conference, 329--334, AFIPS Press, 1979. http://www.csl.sri.com/
neumann/psos.pdf.

25. P. G. Neumann, R. S. Boyer, R. J. Feiertag, K. N. Levitt, and L. Robinson,
A Provably Secure Operating system: The system, its applications, and
proofs," tech. rep., Computer Science Laboratory, SRI International,
Menlo Park, California, May 1980. 2nd edition, Report CSL-116.

26. P. G. Neumann and R. J. Feiertag, PSOS revisited, in Proceedings of the
19th Annual Computer Security Applications Conference (ACSAC 2003),
Classic Papers section, (Las Vegas, Nevada), pp. 208--216, IEEE Computer
Society, December 2003. http://www.csl.sri.com/neumann/psos03.pdf.

27. P. G. Neumann, Robust nonproprietary software, in Proceedings of the
2000 Symposium on Security and Privacy, Oakland, CA, pp. 122--123,
IEEE Computer Society, May 2000. http://www.csl.sri.com/neumann/
ieee00.pdf.

28. C. Gacek, T. Lawrie, and B. Arief, The many meanings of open source,
tech. rep., Department of Computing Science, University of Newcastle
upon Tyne, Newcastle, England, August 2001. Technical Report CS-
TR-737.

29. C. Gacek and C. Jones, Dependability issues in open source
software, tech. rep., Department of Computing Science, Dependable
Interdisciplinary Research Collaboration, University of Newcastle upon
Tyne, Newcastle, England, 2001. Final report for PA5.

30. Department of~Homeland~Security, Strategic principles for securing the
Internet of Things, tech. rep., DHS, December 2016.

31. BITAG, Internet of Things (IoT) security and privacy recommendations,
tech. rep., BITAG Broadband Internet Technical Advisory Group,
November 2016.

32. Committee on Enhancing National Cybersecurity, Report on securing and
growing the digital economy, tech. rep., NIST Publication, 1 December
2016, Gaithersburg MD, 1 December 2016.

CHAPTER 6

Fundamental Trustworthiness Principles in CHERI

Peter G. Neumann

INTRODUCTION

System trustworthiness is a measure of the extent to which a system might
be trusted to satisfy whatever critical requirements are desired. This is often
relating to security, reliability, guarantees of real-time performance and
resource availability, survivability, and more—all in spite of a wide range
of adversities (known and unknown). Trustworthiness depends on hardware,
software, communications media, power supplies, physical environments,
and people in many capacities—requirements specifiers, designers,
implementers, users, operators, maintenance personnel, administrators,
and (unfortunately) the abilities of attackers to exploit weaknesses or
limitations in all of the above.

We examine the extent to which the ongoing *CHERI (Capability Hardware
Enhanced RISC Instructions)* system hardware-software co-design
effort has successfully applied those principles (either intentionally
or serendipitously).[1,2,3,4,5] See chapter 5.

The prototype CHERI Instruction-Set Architecture (ISA) is an extension
of the MIPS-64 ISA that adds capability instructions and capability registers.
The CHERI ISA prototype provides support for strongly typed objects, rapid
domain crossing, very fine grained access controls, and compartmentalization
of software. The clean-slate approach provides remarkably strong security,
including adaptations of FreeBSD and LLVM-based compilers that understand
the capability instructions, and that effectively prevent many of the common
programming errors—or otherwise help programmers avoid them. It provides a
hybrid architecture that allows legacy object code and recompiled source code
(even with potential malware) to co-exist securely with high-security software,
without adverse effects. The hardware and software are open-sourced.
Extensive technology transfer is in progress, currently halfway through year 7
of what is now an 8-year DARPA project (originally scheduled for only four years).

PRINCIPLED SYSTEMS

"Everything should be made as simple as possible, but no simpler" — *Albert Einstein*

A fundamental hypothesis motivating this analysis is that achieving assuredly trustworthy systems requires much greater observance of certain underlying principles than is normally present. We assert that careful attention to such principles can greatly facilitate the following efforts.

- **Principled architectures:** The establishment of predictably composable open distributed-system network-oriented architectures needs to rely on sensible total-system architectures, if the systems are to be capable of fulfilling critical requirements (e.g., for security, reliability, survivability, and performance), while being readily adaptable to widely differing applications, different hardware, heterogeneous software providers, and changing technologies. The term "architecture" here generally implies both the structure of systems and networks, and the design of their functional interfaces and interconnections—at various layers of abstraction. (This is distinct from the so-called hardware instruction-set architecture, which is concerned primarily with precisely defining the hardware interface to the software).

- **Principled system development:** The entire development process needs to be sensibly structured and managed. This may include the development of detailed specifications, principled implementations that follow good coding practices, up-front concerns for trustworthiness, and assurance of trustworthiness for composable interoperable components, with predictable behavior when those components are composed.

- **Principled assurance:** Any meaningful measure of trustworthiness requires serious attention to assurance that the conceptual requirements, abstract specifications, detailed implementations, and operational practices have some realistic justifiable expectation of satisfying the desired mission needs. Thus, attainment of assuredly trustworthy systems and networks that are capable of addressing all relevant critical requirements requires assurance methodologies, which are themselves highly principled and take advantage of the design, development, and operational principles.

The benefits of disciplined and principled system development cannot be overestimated, especially in the early stages of the development cycle. Principled design and software development can stave off many problems later on in implementation, maintenance, and operation. Huge potential cost savings can result from diligently observing and maintaining relevant principles throughout the design and development cycles. However, the primary concept involved is that of disciplined development; there are many methodologies that provide some kind of discipline, and all of those can be useful in some cases. Furthermore, no system can be called "trustworthy" in the absence of meaningful assurance evaluations, with respect to well-defined requirements.

Many of the principles discussed here are fairly well-known in concept, and reasonably well understood by system cognoscenti. However, their relevance is not often appreciated by people with little development or operational experience. Not wishing to preach to the choir, we do not dwell on elaborating the principles themselves, which have been extensively covered elsewhere (as cited below). Instead, we concentrate on the importance and applicability of these principles in the development of systems with critical requirements—and especially secure systems and networks. The clear implication is that disciplined understanding and observance of the most effective of these principles can have enormous benefits to developers and system administrators, and can also aid user communities. However, we also explore various potential conflicts within and among these principles, and emphasize that those conflicts must be thoroughly understood and respected. The challenges in developing trustworthy systems are intrinsically complicated, especially when attempting to meet life-critical or other stringent requirements. For example, it is important to find ways to manage that complexity, rather than mistakenly believing that intrinsic complexity is avoidable by pretending to practice "simplicity."

TRUSTWORTHINESS PRINCIPLES

"Willpower is always more efficient than mechanical enforcement, when it works. But there is always a size of system beyond which willpower will be inadequate."
— *Butler Lampson*

Developing and operating complex systems and networks with critical requirements demands a different kind of thinking from that used in operating system design and routine programming. We consider here various sets of principles, their applicability, and their limitations. We begin with the historically significant Saltzer-Schroeder-Kaashoek principles, followed by several other sets of principles and structural developmental approaches.

Of particular interest are compositions of different elements (e.g., requirements, specifications, implementations, and analyses), and the assurance that can be attributed to systems with requirements for trustworthiness. Critical problems relate to *composability* (preservation of existing properties) and *compositionality* (analysis of emergent properties arising from the compositions) of constituent components, some of which can be extremely difficult to predict. Examples of compositionality include total-system safety and security, which cannot be evaluated component-wise. These properties may be extremely difficult to predict, although failures that result may be evident (e.g., failure to work at all), or subtle, surprising, and very difficult to detect,[6] which is still relevant today—even if outdated). A recent example of surprising extensive failures of compositionality involved the client and server sides of essentially all-popular implementations of the heavily used and very critical cryptographically-based TLS 1.2 protocol.[7]

Saltzer-Schroeder-Kaashoek Security Principles, 1975 and 2009

The ten basic security principles formulated by Saltzer and Schroeder[8] in 1975 are all still relevant today, in a wide range of circumstances. An eleventh principle on minimizing what must be trusted appears in the 2009 book by Saltzer and Kaashoek.[9] (I had included a similar principle on minimizing what has to be trusted to achieve survivable systems in my 2000 ARL report[10] and again in my 2004 DARPA report on problems and approaches related to trustworthy compositions.)[6] In essence, these principles are summarized here, along with CHERI-relevant explanations. In addition, the principle of intentional use has been added as a twelfth basic principle, at the suggestion of Robert Watson. It is an excellent partner for the principle of least privilege, as it adds considerably more refinement to the indirect use of privileges on behalf of other processes (or users).

1. **Economy of mechanism:** Seek design simplicity (wherever and to whatever extent it is effective). CHERI's high-assurance hardware relies on just a handful of capability instructions, and compilers that constructively utilize those instructions, out of which extremely trustworthy systems and applications can be constructed.

2. **Fail-safe defaults:** Deny accesses unless explicitly authorized (rather than permitting accesses unless explicitly denied). CHERI process initializations can minimize what privileges are available. Further CHERI has no Hydra-like amplification of capability privileges, providing strict monotonicity of privileges.

3. **Complete mediation:** Check every access, without exception. CHERI capabilities are unforgeable, and the capability mechanism is non-bypassable. Any attempts to modify a capability results in something that is no longer a capability.

4. **Open design:** Do not assume that design secrecy will enhance security. The CHERI Instruction Set Architectures (for both the 256-bit research capabilities and the 128-bit implementable version) is open-sourced.

5. **Separation of privileges:** Use separate privileges or even multiparty authorization (e.g., two keys) to reduce misplaced trust. The CHERI ISA supports typed objects that enforce strong typing, each type having its own separately defined privileges that are relevant to the particular type.

6. **Least privilege:** Allocate minimal (separate) privileges according to need-to-know, need-to-modify, need-to-delete, need-to-use, and so on to the typed objects. The existence of overly powerful mechanisms, such as *superuser,* is inherently dangerous. The CHERI hardware capability mechanism, in which each capability has its own minimal set of privileges and the hardware-software support for fine-grained compartmentalization, further enhances the least-privilege principle.

7. **Least common mechanism:** Minimize the amount of mechanism common to more than one user and depended on by all users. Avoid sharing of trusted multipurpose mechanisms, including executables and data—in particular, minimizing the need for, and use of, overly powerful mechanisms such as the superuser and non-locally shared buffers. As one example of the flaunting of this principle, exhaustion of shared resources provides a huge source of covert storage channels, whereas the natural sharing of real calendar-clock time provides a source of covert timing channels. CHERI's strongly typed higher-layer objects allow each type to have its own rules and privileges; when reusing any common code, the capability mechanism and the compartmentalization provide suitable isolation to prevent harmful effects. On the other hand, at present covert channels are not considered in the CHERI ISA, and must be dealt with in implementation.

8. **Psychological acceptability:** Strive for ease of use and operation—
    for example, with easily understandable and forgiving interfaces.
    To a considerable extent, issues related to security benefit from being
    largely invisible to casual users. Much of the CHERI capability mechanism
    can be hidden by operating systems and compilers. Optimizing
    performance is likely to be not necessary for users other
    than application developers.

9. **Work factor:** Make cost-to-protect commensurate with threats
    and expected risks. This is a problem in many conventional systems,
    in which attackers need to find only a few exploitable weak links,
    whereas system developers and administrators need to ensure that
    there are very few exploitable weak links that cannot be exploited.
    The work factor is often mistakenly applied to cryptography, when
    exploitable system flaws can totally undermine the belief that the
    cryptography is very strong. We believe that formal analysis of the
    CHERI ISAs can greatly increase the assurance associated with the
    trustworthiness of the hardware, and that the resulting software
    will be significantly less vulnerable to hardware-based attacks.

10. **Recording of compromises:** Provide non-bypassable tamper-proof
    trails of evidence. This is a huge problem in proprietary paperless
    all-electronic voting machines and election support systems. CHERI
    can provide the non-bypassability and tamper-proof trails of evidence
    through compartmentalization and fine-grained least privilege. This is a
    requirement that is made much easier on CHERI-based systems, because
    of the compartmentalization, encapsulation, control-flow integrity, and
    other trustworthiness attributes that can enable forensics-worthy audit
    trails. Thus, this principle is not one that guided the development, but
    rather emerged naturally as a by-product of the system itself.

11. **Minimization of what has to be trustworthy:** Poorly designed systems may have a sense of structural abstraction, but typically do not provide encapsulation (discussed in the next subsection) within each module—which often leads to vulnerabilities. In such systems, higher-layer abstractions can often compromise lower layers. CHERI's ISA and indeed its overall hardware-software system seriously pursue this principle throughout, with encapsulated abstractions that can be enforced with fine-grained least-privilege capability architecture in hardware, and fine-grained compartmentalization within processes in hardware and software—providing an elegant way to respect this principle. The following added principle is also highly beneficial.

12. **Intentional use:** Whenever multiple rights are available to a program, the selection of rights used to authorize work on behalf of the program must be explicit, irrespective of the specific layer of software abstraction. The intent of this principle is to avoid the accidental or unintended exercise of rights that could lead to a violation of the intended policy. It counters what is classically known as "confused deputy" problems, in which a program can unintentionally exercise a privilege that it holds legitimately, but on behalf of another program that does not (and should not) have the ability to exercise that privilege. This principle (implicit in many capability systems) has been applied throughout the CHERI design, including architectural privileges (e.g., the requirement to explicitly identify capability registers used for load or store) and the sealed capability mechanism that can be used to support the CHERI object-capability model. (An attempt to satisfy this principle was found implicitly in PSOS's propagation-limiting capabilities, and has also been applied to CheriBSD.)

With regard to the penultimate principle above (11), appropriate trustworthiness should be situated where it is most needed—suitable to overall system requirements, rather than required uniformly across widely distributed components (with potentially many weak links) or totally centralized (with creation of a single weak link and forgetting other vulnerabilities). Trustworthiness is expensive to implement and to ensure; as a consequence, significant benefits can result from architecturally minimizing the extent to which higher-layer mechanisms have to be trustworthy, especially if they can depend on (and rely on) the trustworthiness of lower layers. This principle can contribute notably to sound architectures. In combination with the economy of mechanism, this suggests avoidance of bloatware and an unfortunate dependence on less trustworthy components.

Remember that these are principles, not hard-and-fast rules. By no means should they be interpreted as ironclad, especially in light of some of their potentially mutual contradictions that require development trade-offs. The Saltzer-Schroeder principles grew directly out of the Multics experience,[11] discussed further at the end of this section. Some of these principles have taken on almost mythic proportions among the security elite, and to some extent buzzword cult status among many fringe parties. Therefore, perhaps it is not necessary to explain each principle in detail—although there is considerable depth of discussion underlying each principle. Careful reading of the Saltzer-Schroeder paper[8] and the Saltzer-Kaashoek book[9] is recommended. Matt Bishop's security books[12,13] are also useful in this regard, placing the principles in a more general context. In addition, chapter 6 of Matt Curtin's book[14] on "developing trust"—by which he might really hope to be "developing trustworthiness"—provides some useful further discussion of these principles. Also, consider the discussion below on additional principles.

There are two fundamental caveats regarding these principles. First, each principle by itself may be useful in some cases and not in others. The second is that when taken in combinations, groups of principles are not necessarily all reinforcing; indeed, they may be mutually in conflict. Consequently, any sensible development must consider the appropriate use of each principle in the context of the overall effort. Examples of a principle being both good and bad—as well as examples of cross-principle interference—are scattered through the following discussion. Various caveats are considered in the penultimate section.

Table 1 summarizes the applicability of each of the Saltzer-Schroeder-Kaashoek principles to the goals of composability, trustworthiness, and assurance (particularly with respect to security, reliability, and survivability-relevant requirements). Although this table is somewhat generic, it is also specifically relevant to CHERI, in light of the CHERI-relevant enumeration of the principles above. An asterisk indicates that CHERI makes constructive use of this principle in the system design (consciously or unconsciously), and thereby enhances trustworthiness. An asterisk in parenthesis implies that this principle was not a driving force in the design, but became easier to satisfy in implementations—as a result of the principled system architecture.

Table 6.1 Relevance of Saltzer-Schroeder to CHERI Goals.

Principle	Composability	Trustworthiness	Assurance
Economy of mechanism *	Beneficial within a sound architecture; requires proactive design effort	Vital aid to sound design; exceptions must be completely handled	Can simplify analysis
Fail-safe defaults *	Some help, but not fundamental	Simplifies design, use, operation	Can simplify analysis
Complete mediation *	Very beneficial with disjoint object types	Vital, but hard to achieve without hardware help	Can considerably simplify analysis; Non-bypassability
Open design *	Documentation of design is very beneficial among multiple developers	Secrecy of design is, a bad assumption; open design requires strong system security	Assurance is mostly irrelevant in badly designed systems; open design enables total-system analysis
Separation of privileges *	Very beneficial if hardware supported	Avoids many common flaws	Focuses analysis more precisely
Least privilege *	Very beneficial if hardware supported	Limits flaws; improves design and operation	Focuses analysis more precisely
Least common mechanism *	Beneficial absent natural polymorphism	Avoids some common flaws	Modularizes analysis
Psychological acceptability	Could help a little if not subvertible	Affects usability and operation	Ease of use can contribute
Work factor *	Relevant especially for cryptography, but not embeddings; may be composable	Misguided if system is easily compromised from below, spoofed, bypassed, etc.	Gives false sense of security under non-algorithmic compromises

Principle	Composability	Trustworthiness	Assurance
Compromise recording (*)	Not an impediment if distributed; needs real-time detection and response	After-the-fact, but useful, easy to attain in secure systems	Not primary contributor to analysis
Minimize what must be trustworthy *	Composability can be significantly improved	Can greatly increase trustworthiness	Formal analysis and flow control can detect flaws
Intentional use of rights *	Simplifies predictable composability	Enhances least privilege	Refines operational assurance

In particular, complete mediation, separation of privileges, and allocation of least privilege are enormously helpful to composability and trustworthiness. Open design can contribute significantly to composability, when subjected to internal review and external criticism. However, there is considerable debate about the importance of open design with respect to trustworthiness, with some people still clinging tenaciously to the notion that security by obscurity is sensible—despite risks of many flaws being so obvious as to be easily detected externally, even without reverse engineering. Indeed, the recent emergence of very good decompilers for C and Java, along with the likelihood of similar reverse engineering tools for other languages, suggest that such attacks are becoming steadily more practical. Overall, the assumption of design secrecy and the supposed unavailability of source code is often not a deterrent, especially with ever-increasing skills among black-box system analysts. However, there are of course cases in which security by obscurity is unavoidable—as in the hiding of private and secret cryptographic keys, even where the cryptographic algorithms and implementations are public.

Fundamental to trustworthiness is the extent to which systems and networks can avoid being compromised by malicious or accidental human behavior and by events such as hardware malfunctions and so-called acts of God. We have considered compromise from outside, compromise from within, and compromise from below, with fairly intuitive meanings.[10] For example, outsiders may penetrate a system, or create denials of service; insiders may be able to masquerade as other users or misuse existing privileges; operating systems may be compromised from below by utilizing hardware quirks, and applications may be compromised by manipulating operating systems. There are cases in theory where weak links can be avoided (e.g., end-to-end encryption for integrity, and zero-knowledge protocols that can establish a shared key without any part of the protocol requiring secrecy), although in practice they may also be undermined by compromises from below.

From its beginning, the Multics development was strongly motivated by a set of principles—some simple ones were originally stated by Ted Glaser and Neumann in the first section of the very first edition of the Multics Programmers' Manual in 1965 (see http://multicians.org). Multics was also driven by disciplined development. For example, with almost no exceptions, coding effort was never begun until a written specification had been approved by the Multics advisory board. With almost no exceptions, all of the code was written in a subset of PL/I just sufficient for the initial needs of Multics, for which the first compiler (early PL, or EPL) had been developed by Doug McIlroy and Bob Morris.

In addition to the Saltzer-Schroeder principles, further insights on principles and discipline relating to Multics can be found in a paper by Corbató, Saltzer, and Clingen[15] and in Corbató's Turing lecture.[16]

Related Principles, 1969 and Later

Another view of principled system development was given by Neumann in 1969,[17] relating to what is often dismissed as merely motherhood— but which is both very profound and difficult to observe in practice. The basic motherhood principles under consideration in that paper (alternatively, you might consider them just as desirable system attributes) included automatedness, availability, convenience, debuggability, documentedness, efficiency, evolvability, flexibility, forgivingness, generality, maintainability, modularity, monitorability, portability, reliability, simplicity, and uniformity. Some of those attributes indirectly affect security and trustworthiness, whereas others affect the acceptability, utility, and future life of the systems in question. Considerable discussion[17] was also devoted to (1) the risks of local optimization and the need for a more global awareness of less obvious downstream costs of development (e.g., writing code for bad—or nonexistent—specifications, and having to debug really bad code), operation, and maintenance; and (2) the benefits of higher-level implementation languages (which prior to Multics were rarely used for the development of operating systems).[15,16]

In later reports,[10] Neumann considered some extensions of the Saltzer-Schroeder principles. Although most of those principles might seem more or less obvious, they are of course full of different interpretations and hidden issues. We summarize an extended set of principles here, particularly as they might be interpreted in the CHERI context.

13. **Sound architectures:** Recognizing that it is much better to avoid design errors early than to attempt to fix them later, the importance of architectures inherently capable of evolvable, maintainable, robust implementations is enormous—even in an open-source environment. The value of a well-thought-out architecture is considerable in open-source systems. The value in closed-source proprietary systems

could also be significant, if it were thought through early on, although architectural foresight is often impeded by legacy compatibility requirements that tend to lock system evolution into inflexible architectures. Good interface design is as fundamental to good architectures as is their structure. Both the architectural structure and the architectural interfaces (particularly the visible interfaces, but also some of the internal interfaces that must be interoperable) benefit from careful early specification. Defense in depth and defense in breadth are both conceptually feasible, but only in the context of the preceding and following principles as they relate to total-system trustworthiness.

14. **Abstraction:** The primitives at any given logical or physical layer should be relevant to the functions and properties of the objects at that layer, and should mask lower-layer detail where possible. Ideally, the specification of a given abstraction should be in terms of objects meaningful at that layer, rather than requiring lower-layer (e.g., machine dependent) concepts. Abstractions at one layer can be related to the abstractions at other layers in a variety of ways, thus simplifying the abstractions at each layer rather than collapsing different abstractions into a more complex single layer. (Horizontal and vertical abstractions and six types of abstractions are discussed in Virgil Gligor's contributed appendix on Visibly Controllable Computing,[6] as this text is an elaboration of David Parnas's "uses" paper.)[18]

15. **Modularity:** Modularity relates to the characteristic of system structures in which different entities (modules) can be relatively loosely coupled and combined to satisfy overall system requirements, whereby a module could be modified or replaced as long as the new version satisfies the given interface specification. In general, modularity is most effective when the modules reflect specific abstractions and provide encapsulation within each module. CHERI takes modularity seriously, and actually provides submodularization particularly

in application software when an application module needs further separation.

16. **Encapsulation:** Details that are relevant to a particular abstraction should be local to that abstraction and subsequently isolated within the implementation of that abstraction and the lower layers on which the implementation depends. One example of encapsulation involves *information hiding*—for example, keeping internal state information hidden from the visible interfaces. Another example involves masking the idiosyncrasies of physical devices from higher-layer system interfaces—and of course from the user interfaces as well. Encapsulation includes but is not limited to information hiding (as in the early work of David Parnas), and also helps maintain integrity of the abstraction in question from manipulation from outside the modular abstraction. The CHERI hardware ISA supports encapsulation in several respects, including within typed objects, and also as a by-product of the Bluespec strongly typed language that has been used to specify our various prototype ISAs.

17. **Layered and compositional assurance:** Protection (and generally defensive design for security, reliability, etc.) should be distributed to where it is most needed, and should reflect the semantics of the objects being protected. Layering (e.g., Multics rings or Dijkstra's THE system) can be very effective without losing efficiency. Compositional separation (compartmentalization) among modules or even within a single application or modular abstraction can also be effective. Structured abstractions can greatly simplify analysis, although the compositions themselves must also be analyzed. With respect to the reality of implementations that transit entities of different trustworthiness, layers of protection are vastly preferable to flat concepts such as single sign-on (that is, where only a single authentication is required). With respect to psychological acceptability,

single sign-on has enormous appeal; however, it can leave enormous security vulnerabilities as a result of compromise from outside, from within, or from below, in both distributed and layered environments. Thus, with respect to the apparent user simplicity provided by single sign-on, psychological acceptability conflicts with other principles, such as complete mediation, separation of privileges, and least common privilege. The hierarchically layered separation of the CHERI hardware and the various software layers as well as the horizontal separations provided by compartmentalization are fundamental to CHERI's trustworthiness.

18. **Constrained dependency:** Improperly guarded dependencies on less trustworthy entities should be avoided. However, it is possible in some cases to surmount the relative untrustworthiness of mechanisms on which certain functionality depends—as in the two-dozen types of trustworthiness-enhancing mechanisms enumerated.[6] In essence, do not trust anything on which you must depend—unless you are entirely satisfied with demonstrations of its trustworthiness. This principle is a generalization of the Biba property,[19] which deals more specifically with multilevel integrity.

19. **Object orientation:** The OO paradigm bundles together abstraction, encapsulation, modularity of state information, inheritance (subclasses inheriting the attributes of their parent classes—e.g., for functionality and for protection), and subtype polymorphism (subtype safety despite the possibility of application to objects of different types). This paradigm facilitates programming generality and software reusability, and if properly used can enhance software development. This is a contentious topic, in that most of the OO methodologies and languages are somewhat sloppy with respect to inheritance. (Jim Horning noted that the only object-oriented language he knows that takes inheritance of specifications seriously was the Digital Equipment Corporation ESL OWL/Trellis, which

was a descendant of Barbara Liskov's CLU language). CHERI supports the separations associated with typed objects, in both hardware and software.

20. **Separation of policy and mechanism:** Statements of policy should avoid inclusion of implementation-specific details. Furthermore, mechanisms should be policy-neutral where that is advantageous in achieving functional generality. However, this principle must never be used in the absence of understanding about the range of policies that might be usefully implemented. There is a temptation to avoid defining meaningful policies, deferring them until later in the development— and then discovering that the desired policies cannot be realized with the given mechanisms. This is a characteristic chicken-and-egg problem with abstraction. However, it is again fundamental to the CHERI total-system architecture.

21. **Separation of duties:** In relation to separation of privileges, separate classes of duties of users and computational entities should be identified, so that distinct system roles can be assigned accordingly. Distinct duties should be treated distinctly, as in system administrators, system programmers, and unprivileged users.

22. **Separation of roles:** Concerning separation of privileges, the roles recognized by protection mechanisms should correspond in some readily understandable way to the various duties. For example, a single all-powerful superuser role is intrinsically in violation of separation of duties, separation of roles, separation of privilege, and separation of domains. The separation of would-be superuser functions into separate roles, as in Trusted Xenix, is a good example of desirable separation. Once again (as with single sign-on, noted above), there is a conflict between principles: the monolithic superuser mechanism provides economy of mechanism, but violates other principles. In practice, all-powerful mechanisms are sometimes unavoidable, and sometimes even desirable despite the negative consequences

(particularly if confined to a secure sub-environment). However, they should be avoided wherever possible.

23. **Separation of domains:** Concerning separation of privileges, domains should be able to enforce separate roles. For example, a single all-powerful superuser mechanism is inherently unwise, and is in conflict with the notion of separation of privileges. However, separation of privileges is difficult to implement if there is inadequate separation of domains. Separation of domains can help enforce separation of privilege, but can also provide functional separation as in the Multics ring structure, a kernelized operating system with a carefully designed kernel, or a capability-based architecture.

24. **Sound authentication:** Authentication is a pervasive problem. Non-bypassable authentication should be applicable to users, processes, procedures, and in general to any active entity or object. Authentication relates to evidence that the identity of an entity is genuine, that procedure arguments are legitimate, that types are properly matched when strong typing is to be invoked, and other similar aspects.

25. **Sound authorization and access control:** Authorizations must be correctly and appropriately allocated, and non-subvertible (although they are likely to assume that the identities of all entities and objects involved have been properly authenticated—see sound authentication, above). Crude all-or-nothing authorizations are often risky (particularly with respect to insider misuse and programming flaws). In applications for which user-group-world authorizations are inadequate, access-control lists and role-based authorizations may be preferable. Finer-grained access controls may be desirable in some cases, such as capability-based addressing and field-based database protection. However, knowing who has access to what at any given time should be relatively easy to determine.

26. **Administrative controllability:** The facilities by which systems and

networks are administered must be well-designed, understandable, well-documented, and sufficiently easy to use without inordinate risks. This both a driving principle of the CHERI architecture and a by-product of sensible use of the systems.

27. **Comprehensive accountability:** Well-designed and carefully implemented facilities are essential for comprehensive monitoring, auditing, interpretation, and automated response (as appropriate). Thus, this principle should an a priori concern, as serious security and privacy issues must be carefully used relating to the overall accountability processes and audit data. CHERI addresses this need through its provisioning of trustworthy hardware and operating systems, and its ability to provide high-integrity application compartmentalization.

Table 2 summarizes the utility of the extended-set principles with respect to the three goals of the CHERI program acronym, as in table 6.1. Once again, an asterisk indicates that CHERI makes constructive use of this principle, and is thereby enhances trustworthiness. An asterisk in parentheses implies that this principle was not a driving force in the design, but became easier to satisfy in implements—as a result of the principled system architecture.

For an extensive further elaboration of abstraction, modularity, dependence, and more, see Virgil Gligor's appendix (Visibly Controllable Computing).[6]

At this point in our analysis, it should be no surprise that all of these principles can contribute in varying ways to many aspects of total-system trustworthiness—safety, security, reliability, survivability, and other -ilities. Ultimately, these properties are emergent properties of the total system, and cannot be determined from the components. Furthermore, many of the principles and -ilities are interrelated. We cite just a few of the interdependencies that must be considered.

Table 6.2 Relevance of Extended-Set Trustworthiness Principles to CHERI Goals.

Principle	Composability	Trustworthiness	Assurance
Sound system architecture *	Huge help for compatibility and compositionality	Can greatly increase trustworthiness	Can increase assurance of design and simplify implementation analysis
Abstraction *	Very beneficial if encapsulated	Very beneficial if composable	Simplifies analysis by decoupling it
Encapsulation *	Very beneficial to integration	Very beneficial if composable; avoids certain bug types	Localizes analysis to abstractions and their interactions
Modularity *	Very beneficial if interfaces & specifications well defined	Very beneficial if if well specified; over-modularization impairs performance	Simplifies analysis by decoupling it and if modules are well specified
Layered and compositional assurance *	Very beneficial, but may impair performance	Very beneficial if uncompromisable above/within/below	Structures analysis according to layers and their interactions
Robust dependency *	Can help avoid compositional conflicts	Beneficial: obviates design flaws from misplaced trust	Robust architectural on structure simplifies analysis
Object/type integrity *	Beneficial; labor-intensive? inefficient?	Can be beneficial; may complicate coding and debugging	Can simplify analysis of design, structuring implementation
Separation of policy/mech. *	Beneficial; must compose	Increases evolution and flexibility	Simplifies analysis
Separation of duties *	Indirectly help as a precursor	Beneficial if well defined/enforced	Can simplify analysis if well-defined

Principle	Composability	Trustworthiness	Assurance
Separation of roles *	Beneficial if non-overlapping	Beneficial if properly enforced	Partitions analysis of design and operation
Separation of domains *	Can improve composition and side effects	Allows finer-grain enforcement and self-protection	Partitions analysis of implementation and operation
Sound authentication (*)	Must be invoked uniformly	Security benefits; aids accountability	Can simplify analysis, improve assurance
Sound authorization (*)	Must be invoked uniformly	Reduces misuse, aids accountability	Can simplify analysis, improve assurance
Administrative control (*)	Composability-> controllability	Good design helps controllability	Control enhances operational assurance
Comprehensive accountability (*)	Composability-> accountability	Beneficial for post-hoc analysis	Can provide feedback for improved assurance

For example, authorization is of limited use without authentication, whenever identity is important. Similarly, authentication may be of questionable use without authorization. In some cases, authorization requires fine-grained access controls. Least privilege requires some sort of separation of roles, duties, and domains. Separation of duties is difficult to achieve if there is no separation of roles. Separation of roles, duties, and domains each must rely on a supporting architecture.

The comprehensive accountability principle is particularly intricate, as it depends critically on many other principles being properly invoked. For example, accountability is inherently incomplete without authentication and authorization. In many cases, monitoring may be in conflict with privacy requirements and other social considerations,[20] unless extremely stringent controls are enforceable. Furthermore, trustworthy forensic evidence requires trustworthy systems in the first place. Separation of duties and least privilege are particularly important here. All accountability procedures are subject to security attacks, and are typically prone to covert channels as well. Furthermore, the procedures themselves must be carefully monitored. Who monitors the monitors? (Quis auditiet ipsos audites?)

CAVEATS ON APPLYING THE PRINCIPLES

"For every complex problem, there is a simple solution. And it's always wrong"
– H.L. Mencken

As we noted above, the principles referred to here may be in conflict with one another if each is applied independently. In certain cases, the principles are not composable. In general, each principle must be applied in the context of the overall development. Ideally, greater effort might be useful to reformulate the principles to make them more readily composable, or at least to make their potential tradeoffs or incompatibilities more explicit. However, this is probably counterproductive, because judicious use of principles is not a cookbook exercise.

There are also various potentially harmful considerations that must be considered—for example, over-use, under-use, or misapplication of these principles, and certain limitations inherent in the principles themselves. Merely paying lip-service to a principle is clearly a bad idea; principles must be sensibly applied to the extent that they are appropriate to the given purpose. Similarly, all of the criteria-based methodologies have many systemic limitations;[21,22] for example, formulaic application of evaluation criteria is always subject to incompleteness and misinterpretation of requirements, oversimplification in analysis, and sloppy evaluations. However, when carefully applied, such methodologies can be useful and add discipline to the development process. Thus, we stress the importance of fully understanding the given requirements and of creating an overall architecture that is appropriate for realizing those requirements, before trying to conduct any assessments of compliance with principles or criteria. And then, the assessments must be taken for what they are worth— just one piece of the puzzle—rather than over-endowed, as definitive results out of context. Overall, there is absolutely no substitute for human intelligence, experience, and foresight.

The Saltzer-Schroeder principle of design simplicity is one of the most popular and commonly cited. However, it can be extremely misleading when espoused (as it commonly is) in reference to systems with critical requirements for security, reliability, survivability, real-time performance, and high assurance—especially when all of these requirements are necessary within the same system environment. Simplicity is a very important concept in principle (in the small), but complexity is often unavoidable in practice (in the large). For example, serious attempts to achieve fault-tolerant behavior often result in roughly doubling the size of the overall subsystem or even the entire system. As a result, the principle of simplicity should really be one of managing complexity rather than trying to eliminate it, particularly where complexity is in fact inherent in the combination of requirements. Keeping things simple is indeed a conceptually wonderful principle, but often not achievable. Nevertheless, unnecessary complexity should of course be avoided. The back-side of the Einstein quote at the beginning of the section on Principled Systems, is indeed both profound and relevant, yet often overlooked in the overzealous quest for perceived simplicity.

An extremely effective approach to dealing with intrinsic complexity is through a combination of the principles discussed here. Particularly abstraction, modularity, encapsulation, and careful hierarchical separation that architecturally does not result in serious performance penalties. It also requires well conceived virtualized interfaces that greatly facilitate implementation evolution without requiring changes to the interfaces or that enable design evolution with minimal disruption, and far-sighted optimization. In particular, hierarchical abstraction can result in relative simplicity at the interfaces of each abstraction and each layer, in relative simplicity of the interconnections, and perhaps even relative simplicity in the implementation of each module. By keeping the components and their interconnections conceptually simple, it is possible to achieve conceptual simplicity of the overall system or networks of systems despite inherent complexity. Furthermore, simplicity can sometimes be achieved through design generality, recognizing that several seemingly different problems can be solved systemically at the same time, rather than creating different (and perhaps incompatible) solutions.

Note that such solutions might appear to be a violation of the principle of least common mechanism, but not when the common mechanism is fundamental—as in the use of a single uniform naming convention or the use of a uniform and non-bypassable capability-based addressing mode that transcends different subtypes of typed objects. It is risky to have multiple procedures managing the same data structure for the same purposes. However, it can be very beneficial to separate reading from writing—as in the case of one process that updates and another process that uses the data. It can also be beneficial to reuse the same code on different data structures, although strong typing is then important.

One further unfortunate common practice that should be considered as an anti-principle is security by obscurity. This involves the fallacious belief that if something is never revealed to the public, it is more likely to remain secure. There are notorious counter-examples, such as Matt Blaze's ability to render the Clipper Chip key-escrow process completely useless by disabling the Law-Enforcement Access Field (LEAF) without any access to the classified algorithms and classified production process. (I recall being told by an ex-NSA person: "Oh, yes, we knew about that vulnerability, but did not think anyone would find it.")

One of the primary goals of system developers should be to make system interfaces conceptually simple while masking complexity so that the complexities of the design process and the implementation itself can be hidden by the interfaces. This may in fact increase the complexity of the design process, the architecture, and the implementation. However, the resulting system complexity need be no greater than that required to satisfy the critical requirements such as those for security, reliability, and survivability. It is essential that tendencies toward bloatware be strongly resisted. (They seem to arise largely from the desire for bells and whistles—extra features—and fancy graphics, but also from a lack of enlightened management of program development.)

A networking example of the constructive use of highly principled hierarchical abstraction is given by the protocol layers of TCP/IP.[23] An early total-system co-design is given by the capability-based Provably Secure Operating system hardware-software design (PSOS),[24,25,26] whose functionality at each of more than a dozen layers was specified formally in only a few pages each, with at least the bottom seven layers intended to be implemented in hardware. The underlying addressing is based on a capability mechanism (layer 0) that uniformly encompasses and protects objects of arbitrary types—including files, directories, processes, and other system- and user-defined types. The PSOS design is particularly noteworthy because a single capability-based operation at layer 12 (user processes) could be executed as a single machine instruction at layer 6 (system processes), with no iterative interpretation required unless there were missing pages or unlinked files that require operating system intervention (e.g., for dynamic linking of symbolic names, as in Multics). To many people, hierarchical layering instantly brings to mind inefficiency. However, the PSOS architecture is an example in which the hierarchical design could be implemented extremely efficiently—because of the power of the capability mechanism, strong typing, and abstraction, and its intended hardware implementation.

We note that formalism for its own sake is generally counterproductive. Formal methods are not likely to reduce the overall cost of software development, but can be helpful in decreasing the cost of software quality and assurance. They can be very effective in carefully chosen applications, such as evaluation of requirements, specifications, critical algorithms, and particularly critical code. Once again, we should be optimizing not just the cost of writing and debugging code, but rather optimizing more broadly over the life cycle. (Properties of the CHERI ISA capability mechanism have been subjected to formal analysis.)

There are many other common pitfalls that can result from the unprincipled use of principles. Blind acceptance of a set of principles without understanding their implications is clearly inappropriate. (Blind rejection of principles is also observed occasionally, particularly among people who establish firm requirements with no understanding of whether those requirements are realistically implementable—and among strong-willed developers with a serious lack of foresight.)

Lack of discipline is clearly inappropriate in design and development. For example, we have noted elsewhere[10,27] that the open-source paradigm by itself is not likely to produce secure, reliable, survivable systems in the absence of considerable principled discipline throughout development, operation, and maintenance. However, with such discipline, there can be many benefits. (See information[28] on the many meanings of *open-source,* as well as a Newcastle Dependable Interdisciplinary Research Collaboration (DIRC) final report[29] on dependability issues in open-source software.)

Any principle can typically be carried too far. For example, excessive abstraction can result in over-modularization, with enormous overhead resulting from intermodule communication and non-local control flow. On the other hand, conceptual abstraction through modularization that provides appropriate isolation and separation can sometimes be collapsed (e.g., for efficiency reasons) in the implementation—as long as the essential isolation and protection boundaries are not undermined. Thus, modularity should be considered where it is advantageous, but not merely for its own sake.

Application of each principle is typically somewhat context dependent, and in particular dependent on specific architectures. Principles should always be applied relative to the integrity of the architecture.

One of the severest risks in system development involves local optimization with respect to components or individual functions, rather than global optimization over the entire architecture, its implementation, and its operational characteristics. Radically different conclusions can be reached depending on whether or not you consider the long-term complexities and costs introduced by bad design, sloppy implementation, increased maintenance necessitated by hundreds of patches, incompatibilities between upgrades, lack of interoperability among different components with or without upgrades, and general lack of foresight. Furthermore, unwise optimization (whether local or global) must not collapse abstraction boundaries that are essential for security or reliability—perhaps in the name of improved performance. As one example, real-time checks (such as bounds checks, type checking, and argument validation generally) should be kept close to the operations involved, for obvious reasons.

As another example, the Risks Forum archives include several cases in which multiple alternative communication paths were specified, but were implemented in the same or parallel conduits—which were then all wiped out by a single backhoe.

Perhaps most insidious is the a priori lack of attention to critical requirements, such as any that might involve the motherhood attributes.[17] Particularly in dealing with security, reliability, and survivability in the face of arbitrary adversities, there are few, if any, easy answers. But if those requirements are not dealt with from the beginning of a development, they can be extremely difficult to retrofit later. One particularly appealing survivability requirement would be that systems and networks should be able to reboot, reconfigure, and revalidate their soundness following arbitrary outages, without human intervention. That requirement has numerous architectural implications.

Once again, everything should be made as simple as possible, but no simpler. Careful adherence to principles that are deemed effective is likely to help achieve that goal.

REVIEWING CHERI'S USE OF THE PRINCIPLES

Most of the principles enumerated here were instrumental (explicitly or even occasionally coincidentally) in the CHERI system hardware-software co-design and implementation—as summarized by the asterisks in the left-hand columns of tables 6.1 and 6.2.

Not surprisingly, the highly principled CHERI total-system architecture has actually succeeded in following most of these principles constructively—in the hardware ISAs, in low-layer software, and in the compilers. This principled approach is enabling considerable advances toward much greater trustworthiness. In particular, the CHERI hardware-software co-design has approached inherently complex problems architecturally, structuring the solutions to those problems as conceptually simple compositions of relatively simple components, with emphasis on the predictable behavior of the resulting systems and networks. We are also engaged in formal analyses of the critical hardware properties, which will enhance the assurance that the formal specifications of the hardware ISA will live up to our expectations. We hope that this carefully documented and highly principled effort will be an inspirational example to others.

In that the basic CHERI prototype hardware instruction-set architecture (256-bit capabilities on the extended MIPS64 ISA) is actually scalable downward (e.g., 128-bit capabilities, and even 64-bit capabilities on a 32-bit platform—without the memory-management unit) suggests a considerable range of applicability to a variety of applications. The high-end would be very applicable to servers, cloud storage, rack computing, and powerful desktops; the medium version could be ideal for laptops and mobile devices; and the low-end more suitable for devices and controllers for the Internet of Things. Thus, we can also envision a comparable range of trustworthy operating systems to match the power and trustworthiness of the capability hardware.

CONCLUSIONS

In theory, there is no difference between theory and practice. In practice, there is an enormous difference. (Many variants of this concept are attributed to various people. This is a personal adaptation.)

What would be extremely desirable in our quest for trustworthy systems and networks is theory that is practical and practice that is sufficiently theoretical. Thoughtful and judiciously applied adherence to sensible principles appropriate for a particular development can greatly enhance the security, reliability, and overall survivability of the resulting systems and networks. These principles can also contribute greatly to operational interoperability, maintainability, operational flexibility, long-term ability to evolve, higher assurance, and many other desirable characteristics.

What are generally called "best practices" are often rather lowest-common-denominator techniques that have found their way into practice, rather than what might otherwise be the "best practices" that would be useful.[30,31,32] Furthermore, the supposedly best practices can be misapplied by very good programmers, and bad programming languages can still be used wisely. Unfortunately, spaghetti code is seemingly always on the menu, and engorged bloatware tends to win out over elegance. Overall, there are no easy answers. Having sensible system and network architectures is generally a good starting point—especially if they observe the principles noted here.

NOTES

1. Saltzer, J. *Protection and the control of information sharing in Multics.* Communications of the ACM 17, 7 (July 1974), 388-402.

2. Salter, J. and Schroeder, M. *The Protection of Information in Computer Systems.* In Proceedings of the IEEE 63, 9 (September 1975], 1278-1308.

3. Wulf, W., Cohen, E., Corwin, W., Jones, A., Levin, R., Pierson, C., and Pollack, F. *HYDRA: the kernel of a multiprocessor operating system.* Communications of the ACM 17, 6 (1974), 337-345.

4. Wilkes, M., and Needham, R. *The Cambridge CAP computer and its operating system.* Elsevier North Holland, New York, 1979.

5. Klein, G., Andronick, J., Elphinstone, K., Heiser, G., Cock, D., Derrin, P., Elkaduwe, D., Engelhardt, K., Kolanski, R., Norrish, M., Sewell, T., Tuch, H., and Winwood, S. *seL4: Formal verification of an operating system kernel.* Communications of the ACM 53 (June 2009), 107-115.

6. Dennis, J. B., and Van Horn, E. C. *Programming semantics for multiprogrammed computations.* Communications of the ACM 9, 3 (1966), 143-155.

7. Levy, H. M. *Capability-Based Computer Systems.* Butterworth-Heinemann, Newton, MA, USA, 1984.

8. Carter, N. P., Keckler, S. W., and Dally, W. J. *Hardware support for fast capability-based addressing.* SIGPLAN Not. 29, 11 (Nov. 1994), 319-327.

9. Neumann, P. G. *Principled assuredly trustworthy composable architectures.* Tech. rep., Computer Science Laboratory, SRI International, Menlo Park, California, December 2004. http://www.csl.sri.com/neumann/chats4. html, .pdf, and .ps.

10. Watson, R. N. M., Anderson, J., Laurie, B., and Kennaway, K. *Capsicum: Practical capabilities for Unix.* In Proceedings of the 19th USENIX Security Symposium (August 2010), USENIX.

11. Mettler, A., Wagner, D., and Close, T. *Joe-E: A Security-Oriented Subset of*

Java. In NDSS 2010: Proceedings of the Network and Distributed System Security Symposium (2010).

12. Szekeres, L., Payer, M., Wei, T., and Song, D. *SoK: Eternal war in memory.* In IEEE Symposium on Security and Privacy (2013).

13. Provos, N., Friedl, M., and Honeyman, P. *Preventing Privilege Escalation.* In Proceedings of the 12th USENIX Security Symposium (2003), USENIX.

14. Kilpatrick, D. *Privman: A Library for Partitioning Applications.* In Proceedings of 2003 USENIX Annual Technical Conference (2003).

15. Reis, C., and Gribble, S. D. *Isolating web programs in modern browser architectures.* In EuroSys '09: Proceedings of the 4th European Conference on Computer Systems (2009), ACM.

16. Watson, R. N. M. *A decade of OS access-control extensibility.* Communications of the ACM 56, 2 (Feb. 2013).

17. Watson, R. N. M., Neumann, P. G., Woodruff, J., Roe, M., Anderson, J., Baldwin, J., Chisnall, D., Davis, B., Joannou, A., Laurie, B., Moore, S. W., Murdoch, S. J., Norton, R., Son, S., and Xia, H. *Capability Hardware Enhanced RISC Instructions: CHERI Instruction-Set Architecture (Version 6).* Tech. Rep. UCAM-CL-TR-907, University of Cambridge, Computer Laboratory, Apr. 2017.

18. Woodruff, J., Watson, R. N. M., Chisnall, D., Moore, S. W., Anderson, J., Davis, B., Laurie, B., Neumann, P. G., Norton, R., and Roe, M. *The CHERI capability model: Revisiting RISC in an age of risk.* In Proceedings of the 41st International Symposium on Computer Architecture (June 2014).

19. Chisnall, D., Rothwell, C., Davis, B., Watson, R. N., Woodruff, J., Vadera, M., Moore, S. W., Neumann, P. G., and Roe, M. *Beyond the PDP-11: Processor support for a memory-safe C abstract machine.* In Proceedings of the 20th Architectural Support for Programming Languages and Operating systems (2015), ACM.

20. Watson, R. N. M., Woodruff, J., Neumann, P. G., Moore, S. W., Anderson, J., Chisnall, D., Dave, N., s Davis, B., Gudka, K., Laurie, B., Murdoch, S. J.,

Norton, R., Roe, M., Son, S., and Vadera, M. *CHERI: A Hybrid Capability-System Architecture for Scalable Software Compartmentalization.* In Proceedings of the 36th IEEE Symposium on Security and Privacy (May 2015).

21. Watson, R. N. M., Chisnall, D., Davis, B., Koszek, W., Moore, S. W., Murdoch, S. J., Neumann, P. G., and Woodruff, J. *Capability Hardware Enhanced RISC Instructions: CHERI Programmer's Guide.* Tech. Rep. UCAM-CL-TR-877, University of Cambridge, Computer Laboratory, 15 JJ Thomson Avenue, Cambridge CB3 0FD, United Kingdom, Nov. 2015.

22. Watson, R. N., Woodruff, J., Chisnall, D., Davis, B., Koszek, W., Markettos, A. T., Moore, S. W., Murdoch, S. J., Neumann, P. G., Norton, R., and Roe, M. *Bluespec Extensible RISC Implementation: BERI Hardware reference.* Tech. Rep. UCAM-CL-TR-852, University of Cambridge, Computer Laboratory, Apr. 2014.

23. Watson, R. N. M., Neumann, P. G., Woodruff, J., Roe, M., Anderson, J., Chisnall, D., Davis, B., Joannou, A., Laurie, B., Moore, S. W., Murdoch, S. J., Norton, R., Son, S., and Xia, H. *Capability Hardware Enhanced RISC Instructions: CHERI Instruction-Set Architecture (Version 5).* Tech. Rep. UCAM-CL-TR-891, University of Cambridge, Computer Laboratory, June 2016.

24. Karger, P. *Limiting the damage potential of discretionary Trojan horses.* In Proceedings of the 1987 Symposium on Security and Privacy (April 1987), IEEE.

25. Neumann, P., Boyer, R., Feiertag, R., Levitt, K., and Robinson, L. A Provably *Secure Operating system: The system, its applications, and proofs.* Tech. rep., Computer Science Laboratory, SRI International, May 1980. 2nd edition, Report CSL-116.

26. Watson, R. N. M., Norton, R. M., Woodruff, J., Moore, S. W., Neumann, P. G., Anderson, J., Chisnall, D., Davis, B., Laurie, B., Roe, M., Dave, N. H., Gudka, K., Joannou, A., Markettos, A. T., Maste, E., Murdoch, S. J.,

Rothwell, C., Son, S. D., and Vadera, M. *Fast protection-domain crossing in the CHERI capability-system architecture.* IEEE Micro 36, 5 (Sept 2016), 38-49.

27. Gudka, K., Watson, R. N. M., Anderson, J., Chisnall, D., Davis, B., Laurie, B., Marinos, I., Neumann, P. G., and Richardson, A. *Clean Application Compartmentalization with SOAAP.* In Proceedings of the 22nd ACM Conference on Computer and Communications Security (CCS 2015) (October 2015).

28. Memarian, K., Matthiesen, J., Lingard, J., Nienhuis, K., Chisnall, D., Watson, R. N., and Sewell, P. *Into the depths of C: elaborating the de facto standards.* In Proceedings of PLDI 2016 (June 2016).

29. Jim, T., Morrisett, J. G., Grossman, D., Hicks, M. W., Cheney, J., and Wang, Y. *Cyclone: A safe dialect of C.* In Proceedings of the USENIX Annual Technical Conference (Berkeley, CA, USA, 2002), USENIX.

30. Nagarakatte, S., Zhao, J., Martin, M. M. K., and Zdancewic, S. *SoftBound: highly compatible and complete spatial memory safety for C.* In Proceedings of the 2009 ACM SIGPLAN conference on Programming language design and implementation (2009), ACM.

31. Necula, G. C., McPeak, S., and Weimer, W. *CCured: Type-safe retrofitting of legacy code.* ACM SIGPLAN Notices 37, 1 (2002), 128-139.

32. Kwon, A., Dhawan, U., Smith, J. M., Knight, Jr., T. F., and DeHon, A. *Low-fat pointers: Compact encoding and efficient gate-level implementation of fat pointers for spatial safety and capability-based security.* In 20th Conference on Computer and Communications Security (November 2013), ACM.

33. Watson, R. N. M., Neumann, P. G., Woodruff, J., Anderson, J., Chisnall, D., Davis, B., Laurie, B., Moore, S. W., Murdoch, S. J., and Roe, M. *Capability Hardware Enhanced RISC Instructions: CHERI Instruction-set architecture.* Tech. Rep. UCAM-CL-TR-864, University of Cambridge, Computer Laboratory, Dec. 2014.

34. Watson, R. N. M., Neumann, P. G., Woodruff, J., Roe, M., Anderson, J., Chisnall, D., Davis, B., Joannou, A., Laurie, B., Moore, S. W., Murdoch, S. J., Norton, R., and Son, S. *Capability Hardware Enhanced RISC Instructions: CHERI Instruction-Set Architecture.* Tech. Rep. UCAM-CL-TR-876, University of Cambridge, Computer Laboratory, 15 JJ Thomson Avenue, Cambridge CB3 0FD, United Kingdom, Nov. 2015.

CHAPTER 7

ISP—Hardware Enforcement of Security Policies

Gregory T. Sullivan, Jothy Rosenberg,
Howard E. Shrobe, and André DeHon

OVERVIEW

The Inherently Secure Processor (ISP) is a new processor architecture that takes security seriously. ISP extends a conventional processor architecture with additional circuitry that applies security policies in lock step with the ordinary execution of application instructions. At a high level, the ISP computer architecture can be viewed as two interlinked processors executing two programs in lock step. The first program, which we call the application, is whatever program is running at the time (web browser, web server, control program for a physical device, etc.), including the operating system. The second program is the set of security policies that were securely installed when the system was powered on.

Security policies that can be enforced by the ISP architecture cover at least 90% of the vulnerabilities enumerated by the Common Vulnerabilities and Exposures (CVE) database.[1]

Existing approaches to cybersecurity deploy ever more complex "security software" systems in an effort to protect our ever more complex and valuable cyber-physical systems from attack. Protecting complex, bug-ridden software systems using other complex, and inevitably bug-ridden software systems, has never worked and never will.

The ISP computer architecture has been designed based on a few core principles:
- Transistors are cheap, small, and plentiful enough that we should dedicate some hardware resources towards enforcing security, in addition to executing application logic.
- Since the preponderance of cyberattacks exploit software vulnerabilities created by defects (bugs), the intent of the program needs to be conveyed to the processor. A processor cannot enforce security policies that it does

not know about. Once the processor knows the size of a buffer, that a data item is a pointer, or that a word is an instruction, then it can enforce rules about those entities.

- Hardware interlocks must ensure that security policy logic and associated metadata is inaccessible to the application code and data. Furthermore, hardware interlocks should ensure that it is impossible to avoid or subvert enforcement of security policies.

- There is no fixed set of security policies that will address all security concerns for all users for all computing platforms forever. Thus, we require the capability to add and customize security policies based on a myriad of priorities and parameters.

The rest of this chapter will go into greater depth on:

- The underlying causes of the poor state of cyber *in-security* in which we find ourselves.

- The ISP security architecture, including how ISP is able to maintain full speed in the common case.

- ISP *micro-policies* and the wide range of security (and safety) policies that can be enforced by the ISP architecture.

- ISP's self-protection mechanisms that prevent the processor and its critical security apparatus from being the victim of an attack itself, including how ISP securely segregates policy code and data from application code and data.

MOTIVATION: OUR POOR STATE OF CYBER "IN-SECURITY"

Our legacy processor architectures are built around what the cybersecurity community calls "Raw Seething Bits"—a description of what it means to have a single undifferentiated memory where the processor cannot tell if a word is an instruction or an integer or a pointer to a block of memory. There is an important reason processors started out having this single undifferentiated memory: It was simple to build. Simple was important when logic was performed by vacuum tubes or, a bit later, by a few expensive transistors.

That architecture—still in use in virtually all our computing devices whether servers, laptops, or embedded devices—is Von Neumann's 1945 stored-program computer (see figure 7.1). Discovering the simplest architecture that worked, the industry started to perfect it, made transistors smaller and smaller, and ultimately started to see a trend that became known as Moore's Law take hold.

Moore's Law stated that every 18 months the number of transistors occupying the same area would double. The reason for the explosion of the Internet, mobile devices, and the rapidly growing Internet of Things, is Moore's Law leveraging this simple architecture and is driven by a mantra of "smaller, cheaper, faster." This has given us an iPhone more powerful than all computers combined that NASA owned when it landed men on the moon. Transistors are now incredibly cheap, and while Moore's Law may have reached its limit, the 2,000 transistors for the first microprocessor in 1971 have become 15 billion transistors in the 2015 Oracle Sparc M7. The combination of (1) dramatically more powerful processors, (2) connecting all of these processors together (thanks to the Internet), and (3) not ensuring security from the ground up, has made cyber threats prevalent and serious.

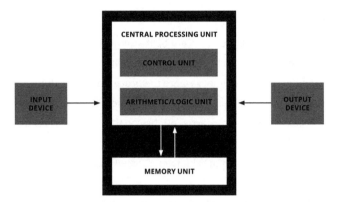

Figure 7.1 The Von Neumann Processor Architecture.

In 1945, Von Neumann and others described a simple but powerful processor architecture with a single internal memory. This architecture continues to dominate the architecture of processors in billions of devices today. The single memory is where instructions, data, pointers and all the data structures needed by an application are stored with no way to tell what is what. It is this memory sometimes called "raw, seething bits" that prevents the processor from co-operating with the program to enforce security.

To implement secure programs, there are important constraints that have to be enforced in every program by every programmer. But those vital constraints can only be enforced when every programmer gets everything right on every single line of code. A single mistake becomes a vulnerability and can sink the ship.

Each of the over 80,000 CVE-related idioms that NIST maintains[2] started out as a bug created by a programmer that turned into a cybersecurity exploit. A single CVE (like not checking buffer bounds) can have many instances (hundreds or thousands in a single program, millions to billions in today's more complex systems). You cannot remove a CVE by fixing one instance—you have to fix it everywhere. If you fix it in N-1 places, there is still one porthole open for the bad guys to get in (and they will). A lot of ships begin sinking.

Since vulnerabilities are inevitable using today's, and the foreseeable future's, programming methods, and they make our systems unsafe by default, how can we win? What if the underlying processor didn't allow the vulnerabilities to become an attack vector? What if the processor was inherently secure even if the software running on it has vulnerabilities? Inherent security means safe by default even when programmers make mistakes.

This is achievable. It is possible to change the architecture of our processors, use transistors for security purposes, and build a new computing foundation that is inherently secure without giving up backwards compatibility to existing processor instruction sets, operating systems, and programming languages.

OVERVIEW OF THE ISP ARCHITECTURE

Building on a $100M DARPA investment from the 2010–2014 CRASH program that focused on basic research to build a "clean-slate" inherently secure processor (ISP), has seen Draper picking up that research. Draper has turned it into a practical, commercially viable, and inherently secure processor that is immune to the software vulnerabilities responsible for the vast majority of serious cyberattacks. In the effort to accelerate maturation and transition,

Draper has spun out a company, Dover Microsystems, funded by external investors and targeting commercial markets such as Industrial Internet of Things (IIOT) and medical devices.

The inherently secure processor being developed at Draper and Dover provably and securely enforces a combination of security policies. A key insight behind the development of ISP:

> *A computer cannot enforce policies it does not know about.*

ISP provides the ability to inform the computer about the policies it should enforce. Using hardware (and therefore unsubvertible) mechanisms, ISP addresses the above insight by providing a securely installed, isolated set of policy rules, as well as the mechanism to maintain per-word metadata to be maintained and examined by the security policies. ISP hardware interlocks ensure that at every instruction the set of installed security policies are checked and not one single instruction will execute that violates any of these policies.

Using a carefully designed cache, ISP is able to avoid slowing processor performance in the common case of seeing a combination of metadata that it has seen before.

We will explain how this works in a moment but first, why aren't Intel, IBM, Oracle/SUN, or ARM doing this?

The short answer is this: they are, and they will do more. But the more nuanced answer is that first, constant pressure to get more performance leads them to use those ever-cheaper transistors to build multi-core chips and deliver more features and performance. Further, the requirement for

100% backward compatibility for millions of applications running on billions of existing devices forces them into an incremental change model. They are coming out with new instructions and other incremental developments that acknowledge security is a problem and it must be addressed, but they cannot move too quickly for fear of breaking their legacy.

Unlike the inevitably vulnerable software-only cybersecurity systems, ISP uses hardware mechanisms to isolate metadata and policy enforcement from attacker code. Unlike policy-specific hardware safety mechanisms demonstrated by Intel and Oracle, ISP supports an infinitely customizable set of security policies than can adapt over time to an evolving cyber landscape.

Draper's approach to creating an inherently secure processor is to add metadata tags to every word in memory (a way to process those tags in parallel with instruction processing) and to define a language of micro-policies that enforce security based on information in the metadata tags. A good way to think about what these security/safety micro-policies do for our current inherently insecure processors is to add an *interlock*.

When you build a nuclear power plant, you include several levels of safety interlocks to prevent the worst things from happening. Interlocks here include temperature sensors to shut things down if they get too hot, and shunt valves to dump reactants. Machines have physical interlock buttons to shut down dangerous cutters if they are opened. Radiation machines have physical interlocks to prevent removal of the shield when the radiation beam is set too high. Even highways have physical guard rails and barriers to prevent drivers from driving off ramps and bridges into oncoming traffic, even if the driver falls asleep. Our goal is to provide a set of interlocks in the processor that detect bad things, which shouldn't happen, and prevent the most egregious things from happening. Let's look in some detail now at the three key ideas that create these security interlocks: Programmable metadata tags, a Programmable Interlock for Policy Enforcement, and a set of micro-policies.

Programmable Metadata Tags

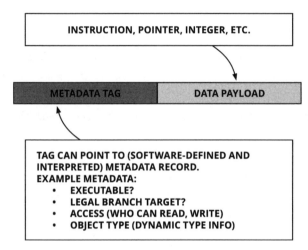

Figure 7.2 Metadata tags are on every word.

Associated with every word is a metadata tag. The word may be an instruction, a pointer, an integer or any other data item. The metadata can point to a software-defined and interpreted record. That record indicates certain properties of the data payload. Properties might include the provenance of the data, the fine-grained access control associated with the data, what type the data is, whether it is an instruction or data, or a legal branch target, and more.

The first architectural modification to the processor is programmable metadata tags. Here is where we use the most silicon (transistors) to support security. A metadata tag is a word of memory attached to and permanently associated with a "normal" word of memory. Call that normal word the *payload*. A payload might be an instruction for the processor, a value to be processed, or a pointer to data structures stored in memory. A tag attached to a payload word of memory is not a new concept. LISP machines used it for identifying types. A machine made by a computer company called Burroughs had a tag bit in each word to identify the word as a control word or numeric word. This was partially a security mechanism to stop programs from being able to corrupt control words on the stack. Later, it was realized that the 1-bit control word/numeric distinction was a powerful idea, and this was extended to three bits outside of the 48-bit native word into a more general tag used for things like "this is the top of the stack," "this is a return address," "this is code," "this is data," "this is the index value for a loop," and so on. Tagged architectures have been the subject of many research papers.

The ISP architecture employs a comprehensive approach to metadata tagging as shown in figure 7.2. These tags can point to software-defined and interpreted metadata records. This metadata can express provenance (where and whom the data came from), access control (who can read or write the payload word), executability (the payload for an instruction), legal branch target (the payload for an address that it is legal for the program to branch to), and any other dynamic data that can be collected during program runtime. Most important is the fact that these metadata tags are permanently bonded to the payload word, are uninterpreted by the hardware, can be a pointer to an arbitrary data structure, and are not accessible from the application. The hardware component that will process these tags is called a Processor Interlock for Policy Enforcement (PIPE).

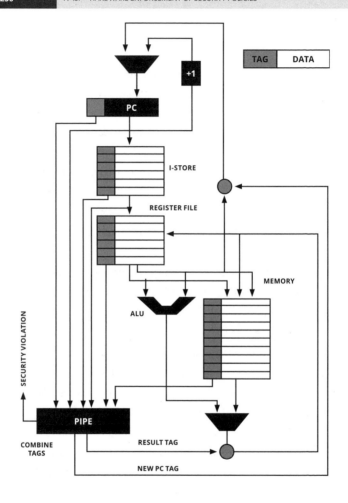

Figure 7.3 Addition of tags and PIPE to processor.

Tags are shown in green and are placed on the PC, the Instruction Store,

the registers, and all words in memory. In parallel with the ALU performing the

computation, the PIPE determines if the micro-policy for that operation will allow

that instruction to complete or whether or not it is a policy violation.

Processor Interlock for Policy Enforcement (PIPE)

To process these tags in parallel with the standard Arithmetic Logic Unit (ALU)—the heart of the processing pipeline of any standard processor—we create a PIPE, the second architectural modification to the processor, and add it into the instruction processing pipeline, such that it operates in parallel with the ALU (see figure 7.3). Note that in the diagram the Program Counter (PC), the Instruction Store, the Register File, and all the general-purpose memory have the extra word of metadata associated with them shown in green. As the ALU executes an instruction, the PIPE operates in parallel checking and updating appropriate tags. The hardware makes sure that payloads are sent to the ALU while tags are sent to the PIPE so that parallel processing of tags happens at the same speed as instruction processing.

To propagate tags efficiently, the PIPE is augmented with a rule cache that operates in parallel with instruction execution. On a rule cache miss, control is transferred to a trusted miss handler (executing policy code) which, given the tags of the instruction's arguments, decides whether the current operation should be allowed and, if so, computes appropriate tags for its results. It then adds this set of argument and result tags to the rule cache, so that when the same situation is encountered in the future, the rule can be applied without slowing down the processor.

In performance tests on accurate machine simulators, the overall performance overhead for security enforcement is less than 10%.

INTRODUCTION TO MICRO-POLICIES

Metadata tags and the PIPE give us a general mechanism for securely and efficiently maintaining and checking complex metadata in parallel with application execution. But how do we specify the set of policies that we want enforced? *Micro-policies* (abbreviated as μ-policies hereon in) allow us to specify the metadata that should be maintained during execution, and exactly when that metadata may indicate a security violation. Furthermore, ISP's μ-policy framework composes multiple μ-policies together into one optimized global policy.

Examples of μ-policies and what they protect against include:

Memory Safety	Protecting buffers in memory from over-read or over-write.
Control-flow Integrity	Guaranteeing that only jumps to program-defined locations are made at run-time.
Taint Tracking / Information Flow Control	Tracking the influences of values through a computation to prevent untrusted values from influencing critical decisions and to limit the flow of sensitive data (e.g., guarantee encryption if data leaves the system).
Access Control	Fine-grained control over who has what kind of access to a piece of data.
Type Safety	Making sure types declared in the program are manipulated, as those types not just as raw data.
Instruction Permission	Protects special sections of code from being executed by user level applications, which is a part of the ISP self-protection mechanism.

As the PIPE processes tags associated with an instruction, it takes the relevant metadata and sends it to the installed set of software-defined μ-policies, where the metadata is checked against those policies and, if the instruction is allowed to complete, determines the result tags. Like an inline security auditor, if the result is not allowed by policy, the PIPE flags a security violation that causes the current instruction to fail which may kill the execution thread (or could be handled by the application's exception handler if the programmer provided such).

μ-policies Enforce Security

The programming model for μ-policies involves abstracting the hardware. At the hardware level, as we have shown, there are metadata bits attached to each word and there is a hardware PIPE whose job it is to resolve this metadata. It is important that the programmer should not have to worry about limits, such as the number of bits of metadata or the complexity of the rule logic inside the PIPE. For generality, the metadata tag will be viewed as a pointer that can point to a data structure of arbitrary size.

A policy is a collection of rules that take the form:

$$(opcode,\ PC_{tag},\ INST_{tag},\ OP1_{tag},\ OP2_{tag},\ MR_{tag}) \rightarrow (allow?,\ PC'_{tag},\ Result_{tag})$$

This is a transfer function processed by the PIPE (diagrammed in figure 7.4).

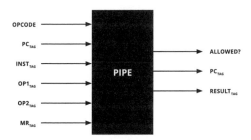

Figure 7.4. Abstract Function of the PIPE.

The PIPE performs a transfer function based on the Opcode and the tags on the Program Counter, the Instruction, operand 1, operand 2, and memory reference, if those elements exist for this particular instruction. The result of the PIPE's operation is whether this instruction is allowed to complete or not, and, if so, creates new tags for the PC and the Result.

The *opcode* indicates what sort of instruction is being executed (e.g., an ADD instruction, or a LOAD, or a BRANCH). All the remaining arguments—PC, INST, OP1, OP2, MR—are the *tags* of the Program Counter, the Instruction, operand 1, operand 2, and memory reference, respectively, if those elements exist for the current instruction. To better understand how μ-policies work, we will examine memory safety, control-flow integrity, and taint tracking μ-policies.

Example μ-policies

Memory Safety – Protects Against Buffer Overflow Attacks

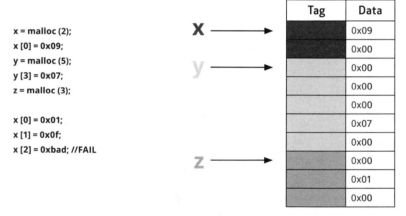

Figure 7.5 Memory Safety μ-Policy.
Pointers x, y, and z are created through calls to the runtime routine malloc. Malloc is given the number of bytes to allocate, which it colors using the next color value available. It also colors the pointer to the beginning of the buffer before it returns that pointer. The μ-policy demands that the memory cells in all memory operations match the color of the pointer used for access. In the sample code note that x[2] is outside the range of the buffer pointed to by x so that the assignment will fail.

In the rankings of the top vulnerability categories of 2016, according to Verizon,[3] the top 10 CVEs accounted for 85% of all exploits, and 7 of those 10 were memory errors. Consequently memory safety is the first and probably most important μ-policy to consider. What we will outline here is a simplified version of our actual memory safety policy.

This policy will work for heap-allocated data such as what is created by calls to the runtime function *malloc*. We want this policy to protect against both spatial safety violations (e.g., accessing an array out of its bounds) and temporal safety violations (e.g., referencing through a pointer after the region has been freed). Such violations are a common source of security vulnerabilities, such as heap-based buffer overflows, confidential data leaks, exploitable use-after-free, and double-free bugs.

The method we will use, shown in figure 7.5, is to give each pointer a unique "color" and then to color each memory slot in the allocated buffer with the same color. A "color" is just a numeric value of size $2^{number-of-bits}$, where number-of-bits is the size of the metadata tag available for this purpose (typically 32-bits, which provides over 4 billion unique values).

Some μ-policies track a fixed set of tag values. For example, a simple taint-tracking policy may only track "tainted" versus "not tainted." Or a dynamic type checking policy may distinguish between a fixed set of types (e.g., "pointer" versus "integer" versus "instruction").

Other policies dynamically allocate new tag values based on runtime behavior. The heap memory safety micro-policy is an example of dynamic tag generation, where a newly allocated block of memory is "colored" with a newly generated color/integer.

A core principle of ISP's design is that user-land (including the operating system code) cannot inspect either tag metadata or policy code. Similarly, micro-policy code cannot directly reach into user-land memory. As a result, runtime code cannot simply create a new tag and apply it to a word in the machine. Instead, user-land code "signals" the micro-policy code by accessing specially tagged words in memory and/or by executing specially tagged instructions.

The transfer function for the heap memory safety μ-policy, for LOAD instructions, is:

$$(LOAD, \text{-}, \text{-}, (\text{-}, R1PtrColor), \text{-}, (MemRegionColor, MemPtrColor)) \rightarrow$$
$$(R1PtrColor == MemRegionColor, \text{-}, (RegisterColor, MemPtrColor))$$

To understand this rule, note that, for the memory safety policy, every location actually has a *pair* of colors (*RegionColor*, *PtrColor*) associated with it. The *RegionColor* color is the location in memory in which the value lives. For registers, *RegionColor* is a constant *RegisterColor*. *PtrColor* is the color, if the value is a pointer, into which the pointer is allowed to dereference. For non-pointer values, *PtrColor* is a constant *ValueColor*.

The rule says that the LOAD instruction will be allowed to complete only if the *PtrColor* component of the register R1 is the same (represented as "==") as the *RegionColor* component of the tag on the memory location being dereferenced. If that condition is true, then the register receiving the value loaded from memory gets the *PtrColor* from the memory cell.

We might additionally require that the PC *PtrColor* matches the color of the block to which the PC points. This would ensure that the PC cannot be used to leak information about inaccessible frames by loading instructions from them.

All other slots in the formula are designated by "hyphens"; a "hyphen" on the left-hand side means "do not care," and "hyphen" on the right-hand side means "keeps same value."

We want to allow adding and subtracting integers from pointers since C/C++ does this frequently. The result of such pointer arithmetic is a pointer with the same color. The new pointer is not necessarily in bounds, but the rules for LOAD and STORE opcodes will prevent invalid accesses. (Computing an out-of-bounds pointer is not a violation per se; however, reading or writing through it is, and will be, handled by the rules for LOAD and STORE.)

This simple µ-policy, in conjunction with support from the runtime system's **malloc** and **free**, and from the compiler (as it creates stack frames for each function called), provides memory safety, preventing buffer overflows when both reading and writing into memory.

Memory safety is so critical that the major processor vendors are starting to address the issue themselves. Intel is introducing new MPX (Memory Protection Extensions) instructions as a set of extensions to the x86 instruction set architecture.[4] With compiler, runtime library, and operating system support, these instructions are designed to prevent accidental (or malicious) out-of-bounds pointer references. With MPX there are new bounds registers, and new instruction set extensions that operate on these registers. The result is x86 support for memory protection that, once compilers are modified to use them, will protect against buffer overflows.

In addition, Oracle/SUN announced the Sparc M7, which uses the highest four bits of a pointer (a tag of sorts), to keep track of 2^4 (or 16) different regions of memory (buffers) and protect them from reads or writes going out of bounds on them. This is a step in the right direction but only the simplest program creates only 16 distinct buffers, so this does not sufficiently address the buffer overflow vulnerability. While both these developments are encouraging—because it means the major vendors are cognizant of the huge problem—they have a long way to go in addressing all of the other identified NIST Common Vulnerabilities and Exploits.

Control Flow Integrity - Protects Against Return-Oriented Programming Attacks

A simple security mechanism that has become popular on current architectures and operating systems is the use of an NX ("No eXecute") bit. An NX bit is a page-level marker used to distinguish between unwritable memory that contains executable instructions and writeable memory that contains non-executable data. The NX scheme defeats simple binary code injection attacks (in which the attacker injects their own code into a target system), and, as a result, attackers have devised more subtle methods of taking control over the code that is running on a victim's machine. In particular, a general approach called *code reuse attacks* (or *control flow hijacking*) changes the order in which application code is executed, thus repurposing the application's code to do the attacker's bidding.

A prevalent form of code reuse attack is called *Return-Oriented Programming (ROP)*. In this technique, an attacker first identifies a set of machine instruction sequences (called *gadgets*) from within the targeted application, where each gadget ends with a RETURN statement. In the second phase of a ROP attack, the attacker overwrites the area on the program stack that controls where active functions return. By writing a sequence of return addresses to the stack, the attacker can execute any sequence of gadgets, and thus any sequence of instructions, which is equivalent, from the attacker's perspective, of having injected their own code. To understand a control flow integrity policy that prevents ROP attacks, it is important to understand that these attacks work by returning into the middle of sequences of code—returns (i.e., control-flow-branches) that did not exist in the original program. Current processors will blindly run the code for the attacker.

The control flow integrity (CFI) μ-policy presented below dynamically enforces that all control transfers (including indirect jumps) adhere to a fixed control flow graph (CFG) emitted by a compiler. This policy is another *interlock* that prevents control-flow-hijacking attacks by locking down control transfers to *only* those intended by the program.

The sample code we will use to illustrate this is shown in figure 7.6. While in function foo(), function bar() is called. The address at which that call occurs is t1. The address where bar() begins is t2 (this relationship is shown with a solid arrow). The address in bar() where it is about to return to its caller is t3. Somewhere else in the program assume bar() is also called from address t42 as well as a few other places. Thus, the full list of legal address locations bar() can be called from includes t1, t42, and a few others (as shown at the bottom of the figure). This list of legal locations from which bar() can be called (shown coming from the dashed arrow), is maintained in the tag on the instruction at address t2. As you will see, CFI uses tags to distinguish the memory locations containing instructions and the sources and targets of jumps, while using the PC tag to track execution history (the sources of indirect jumps).

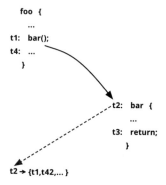

Figure 7.6 Control-flow integrity example.

Function foo() calls bar() from location t1. The call results in a jump to location t2 where bar() begins. The only return from bar() occurs at t3. The complete list of legal ways to get to bar() are listed with t2. Here we show t1, (where bar() is called from foo()), as well at t42 not shown here.

On a call to the function bar(), the µ-policy rule that governs what happens is described by the following transfer function:

$$(CALL, none, INST_{tag}, -, -, -) \rightarrow (true, INST_{tag}, -)$$

This declares that, when the PC tag is *none* (not already in the middle of a call), the tag from the call instruction ($INST_{tag}$) is copied to the tag for the PC as a result of the CALL instruction. The second half of control flow integrity enforcement comes from the following transfer function:

$$(\neg CALL, PC_{tag}, INST_{tag}, -, -, -) \rightarrow (PC_{tag} \ \varepsilon \ INST_{tag}, none, -)$$

This says that whenever the processor is not executing a CALL instruction and the PC is tagged (with the tag of the calling instruction), check that the tag on the PC is in the list of "legal caller tags" on the current instruction. The PIPE also untags the PC as shown by the *none* in the PC tag spot on the right-hand side of the transfer function. The CFI policy applies the same approach to RETURNs. In the example in figure 7.6, when control transfers from t3 back to t4, the PC is tagged with the tag of the instruction at t3 and the tag of the instruction at t4 must contain the tag from t3, as an allowed jump-from address. This set of transfer functions direct the PIPE to strictly enforce the CFG and only allow control transfers to those locations specified in the program, thus creating another interlock that thwarts return-oriented programming attacks.

It is worth noting the flexibility allowed by this architecture. We can implement a coarse-grained CFI μ-policy by merely labeling instructions that are legal control flow transfer targets; that is, not even restrict jumps according to legal (from, to) pairs. We can implement a slightly finer-grained CFI policy by labeling all call (and return) sites in a function with the same tag, in which case the CFI policy will only check that a control flow transfer is between legal (from, to) function pairs. Finally, if each possible transfer site has a unique tag, we get a more fine-grained CFI policy. This sort of flexibility allows ISP customers to fine-tune the balance between policy granularity and performance.

Taint Tracking—Track the Influence of Data Values as they Flow through a Computation

Here we will show how a taint tracking μ-policy can be used to track integrity (or provenance or secrecy) of data throughout the system, preventing classes of attacks, including exfiltration of sensitive data and "improper neutralization" (e.g., "SQL injection" attacks). In a SQL injection attack, data from outside the system is used to construct a command that is sent to the back-end database system. If the incoming data is not sent through a "neutralization" routine, potentially harmful commands can be sent to the database. A simple taint tracking policy assigns a *taint* to data coming from outside of the system, and blocks use of tainted data in calls to the database system. Only a privileged neutralization (sometimes called "sanitization") function can remove taint. Taint propagation is straightforward, with the taint of the output of any instruction being the union of the taint of any of the input values. In other words, if any operands to an instruction are tainted, the result is tainted. Another rule that taint tracking can enforce is "if the data is not public it may not leave the system un-encrypted."

The policy, as applied to the ADD instruction, would be represented by the following transfer function:

$$(ADD, PC_{tag}, INST_{tag}, OP1_{tag}, OP2_{tag}, \text{-}) \rightarrow (true, PC_{tag}, union(PC_{tag}, INST_{tag}, OP1_{tag}, OP2_{tag}))$$

Here, the tag on the Result is formed from the union of the tag on all the operands including the PC, INST, OP1 and OP2.

Figure 7.7 A tag can point to an array of metadata structures

To implement composite policies, we can think of a tag as pointing to an array of record structures, where each structure is maintained by one μ-policy.

Composite Policies—To Allow an Arbitrary Number of Policies be Enforced

It is important that ISP be able to enforce multiple policies simultaneously. An arbitrary number of policies may be required and this is supported in our model by using the tag as a pointer to a tuple of μ-policy metadata records. There is no hardware limit on the number of μ-policies supported in this fashion. For example, figure 7.7 represents a tag pointing to metadata that supports a combination of dynamic type checking, memory safety, control flow integrity, and taint tracking.

A partial list of the types of safety and security policies that can be implemented using the mechanisms just described is listed in table 7.1.

Returning to the analogy of metadata+PIPE+μ-policies being *interlocks*, one of their advantages is that policies are small (few 100s to 1000 lines of code), but they are protecting millions of lines of code. While a programmer has no chance of having millions of lines of code being bug-free, they do have a chance of making the interlocks be bug-free. Just to be certain, since these bits of software are small *and* highly important, they are amenable to and worth verifying formally.

Table 7.1 A partial list of micro-policies supported by the ISP

• Type Safety	• Mandatory Access Control
• Memory Safety	• Classification levels
• Control-Flow Integrity	• Lightweight compartmentalization
• Stack Safety	• Software Fault Isolation
• Unforgeable Resource Identifiers	• Sandboxing
• Abstract Types	• Access control
• Immutability	• Capabilities
• Linearity	• Provenance
• Units	• Full/Empty Bits
• Signing	• Concurrency: Race Detection
• Sealing	• Debugging
• Endorsement	• Data tracing
• Taint	• Introspection
• Confidentiality	• Audit
• Integrity	• Reference monitors
• Bignums	• Garbage collection

CONCLUSION AND FUTURE

Despite heroic efforts to secure our critical software systems using better programming processes or adding additional "security" software, our systems remain plagued with vulnerabilities. The Inherenty Secure Processor (ISP) architecture development incubated at Draper and now spun off into commercial startup Dover Microsystems, enables the reliable enforcement of software-defined security and safety policies. The ISP dedicates some amount of hardware memory and logic to the task of enforcing these policies, but we argue that this cost is worth the enormous increase in security and confidence that results. The ISP allows per-customer customization of the set of policies enforced, enabling adaptation to an ever-changing cybersecurity landscape.

NOTES

1. Common Vulnerabilities and Exposures (CVE) database: https://cve.
    mitre.org/

2. National Vulnerability Database (NVD): https://nvd.nist.gov/

3. Verizon Data Breach Investigations Report: http://www.
    verizonenterprise.com/verizon-insights-lab/dbir/

4. Intel Memory Protection Extensions: https://software.intel.com/en-us/
    isa-extensions/intel-mpx

CHAPTER 8

Stealing Reality: When Criminals Become Data Scientists

Yaniv Altshuler, Nadav Aharony, Yuval Elovici,
Alex Pentland, and Manuel Cebrian

INTRODUCTION

We live in the age of social computing. Social networks are everywhere, exponentially increasing in volume, and changing everything about our lives, the way we do business, and how we understand ourselves and the world around us. The challenges and opportunities residing in the social oriented ecosystem have overtaken the scientific, financial, and pop-ular discourse. With the growing emphasis on personalization, personal recommendation systems, and social networking, there is a growing interest in understanding personal and social behavior patterns. This trend is manifested in the growing demand for "data scientists" and data-mining experts in the commercial ecosystem, which in turn is derived from the increasing number of social data-driven start-up companies, as well the social inference related research sponsored by other commercial entities and various NGOs.

This work is somewhat of a "what if" exploration: History has shown that whenever something has a tangible value associated with it, there will always be those who will try to steal it for profit. Along this line of thought—based on these current trends of the data ecosystem coupled with the emergence of advanced tools for social and behavioral pattern detection and inference—we ask the following : What will happen when the criminals become data scientists?

We conjecture that the world will increasingly see malware integrating tools and mechanisms from network science into its arsenal, as well as attacks that directly target human-network information as a goal rather than a means. Paraphrasing Marshall McLuhan's "the medium is the message" we have reached the stage where "the network is the message."

Specifically, we point out a new type of information security threat—a class of malware, the goal of which is not to corrupt the machines it infects, take control of them, or steal explicit information stored on them (e.g., credit card information and personal records). Rather, the goal of this type of attack is to steal social network and behavioral information through data collection and network science inference techniques. We call this type of attack a "Stealing Reality" attack.

After characterizing the properties of this new kind of attack, we analyze the ways it could be carried out — we show the optimal strategy for attackers interested in learning a social network and its hidden underlying social principles. Remarkably, our analysis shows that such an optimal strategy should follow, in many cases it is an extremely slow spreading pattern. Counterintuitively, such attacks generate far greater damage in the long term compared to more aggressively spreading attacks. In addition, such attacks are likely to avoid detection by many of today's network security mechanisms, which tend to focus on detecting network traffic anomalies such as traffic volume increase. We demonstrate this surprising new discovery using several real world social networks datasets.

In this chapter we discuss related work and the threat model of the Stealing Reality social attack. We present the analysis of the attack, as well as the optimal attack strategy and concluding remarks.

BACKGROUND AND RELATED WORK

In recent years, the social sciences have been undergoing a digital revolution, heralded by the emerging field of "computational social science." Lazer, Pentland, et al.[1] describe the potential of computational social science to increase our knowledge of individuals, groups, and societies, with an unprecedented breadth, depth, and scale. Computational social science combines the leading techniques from network science[2,3,4] with new machine learning and pattern recognition tools specialized for the understanding of people's behavior and social interactions.[5,6]

The pervasiveness of mobile phones in the world has made them ubiquitous social sensors of location, proximity and communications. The term "Reality Mining"[7] describes a collection of sensor data pertaining to human social behavior. Using call records, cellular-tower IDs, and Bluetooth proximity logs, collected via mobile phones at the individual level, the subjects' social networks can be accurately detected, as well as regular patterns in daily activity.[5,7] Mobile phone records from Telecos have proven to be quite valuable for uncovering human level insights: cell-tower location information can be used to characterize human mobility.[8] Eagle et al. find that the diversity of individuals' relationships is strongly correlated with the economic development of communities.[9] Madan[10] expands upon Eagle and Pentland's work,[7] showing how mobile social sensing can be used for measuring and predicting the health status of individuals, based on mobility and communication patterns.

In later works it was shown that social sensing can be extracted not only from mobile-based data, but also from a variety of other platforms such as financial investments. The ability to detect dynamic "trend setters," as well as mapping their dynamic influence on a crowd of investors, was discussed in various papers.[11,12,13] The trade-off between the size of the community and the difficulty in modeling it using network analysis tools was also discussed,[14] whereas the implications of the identity of these "trend setters" on the overall behavior of the "herd" was discussed in another paper.[15]

Already, companies like Sense Networks are putting such tools to use in the commercial world to understand customer churn, enhance targeted advertisements, and offer improved personalization and other services. The technical advancements in mobile phone platforms and the availability of mobile software development kits (SDKs) are making the collection of Reality Mining data easier than ever before.

STEALING REALITY — THREAT MODEL

In our discussion, we refer to "Reality" information as inferred information about personal and social behavior. This includes (1) Information on individuals, which we refer to as "node information" (including any parameter on a node that can be learned from available data—such as occupation, level of income, health state, personality type); (2) Diadic information— information on relationships and other parameters connecting two nodes (referred to as "edge information"); (3) Network level information— information on groups of nodes, communities, and general network properties and information. The full network information includes all data on nodes and edges as well. As mentioned above, we do not refer here to explicitly stated information that can be found in (and stolen from) existing databases, such as names, social security, or credit card numbers. In the same way that Reality Mining is the legitimate collection and analysis of such information, Reality Stealing is the illegitimate accrual of it.

Motivation for Attackers

There already exist secondary markets for the resale of stolen identities, such as www.infochimps.com, or black market sites and chat-rooms for the resale of other illegal datasets.[16] It is reasonable to assume that an e-mail address of a "social hub" would be worth more to an advertiser than that of a "social leaf," and that a person meeting the profile of a student might be priced differently than that of a corporate executive. There are already companies operating in this area, engaged in the collection of e-mail and demographic information with the intention of selling it. Methods of social network analyzing and trends recognition were already published in many leading venues.[17] Why work hard when one can set loose automatic agents that would collect the same, and possibly much higher quality information? Stolen Reality information could be used for several malicious goals:

- Selling to highest bidder—both "legit" bidders, advertisers, etc., or in the black market to other attackers.

- Bootstrapping other attacks—as part of a complex "Advanced Persistent Threats" (APT) attack.[18,19]
- Business espionage—e.g., analyzing a competitor's customer base and profiling high-yielding customers for targeted marketing[20] or producing high quality prediction.[21]

Why Are Reality Stealing Attacks so Dangerous

Communication network topologies and networked device identifiers can be modified with the press of a button. The same goes for passwords, usernames, or credit cards numbers. E-mail and online accounts could be easily replaced, and the user's contacts can be quickly warned of the breach. However, it is much harder to change one's social network, person-to-person relationships, friendships, or family ties. If a chronic health condition is uncovered through such an attack, there is no going back. The victim of a "behavioral pattern" theft cannot change her behavior and life patterns. This type of information, once out, would be very hard to contain.

A second component accentuating this danger is that real-life information can be deduced from seemingly "safe" data, like accelerometer and location information, which users already freely allow many mobile applications to access.

Since we believe this threat is concrete, this paper's goal is to analyze potential attacks from the attackers' perspective, so that they could be better understood and proper defenses can be developed.

Past Attacks on Real-World Information

To help understand the risk in attacks on inferred real-world information, we review prior attacks on explicit data. In 2008, identity information of millions of Korean citizens was stolen in a series of malicious attacks and posted for sale. In 2007, Israel Ministry of Interior's database, with information on every Israeli citizen, was leaked and posted on the Web.[22] These days, a court still has to rule whether the database of a bankrupt gay dating site for teenagers will be sold to raise money for repaying its creditors (the site includes personal information of over a million teenage boys).[23] In all of these cases, once the information is out, there is no way back, and the damage is felt for a long time thereafter. In a recent *Wall Street Journal* interview, former Google CEO Eric Schmidt referred to the possibility that people in the future might choose to legally change their name to detach themselves from embarrassing "reality" information and publicity exposed in social networking sites. This demonstrates the sensitivity and challenges in recovering from leakage of real-life information, whether by youthful carelessness or by malicious extraction through an attack.[24]

Many existing viruses and worms use primitive forms of "social engineering"[25] as a means of spreading, to gain the trust of their next victims and cause them to click on a link or install an application. For example, "Happy99" was one of the first viruses to attach itself to outgoing e-mails, thus increasing the chances of having the recipient open an attachment to a seemingly legitimate message sent by a known acquaintance. More information concerning security and privacy leakage in social networks can be found in Information revelation and privacy in online social networks and Link privacy in social networks.[26,27]

SOCIAL ATTACK MODEL

We shall model the social network as an undirected graph $G(V, E)$. A Stealing Reality attacker's first goal is to inject a single malware agent into one of the network's nodes. Upon such injection, the agent starts to "learn" this node (and its interactions with its neighbors). Periodically, the agent tries to copy itself into one of the original node's neighbors. The probability that an agent tries to copy itself to a neighboring node at any given time step is called the "aggressiveness" of the attack, and is denoted as p. Namely, aggressive agents have higher values of p (and hence take shorter periods of time between each two spreading attempts), whereas less aggressive agents are less likely to try and spread at any given time, and will then wait, on average, longer between trying to copy themselves to one of the neighbors of their current host.

As the information about the network itself has become worthy cause for an attack, the attacker's motivation is stealing as much properties related to the network's social topology as possible. We shall denote the percentage of vertices-related information acquired at time t by $\Lambda_V(t)$ and the percentage of edges-related information acquired at time t is by $\Lambda_E(t)$.

The duration of the learning process of the Stealing Reality attack refers to the time it takes the attacking agent to identify with high probability the properties of a node's behaviors, or of some of its social interactions. We model this process using a standard Gompertz function in the parametric form of $y(t) = ae^{be^{ct}}$ (for some parameters a, b, and c). This model is flexible enough to fit various social learning mechanisms, while providing the following important features : (a) Sigmoidal advancement, namely—the longer such an gent operates, the more precise its conclusions will be. (b) The rate at which information is gathered is smallest at the start and end of the learning process. (c) Asymmetry of the asymptotes, implied from the fact that for any value of T, the amount of information gathered in the first T time steps is greater than the amount of information gathered at the last T time steps.

The applicability of the Gompertz function for the purpose of modeling the evolution of locally "learning" the preferences and behavior patterns of users was demonstrated,[28] where a prediction of the applications mobile users will chose to install on their phones was generated using an ongoing learning process. This experiment has shown that this process can be best modeled using the function $1 - e^{-x}$. As we know that $1 - t \le e^{-t}$ (achieving very tight results for most $t < 1$) we can clearly see that : $1 - e^{-x} \approx e^{-e^{-x}}$ which is an instance of the *Gompertz function* (for $a = 1$, $b = c = -1$).

An aggressive spreading pattern is more likely to be detected by users or administrators, resulting in the subsequent blocking of the attack. On the other hand, attacks that spread slowly may evade detection for a longer period of time, although the amount of data they gather would be limited. To predict the detection probability of the attack at time t we shall use Richard's Curve — a generalized logistic function often used for modeling the detection of security attacks:[29]

$$p_{detect}(t) = \frac{1}{\left(1 + e^{-\rho(t-M)}\right)^{\frac{1}{\rho}\sigma}}$$

where ρ is the attack aggressiveness, σ is a normalizing constant for the detection mechanism, and M denotes the normalizing constant for the system's initial state.

Let $I_u(t)$ be the infection indicator of u at time t, Tu be the initial infection time o, and $p(u, t)$ the Gompertz function, defining $\Lambda_V(t) = \frac{1}{|V|} \sum_{u \in V} I_u(t) \cdot p(u, t - T_u)$ we get:

$$\Lambda_V(\rho) = \int_0^{\infty} \left(\frac{\partial \Lambda_V(t)}{\partial t} \cdot (1 - p_{detect}(t)) \right) dt$$

"SOCIALLEARNABILITY" — OBTAINING THE SOCIAL ESSENCE OF A NETWORK

In this section, we define a mathematical measure that predicts the ability of an attacker to "steal," or acquire, a given social network, we call the "sociallearnability" of a network. The measure reflects both the information contained in the network itself, as well as the broader context from which the network was derived. Once presenting the mathematical formulation of this measure, we demonstrate its importance by showing how it can sort several real world social networks according to their complexity (which is known), and even group two very different social networks that were generated by the same group of people. We conclude by showing that the optimal learning process with respect to this new measure involves in many cases extremely non-aggressive attacks.

Information Complexity of Social Networks

Let us denote by K_E the *Kolmogorov Complexity*[30] of the network, namely the minimal number of bits required to "code" the network in such a way that it could later be completely restored. The Kolmogorov Complexity of a network represents the basic amount of information contained in a social network. For example, a military organization's network has very homogeneous links and hierarchical structures repeated many times over. We would expect it to require a much shorter minimal description than, say, the social network of the residents of a metropolitan suburb.

In the latter, we would expect to see a highly heterogeneous network, composed of many types of relationships (such as work relationships, physical proximity, family ties, and other intricate types of social relationships and group affiliations).

Social Entropy of Social Networks

At this point, let us recall that every social reality network belongs to one, or more, "social family", each of which has its own consistency (or versatility). Some families may contain a great variety of possible networks, each having roughly a similar probability to occur, while another may consist of a very limited number of possible networks.

Notice that the complexity of each network does not necessarily correlate with its entropy. There may exist families of low variety of highly complicated networks, while other families may contain a great variety of relatively simple networks.

Let us define G_n to contain n random instances of networks of $|V|$ nodes that belong to the same social family as G. Let X_n be a discrete random variable with possibility values $\{x_1, x_2 \ldots, x_{2^{\frac{1}{2}} |V|(|V|-1)}\}$ (corresponding to all possible graphs over $|V|$ nodes), taken according to the distribution of G_n. The normalized social entropy of the network G would, therefore, be calculated by dividing the entropy of the variable X_n by the maximum entropy for graphs of $|V|$ nodes:

$$\lambda_n(G) \triangleq \frac{H(X_n)}{\log_2 \zeta_{|V|}}$$

where $\zeta|V|$ denotes the number of distinct non-isomorphic simple graphs of $|V|$ nodes $\lambda(G)$ is then defined as $\lim_{n\to\infty} \lambda_n(G)$.

Stealing the Social Essence of a Network

At this point let us recall Reed's Law, which asserts that the utility of large networks (and particularly social networks), can scale exponentially with the size of the network. This observation is derived from the fact that the number of possible sub-groups of network participants is exponential in N (where N is the number of participants), stretching far beyond the N^2 utilization of Metcalfe's Law (that was used to represent the value of telecommunication networks).

Extending this notion we assert that a strong value emerges from learning the 2^I "social principles" behind a network, denoting by I the information that is encapsulated in a network.

Assuming that at time t an attacker has stolen $|E|\Lambda_\varepsilon(t)$ edges, then taking K_ε as the maximum amount of information that can be coded in the network G, we normalize it by the fraction of edges acquired thus far. As K_ε is measured in bits, the appropriate normalization should maintain this scale. Multiplied by $\lambda(G)$, the normalized social entropy of the network G, the network information can be written as follows:

$$\mathcal{I} = \lambda(G) \cdot K_E \cdot \frac{\log_2\left(|E|\Lambda_E(t)\right)}{\log_2 |E|}$$

After normalizing by the overall "social essence" of the network (received for $\Lambda_\varepsilon = 1$) the following measurement for the social essence of the sub-networked acquired is achieved:

$$\Lambda_S(t) = \frac{2^{\lambda(G) \cdot K_E \cdot \frac{\log_2\left(|E|\Lambda_E(t)\right)}{\log_2 |E|}}}{2^{\lambda(G) \cdot K_E}} = 2^{\lambda(G) \cdot K_E \cdot \frac{\log_2 \Lambda_E(t)}{\log_2 |E|}}$$

which after some arithmetics yields:

$$\Lambda_S(t) = \Lambda_E(t)^{\frac{\lambda(G) \cdot K_E}{\log_2 |E|}}$$

Note that K_ε represents the network complexity, whereas $\lambda(G)$ represents the complexity of its social family.

At this point we assert that our sociallearnability measure presented above is indeed a valuable property for measuring network attacks. For this, we demonstrate the values of this measure for several different real world networks. Figure 1 presents an analysis of the networks derived from the Social Evolution experiment,[10] the Reality Mining network,[5] and the Friends and Family[31] experiment. One can easily see the logic behind the predictions received using the sociallearnability measure concerning the difficulty of learning each of the networks. Specifically, the Social Evolution network is predicted to be harder to steal compared to the Reality Mining network, however easier to steal compared to the networks of Friends and Family. This can be explained when looking closely at the details of the three experiments. Whereas the Reality Mining experiment tracked people within a relatively static work environment, the Social Evolution experiment took place at an MIT undergraduate dorm involving students with (apparently) much more complicated mobility and interactions patterns. The Friends and Family dataset involved even more complicated interactions, as it includes a heterogeneous community of couples, increasing the amount of information encapsulated within the network.

In addition, notice how the sociallearnability measure places the two Friends and Family networks directly on top of each other, despite the fact that the two networks contain significantly different information (of volume, meaning and network information). Still, as the two networks essentially represent the same social group of people, their sociallearnability measure has a very similar value.

The importance of the social entropy of a network is demonstrated in figure 8.3, analyzing the Reality Mining network[5] for various possible values of social entropy. The value for the Kolmogorov Complexity of the network was approximated using an *LZW* compression of the network.

Figure 8.2 demonstrates the progress of the network essence stealing process, for a variety of network complexity values. Notice how as the amount of information contained in a network increases (in other words, the network represents more complicated social structures) the network becomes much more difficult to acquire.

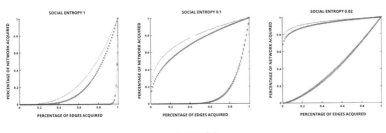

Figure 8.1

Figure 8.1 is an illustration of the reality stealing process for three different values of social entropy $\lambda(G)$ (0.02, 0.1, and 1), for four different networks — the Random Hall network,[3] Reality Mining networks,[4] Friends and Family[5] self-reporting network and Friends and Family Bluetooth network.[5] Using this example, we can see that the Reality Mining network is easier to steal than the Random Hall network, which in turn is easier to steal compared to the Friends and Family networks.

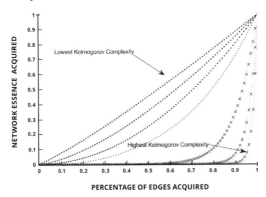

Figure 8.2

Figure 8.2 is an analytic illustration of the evolution of Λ_s as a function of the overall percentage of edges acquired, for networks of same number of edges ($|E|$ = 1,000,000), assuming the same social entropy $\lambda(G)$ = 0.1, with different levels of Kolmogorov complexity.

EXPERIMENTAL RESULTS

We evaluate our model on data derived from a realworld cluster
of mobile phone users, drawn from the call records of a major city within
a developed western country, comprised of approximately 200,000 nodes
and 800,000 edges.

Figure 8.4 demonstrates the attack efficiency (namely, the maximum amount
of network information acquired) as a function of its "aggressiveness" (i.e.,
the attack's infection rate). The two curves represent the overall amount of
information (edges related and vertices related) that can be obtained as a
function of the aggressiveness value p. It can be seen that although a local
optimum exists for an aggressiveness value of little less than $p = 0.5$ (namely,
a relatively aggressive attack), it is preceded by a global optimum achieved by
a much more "subtle" attack, for an aggressiveness value of $p = 0.04$.

To extensively further validate our analytic model for predicting the success
of Stealing Reality attacks, we have simulated attacks for random sub-
networks of our real world 200,000 nodes mobile network using a large
variety of attack aggressiveness values, which use numerous sets of values
for the attack properties (for each of which we have empirically measured
the overall expected amount of information that is stolen by the attack).

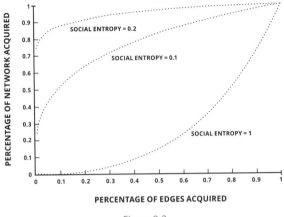

Figure 8.3

Figure 8.3 is a demonstration of the importance of a network's social entropy λ(G), illustrated for the Reality Mining network.[5] The curves represent an approximation of the social essence measure calculated using an LZW compression of the Reality Mining network. It can be seen that, if we assume that the network is derived from a family of the maximum entropy (namely, having a uniform distribution of all possible networks), the evolution of the Stealing Reality attack differs significantly than for networks that were derived from a family of a lower social entropy. Even for λ(G) = 0.1 stealing the network would be materially easier, having additional information out of any edge acquired.

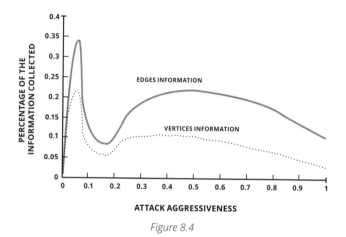

Figure 8.4

Figure 8.4 is an analytical study of the overall amount of data that can be captured by a Stealing Reality attack, illustrating the phenomenon where the most successful attack possible (namely, an attack that is capable of stealing the maximum amount of information) is produced by a very low value of the attack aggressiveness p. The upper curve represents $\Lambda_\varepsilon(p)$, the overall percentage of edges related information stolen. The lower curve represents $\Lambda_v(p)$, the overall percentage of vertices related information stolen. Notice the local maximum around $p = 0.5$ that is outperformed by the global maximum at $p = 0.04$.

Although the actual percentage of stolen information had varied significantly between the various simulations, demonstrating the influence of changes made to the attack's properties, many of them had displayed the same interesting phenomenon—a global optimum for the performance of the attack, located around a very low value of p. Some of these scenarios are presented in figure 8.5.

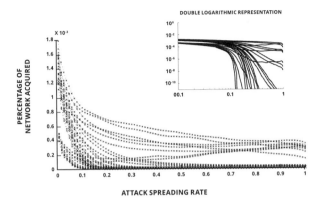

Figure 8.5

Figure 8.5 is an extensive study of a real-life mobile network, simulating Stealing Reality attacks. The performance of each scenario is measured as the percentage of information acquired, as a function of the infection rate ρ. The scenarios that are presented in this figure demonstrate a global optimum of the attack performance for very low values of ρ, stressing the fact that, in many cases, an extremely non-aggressive attack achieves the maximum amount of stolen information.

To further validate our theoretical attack model, we used a small-scale, realworld social network that was obtained from the Friends and Family study,[31] containing data that was derived from a multitude of mobile mounted sensors (e.g., call logs, accelerometer, Bluetooth and WiFi interaction). Using this data, we have confirmed our assumptions concerning the learning process.[28] The authors are currently working on a paper focusing on the empirical implementation and measurement of the model presented in this work.

DISCUSSION AND CONCLUDING REMARKS

In this chapter, the concept of a Stealing Reality attack was presented, an attack aiming towards acquiring implicit social information rather than explicit personal data. We have shown a novel social network measure called sociallearnability, and demonstrated its importance by validating it with several real-world social networks. We then showed that to maximize this measure, an attack must often resort to slow and subtle spreading patterns, rather than aggressive ones, thus achieving maximum learning of the network, while going undetected. We have then validated this theoretical result experimentally, using a real world mobile based social network.

The new concept of Stealing Reality attacks might provide explanation for observed evidence in the process of investi-gating recent Advanced Persistent Threats (APT) attacks, as well as suggest that such attacks might have happened in the past and gone undetected. The reason for the "stealthiness" of the Stealing Reality attack is the limitation of most existing network monitoring methods that are focused on detecting "noisy" attack attempts. Systems such as the Network Telescope[32] are designed to detect activity in IP segments that are supposed to contain no such activities. Other widely-used methods rely on the detection of anomalies in network activity[33,34]—for which a considerable amount of data is required. As a result, a non-aggressive attack is expected to "stay beyond the radar" and avoid detection by such systems.

Finally, it is interesting to note the sensitivity of the attack to the accuracy of the selection of the optimal aggressiveness value (figure 8.4), further hinting at the usefulness of the attack for entities such as global hacking organizations or national defense agencies, having the resources needed to gather the information required for such accurate estimation.

NOTES

1. D. Lazer, A. Pentland, L. Adamic, S. Aral, A.L. Barabasi, D. Brewer, N. Christakis, N. Contractor, J. Fowler, M. Gutmann, T. Jebara, G. King, M. Macy, D. Roy, and M. V. Alstyne, *"Social Science: Computational Social Science,"* Science, 323(5915), 721–723, (2009).

2. A.L. Barabasi and R. Albert, *"Emergence of Scaling in Random Networks,"* Science, 286(5429), 509–512, (1999).

3. D. Watts and S. Strogatz, *"Collective Dynamics of 'Small World' Networks,"* Nature, 393(6684), 440–442, (1998).

4. M. Newman, *"The Structure and Function of Complex Networks,"* SIAM Review, 45, 167–256, (2003).

5. N. Eagle, A. Pentland, and D. Lazer, *"Inferring Social Network Structure using Mobile Phone Data,"* Proc. of the National Academy of Sciences, 106(36), 15274–15278 (2009).

6. C. man Au Yeung, M. Noll, C. Meinel, N. Gibbins, and Shadbolt, *"Measuring Expertise in Online Communities,"* Intelligent Systems, IEEE, 26(1), 26–32 (2011).

7. N. Eagle and A. Pentland, *"Reality Mining: Sensing Complex Social Systems,"* Personal and Ubiquitous Computing, 10, 255– 268, (2006).

8. M. C. Gonzalez, C. A. Hidalgo, and A.-L. Barabasi, *"Understanding individual human mobility patterns,"* Nature, 453(7196), 779–782, (2008).

9. N. Eagle, M. Macy, and R. Claxton, *"Network Diversity and Economic Development,"* Science, 328(5981), 1029–1031, (2010).

10. A. Madan, M. Cebrian, D. Lazer, and A. Pentland, in *"Social sensing for epidemiological behavior change,"* Proc. of the 12th ACM International conference on Ubiquitous computing (New York, NY, USA, 291–300, (2010)).

11. Altshuler, Y., Pan, W. and Pentland, A, Trends Prediction Using Social Diffusion Models, International Conference on Social Computing, Behavioral-Cultural Modeling and Prediction, 97-104, 2012

12. Pan, W., Altshuler, Y., and Pentland, A., Decoding social influence and the wisdom of the crowd in financial trading network, Privacy, Security, Risk and Trust (PASSAT), 2012 International Conference on and 2012 International Confernece on Social Computing (SocialCom), 203-209, 2012

13. Liu, Y., Nacher, J., Ochiai, T., Martino, M., and Altshuler, Y., Prospect Theory for Online Financial Trading, PloS one, 9(10), 2014

14. Altshuler, Y., Fire, M., Aharony, N., Elovici, Y. and Pentland, A, How Many Makes a Crowd? On the Correlation between Groups' Size and the Accuracy of Modeling, International Conference on Social Computing, Behavioral-Cultural Modeling and Prediction, 43-52, 2012

15. Altshuler, Y., Pentland, A., and Gordon, G., Social Behavior Bias and Knowledge Management Optimization, Social Computing, Behavioral-Cultural Modeling, and Prediction, 258-263, 2015

16. C. Herley and D. Florencio, in *"Nobody Sells Gold for the Price of Silver: Dishonesty, Uncertainty and the Underground Economy,"* Economics of Information Security and Privacy, edited by T. Moore, D. Pym, and C. Ioannidis (Springer US, 2010) pp. 33–53.

17. D. Barbieri, D. Braga, S. Ceri, E. D. Valle, Y. Huang, V. Tresp, Rettinger, and H. Wermser, *"Deductive and Inductive Stream Reasoning for Semantic Social Media Analytics,"* IEEE Intelligent Systems, 99, 32–41 (IEEE Computer Society, 2010).

18. Solutionary, *"White paper: The advanced persistent threat (apt),"* (2011).

19. B. E. Binde, R. McRee, and T. J. O'Connor, Assessing Outbound Traffic to Uncover Advanced Persistent Threat, Tech. Rep. (Sans Institute, 2011).

20. M. Brunner, H. Hofinger, C. Krauss, C. Roblee, P. Schoo, and S. Todt, Infiltrating Critical Infrastructures with Next Generation Attacks, Tech. Rep. (Fraunhofer Institute for Secure Information Technology SIT Munich, 2010).

21. L. Tang and H. Liu, *"Toward collective behavior prediction via social*

dimension extraction," IEEE Intelligent Systems, 99, 1– 17 (IEEE Computer Society, 2010).

22. N. Jeffay, *"Israel poised to pass national i.d. database law, www.forward. com/articles/112033/,"* The Jewish Daily For- ward (2009).

23. D. Emery, *"Privacy fears over gay teenage database, http://www.bbc.co.uk/ news/10612800,"* BBC News (2010).

24. R. M. Stana and D. R. Burton, Identity Theft: Prevalence and Cost Appear to be Growing, Tech. Rep. (GAO-02-363, U.S. General Accounting Office, Washington, D.C, 2002).

25. S. Granger, *"Social engineering fundamentals, part i: Hacker tactics. www. securityfocus.com."* Symantec (2001).

26. R. Gross and A. Acquisti, in *"Information revelation and privacy in online social networks,"* Proc. of the 2005 ACM work- shop on Privacy in the electronic society, WPES, 71–80 (2005).

27. A. Korolova, R. Motwani, S. U. Nabar, and Y. Xu, in *"Link privacy in social networks,"* Proc. of the 17th ACM conference on Information and knowledge management, CIKM, 289–298 (2008).

28. W. Pan, N. Aharony, and A. Pentland, in *"Composite Social Network for Predicting Mobile Apps Installation,"* Proc. of the 25th Conference on Artificial Intelligence (2011) pp. 821 – 827.

29. N. A. Christakis and J. H. Fowler, *"Social Network Sensors for Early Detection of Contagious Outbreaks,"* PLoS ONE, Public Library of Science, 5, e12948 (2010).

30. A. Kolmogorov, *"Three Approaches to the Quantitative Definition of Information,"* Problems Information Transmission, 1(1), 1–7, (1965).

31. N. Aharony, W. Pan, C. Ip, I. Khayal, and A. Pentland, in *"The Social fMRI: Measuring, Understanding and Designing Social Mechanisms in the Real World,"* Proc. of the 13th ACM international conference on Ubiquitous computing (to appear), Ubicomp '11 (ACM, 2011).

32. D. Moore, V. Paxson, S. Savage, C. Shannon, S. Staniford, and N. Weaver,

"Inside the Slammer worm," Security Privacy, IEEE, 1(4), 33–39 (2003).

33. F. Apap, A. Honig, S. Hershkop, E. Eskin, and S. Stolfo, *"Recent advances in intrusion detection,"* (Springer Berlin Heidelberg, 2002) Chap. Detecting Malicious Software by Monitoring Anomalous Windows Registry Accesses, pp. 36–53.

34. R. Moskovitch, S. Pluderman, I. Gus, D. Stopel, C. Feher, Y. Parmet, Y. Shahar, and Y. Elovici, in *"Host Based Intrusion Detection using Machine Learning,"* IEEE Intelligence and Security Informatics (2007) pp. 107–114.

.

CHAPTER 9

Moving Target Techniques: Cyber Resilience through Randomization, Diversity, and Dynamism

Hamed Okhravi and Howard Shrobe

INTRODUCTION

Overview

The static nature of computer systems makes them vulnerable to cyberattacks. Consider a situation where an attacker wants to compromise a remote system running a specific application. The attacker needs only find one vulnerability in a local copy of that application. Since all copies of that application are identical and static, the attacker can leverage that vulnerability to exploit the application on a remote machine. Worse yet, the same vulnerability can be exploited to attack thousands or millions of other machines that run the same application. Additionally, since the internals of the system changes little over time, the same attack is likely to succeed for a long time. The situation is exacerbated by the fact that any reconnaissance information collected on the system by the attackers will also be valid for a long time. This creates an imbalance in favor of attacks.[1]

A promising approach to cyber resilience that attempts to rebalance the cyber landscape is known as *cyber moving target* (MT, or just moving target) techniques[2]. Moving target techniques change the static nature of computer systems to increase both the difficulty and the cost (in effort, time, and resources) of mounting attacks. Simply put, these techniques turn systems into MTs that will be hard for cyberattackers to compromise.

MT techniques leverage randomization, diversity, and dynamism to achieve resilience. Randomization refers to introducing non-determinism to the internal structures of a system while preserving its correct functionality. Diversity refers to introducing heterogeneity among computer systems so that they cannot be compromised by the same attack. Lastly, dynamism refers to changing the properties of a system over time so that the same attack cannot compromise it in the future. MT technique can implement any subset of these three goals.

To understand the different domains of MT techniques, we focus on the component that is subject to movement. For ease of design and implementation, a computer often consists of multiple layers of software and hardware, commonly referred to as the software stack (although the stack includes the hardware elements as well). Each layer relies on other layers for its proper operation and function.

Figure 9.1 presents one representation of such a layered design. At the very bottom of the software stack are the hardware components of the machine. These include the processor, the motherboard, the memory cards, and other peripheral devices and cards such as the sound card and video card. Above this layer resides the operating system, which is responsible for controlling and managing the hardware components and providing an abstraction of them to the application. The abstraction provided by the operating system is the key in interoperability and compatibility of the applications because the applications do not typically interact directly with the hardware components. Rather, they use the provided operating system abstraction. The abstraction layer, which is the interface that the operating system provides to the application, is sometimes referred to as the *runtime environment*. The hardware and operating system of a machine are collectively called the *platform*. Above the operating system reside the applications which are used to process and present data. The data and its representation can be considered a layer atop the application. Finally, many machines in today's systems are not isolated devices, and in fact, they are connected to other machines through a *network*. Generally, five domains of MT techniques address dynamically changing the abovementioned software stack layers.

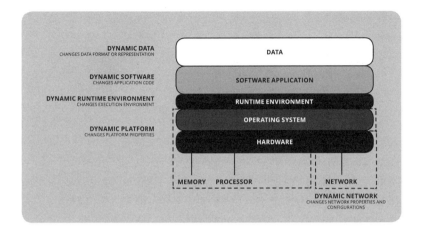

Figure 9.1 Different domains of cyber moving target techniques.

Dynamic Network

Techniques in the dynamic network domain change the properties of the network to complicate network-based attacks. One such technique frequently changes the Internet Protocol (IP) addresses of the machines in an enterprise network.[3] This IP rotation technique can thwart rapidly propagating worms that use a fixed hit list of IP addresses to infect a network. Another technique, known as an overlay network, creates dynamically changing encrypted tunnels (i.e., encrypted communication connections over public networks).

Dynamic networks is an appealing class of techniques to reduce an adversary's ability to conduct reconnaissance on a network, map a defended network, or select specific hosts for a targeted attack. However, these techniques face two important obstacles to deployment.

First, because many dynamic network techniques lack a well-articulated threat model, it may be unclear to inform defenders what threat needs to be mitigated and how best to deploy the defensive technique. Consider a technique that isolates a small group of machines from the larger network (or Internet). If hosts within the isolated network can still communicate to hosts beyond the isolated network, protected hosts may be vulnerable to any number of client-side attacks that exploit vulnerabilities within the unprotected hosts' web browsers or document viewers. For example, targeted spear phishing (fraudulent e-mail messages that try to elicit information, such as passwords to Internet accounts) could penetrate a protected network through the network's connections to unprotected hosts. Dynamic network–based MT techniques do not address these types of attacks.

Second, many dynamic network techniques introduce randomization into the fundamental protocols that are used on the Internet. However, the effectiveness of this randomization at stopping attacks is unclear. Suppose an MT technique randomizes network identifiers (such as an IP address). If service discovery protocols such as the domain name service (DNS) are used to convert human-readable domain names to machine-readable IP addresses, these services may undo any potential security benefit obtained through the MT technique itself, provided that the attacker can issue DNS queries.

Dynamic Platform

The dynamic platform domain consists of cyber defensive techniques that dynamically change the properties of the computing platform. Consider a system that runs a given application on top of multiple operating systems and hardware architectures. For example, the application can run on top of a platform consisting of the Fedora operating system and x86 processor architecture or a different platform consisting of the FreeBSD operating system and ARM processor architecture. Such a system can be implemented, for instance, by compiling the application to different processor architectures and implementing a platform-independent checkpointing mechanism to preserve the current state of the application during platform change.[4] Such a system constitutes a dynamic platform moving target technique. Other examples of dynamic platform techniques include a voting system that runs an application on top of different platforms—each platform voting on the output of the system[5]—or a system that randomizes the internals of the operating system that are unimportant for the correct functionality of the application.

The major benefit of the dynamic platform techniques is preventing platform-dependent attacks. Crafting a successful exploit against a system usually requires that an attacker consider the exact platform of that system. This is similar to the process of developing software for a given system. As a result, by changing the computing platform, an MT technique can mitigate attacks that are platform-dependent. An attacker can develop a stronger attack by incorporating different exploits against different platforms, but this will increase the cost and workload of the attack, which is the main goal of MT techniques. Note that dynamic platform techniques cannot mitigate attacks that target a higher-level application logic flaw and do not depend on the platform. For example, SQL injection attacks,[6] which are attacks that inject a malicious command into a database application using a flaw in the high-level logic of the application, are typically not mitigated by dynamic platform techniques.

While dynamic platforms MT techniques offer the potential to defeat platform-dependent attacks, they can increase the complexity of the overall system, are generally difficult to effectively manage, and can actually be detrimental to security if used inappropriately.[7] Perhaps the greatest challenge from a system complexity and management perspective is the synchronization of application state across the set of diverse platforms. Examples of such program state could include open data files, user input from a keyboard or mouse, or network traffic that needs to be correctly delivered to a specific running process (while correctly maintaining connection-specific state in the kernel). Synchronizing these resources among the dynamic platforms in real-time requires a complex management infrastructure that can migrate state with speed and agility. Reasoning about the correctness of this management infrastructure may be challenging in practice, but at the very least, the necessity to keep program state synchronized across several distinct platforms increases system complexity considerably.

Another potential limitation of dynamic platforms is that requiring multiple distinct platforms can actually increase the attack surface of the system. Attack surface refers to components of the system that are exposed to a potential attacker and can be the target of the attack. Suppose that a dynamic platform MT technique migrates an application between three platforms: Linux, Windows, and Mac. If the attacker has an exploit that works on the Windows host, the attacker simply needs to wait until the application migrates to the Window host to launch the exploit and compromise the application. Making the program migration less predictable can help, provided that the attacker cannot reliably guess which platform is running the application. As a result, dynamic platform techniques are only effective in cases where the diversity is *in-series* and not *in-parallel*. In other words, the successful attack must require all platforms to be compromised, not any platform. For instance, if the attack requires a long time to succeed (long duration of disruption of service), a dynamic platform can be helpful. Otherwise, for short-duration attacks, it can be detrimental to security.

Dynamic Runtime Environment

Techniques in the dynamic runtime environment domain dynamically change or randomize the abstraction provided by the operating system to the applications, without hindering any important functions of the system. One of the most important abstractions in a computer system is memory. For various reasons including isolation of different applications, compatibility, and interoperability, memory locations presented to an application in most modern computer systems is not a direct representation of the actual physical memory. Rather, a redirection is applied by the operating system in an abstraction known as the virtual memory. A well-known dynamic runtime environment MT technique randomizes what addresses in the virtual memory are used by the application. The technique is typically referred to as Address Space Layout Randomization (ASLR)[8] and is implemented in most modern operating systems including Linux, Windows, Mac OSX, Android, and iOS. By randomizing the addresses, ASLR makes exploit development more difficult for an attacker because attackers do not know where to place their malicious code on the system. Other dynamic runtime environment techniques include those that change the processor instruction encoding (a.k.a. Instruction Set Randomization -- ISR), or finer-grained variants of ASLR in which smaller regions of memory are randomized.

Dynamic runtime environments are among the most practical and widely deployed MT techniques. Yet, despite their successes, there are two important weaknesses than can allow an attacker to circumvent the defense.

First, ASLR requires memory secrecy. That is, if the contents of memory are disclosed or leaked to an attacker, the attacker may be able to use this information to defeat ASLR. Such memory disclosures are possible via separate vulnerabilities (known as buffer over-read vulnerabilities), where the contents of memory are read beyond the allowed boundary, disclosing how memory has been randomized. Without strict memory secrecy, an attacker can still circumvent the protections provided by ASLR to launch code injection or code reuse attacks (e.g., ROP).[9]

Second, the granularity of randomization in many ASLR implementations is low, which reduces the overall protection provided by the technique. For example, in Linux only the start location of certain memory regions is randomized by default. The executable program code itself is often not compiled with ASLR support. As such, this section of the program's memory is not protected and can be a vector of exploitation.

Dynamic Software

Techniques in the dynamic software application domain (or simply the dynamic software domain) randomize or diversify the internals of the software application. One technique from this domain is called the multi-compiler,[10] which creates different versions of software executables (binaries) from the same source code (e.g., written in C) that perform the same function, but are different internally. The different internals can arise from different actual processor instructions that are used during the compilation process or using the same instructions in different locations inside the executable. Note that a given copy of the executable with a given set of internals may never change, but various machines in an enterprise run different executables. In other words, this technique can create spatial diversity (diversity among many machines) as opposed to temporal diversity (diversity of one machine over time). The major benefit of dynamic software techniques is to mitigate the impact of large-scale attacks. If an exploit is crafted against a given variant of the executable, it will have a small chance of working against other variants of that executable. Hence, an attacker cannot compromise many machines at once. This is contrary to many existing systems where, if an attacker develops malware, it can successfully compromise millions of machines running the same target application. In recent sophisticated attacks, attackers reuse parts of the benign code of the target application itself to achieve malicious behavior. Known as code reuse attacks or return-oriented programming (ROP) attacks,[9] these attacks can successfully bypass existing defenses that detect or stop foreign pieces of code to mitigate attacks. Dynamic software techniques can be effective against such attacks by making the benign application code diverse.

Dynamic software techniques often use specialized compiler techniques to produce executable software variants with different and unpredictable memory layouts. These variants could use padding to make the size of memory regions unpredictable, or insert no-operation (NOP) instructions within executable code that do not perform any operation, but can make code reuse attacks harder to launch because they change the location of other instructions. However, these techniques suffer from a variety of weaknesses.

First, recompilation to produce a software variant requires access to a program's source code, and is not compatible with proprietary, third-party software for which source code is not made available. Furthermore, reasoning about the correctness of the compiled variant can be challenging, since one cannot simply verify a cryptographic measurement of the executable file to ensure that the code has not been (maliciously) modified.

Second, software is often compiled with special optimization flags that reduce the space and/or computational complexity of the compiled binary code. MT techniques that explicitly compile the software to introduce randomness in the memory layout may not be compatible with space saving or compute-time saving optimization passes performed by the compiler. Consequently, the dynamic software is unlikely to maintain the same performance properties as the ideally optimized compiled code.

Third, dynamic software techniques that use execution monitors to instrument and compare multiple versions of an executable introduce significant performance costs. For example, if an MT technique has two variants, there is at least a 2x performance cost relative to native execution of the application (in terms of processor, memory, and I/O utilization). This cost may be reasonable for protecting one or two applications where the highest degree of security is required, but likely does not scale to protect all applications running on a host.

Fourth, information leakage attacks can also be used against dynamic software techniques (similar to dynamic runtime environment techniques) to bypass them.[11] If attackers can leak how an executable has been diversified, they can attack it as if it was not diversified at all.

Dynamic Data

Techniques in the dynamic data domain change the format, syntax, representation, or encoding of the application data to make attacks more difficult. In this domain, the diversity can be temporal or spatial as well. One technique in this domain dynamically changes the representation of the user identifier (UID) in Linux operating systems. This identifier is used to determine what access rights a user has. One type of attack tries to increase the access level of a user to gain access to otherwise sensitive resources by changing the UID value to that of an administrator. This type of attack is an example of a larger class of attacks known as privilege escalation attacks. The UID randomization dynamic data technique can mitigate such an attack.

Dynamic data techniques offer the promise of protecting data from theft or unauthorized modification, but these techniques also suffer from two important weaknesses.

First, there can be a lack of diversity in the number of acceptable data encodings. For example, to encode binary data, one could use base-64 or hexadecimal, which are both commonly used in practice, but there are few other accepted standards for data encoding. Additional non-standardized encodings are certainly possible, but may increase the complexity of interoperating with other system components.

Second, the use of additional data encodings may also increase the attack surface of the software. For each encoding type, the software must have the proper parsing code to encode and decode the data. The additional parsing code itself could have security-relevant software bugs.

Summary

One way of understanding the benefits of MT techniques is by looking at the steps of a cyberattack that they are trying to mitigate. To successfully compromise a system, an attacker must progress through several steps, as depicted in table 9.1.

The first step is reconnaissance during which an attacker collects information about the target. The second step is accessing the victim during, which the attacker collects enough information about the configurations, applications, and software versions that are running on the target machine to develop an attack against it. During the third step, the attacker develops an exploit against a vulnerability in the target machine. Then the attack is launched in the next step, which may include, for example, a malicious network packet sent to the target machine or luring the user to click on a maliciously crafted link or using a malicious thumb drive. After the attack is launched and verified, the attackers may take additional steps to maintain their foothold on the target machine (i.e., persistence). Together these steps are referred to as the *cyber kill-chain*. Table 9.1 illustrates the main step of the cyber kill-chain that each domain of MT techniques tries to mitigate.

Table 9.1 Attack phases disrupted by each MT domain.

MT Domain	Attack Phases				
	RECONNAISSANCE	ACCESS	ATTACK DEVELOPMENT	ATTACK LAUNCH	PERSISTENCE
Dynamic Network	✓			✓	
Dynamic Platforms		✓	✓		✓
Dynamic Runtime Env.			✓	✓	
Dynamic Software			✓	✓	
Dynamic Data			✓	✓	

EFFECTIVENESS OF MOVING TARGET TECHNIQUES

Weaknesses of existing MT techniques motivated us to develop a set of criteria for evaluating their effectiveness. By studying attacks against well-known MT techniques we identified three major problems that contribute to the weaknesses of such techniques. First, in some cases the dynamic change in the system is too slow. In such cases, an attacker can observe the current state of the system using information leakage attacks, craft an attack against the current state, and compromise the system by launching the attack, all within the interval between the two system changes. Second, in some other cases, the space of movement is too small. For example, consider a system that has two possible states. While attackers may not know the current state of the system, they will have 50% chance of success in attacking the system by pure guessing. In many MT techniques, attackers can also reduce the amount of uncertainty they are facing by quickly testing every possibility. This is also known as the *brute force* attack. Third, in some MT techniques, parts of an attack surface are dynamic, whereas other parts remain static. The static parts become a target of attack because they do not present any uncertainty for the attacker.

Using the above insights, we developed three criteria for evaluating an MT technique: *timeliness*, *unpredictability*, and *coverage*.

- **Timeliness:** The extent to which a movement can be applied between the time an attacker makes an observation and time an attack is completed.
- **Unpredictability:** The extent to which the outcome of current or future movements of the attack surface are indeterminable by an attacker.
- **Coverage:** The extent to which all elements of a defended attack surface are subject to movement.

Timeliness evaluates how fast the system moves. The actual time between movements depends on the attack model of concern for the technique. Hence, the definition of timeliness considers the possible attacker observations. In fact, an optimal MT technique should tie movement events to possible actions that can leak information to an attacker.[12]

Unpredictability evaluates the uncertainty faced by an attacker. A quantitative metric for unpredictability is entropy.

Coverage evaluates whether or not the MT technique moves every element of an attack surface. If some parts of the attack surface remain static, they can become the target of attacks.

We have also developed rigorous, quantitative metrics for these criteria,[13] the discussion of which is beyond the scope of this book chapter. We use these metrics to evaluate MT techniques and analyze the protection they provide against cyber attacks.

PRACTICAL CONSIDERATIONS

When deciding to deploy an MT technique, there are many practical issues to consider. The defender should understand the potential performance impact of the MT technique on the system. Many MT techniques offer security against strong adversaries, but incur performance penalties, which could be prohibitively high, depending on the application. Understanding the performance requirements of the system and the expected performance costs of the MT technique can help defenders make the right decision about deploying MT defenses.

Moreover, the defender should understand the effectiveness of the MT technique before it is deployed. Techniques that offer high effectiveness against realistic attack models should be selected before those that suffer from false positives or negatives, or those that protect against an unrealistic threat. Hence, an important part of this consideration is having a well-defined attack model that describes the exact types of attacks that are of concern and that are relevant to the system being protected.

Finally, the defender should understand the composability of MT and non-MT techniques. MT techniques do not solve all security problems, but rather are best suited toward defending against specific threat models. For example, a defender may want to defend against code injection attacks using ASLR. But to achieve in-depth defense, signature-based network monitoring can be used to examine network traffic in real time and drop all packets that appear to contain code injection payloads. Understanding how well MT and non-MT techniques can be composed to achieve the necessary protection is paramount to effective cyber resilience.

NOTES

1. D. Kaufman, An Analytical Framework for Cyber Security, Defense Advanced Research Projects Agency, 2011, available at www.dtic.mil/dtic/tr/fulltext/u2/a552026.pdf.

2. H. Okhravi, T. Hobson, D. Bigelow, and W. Streilein, "Finding Focus in the Blur of Moving Target Techniques," IEEE Security & Privacy, vol. 12, no. 2, 2014, pp.16–26.

3. S. Antonatos, P. Akritidis, E.P. Markatos, and K.G. Anagnostakis, "Defending Against Hitlist Worms Using Network Address Space Randomization," Computer Networks: The International Journal of Computer and Telecommunications Networking, vol. 51, no. 12, 2007, pp. 3471–3490.

4. H. Okhravi, A. Comella, E. Robinson, and J. Haines, "Creating a Cyber Moving Target for Critical Infrastructure Applications Using Platform Diversity," International Journal of Critical Infrastructure Protection, vol. 5, no. 1, 2012, pp. 30–39.

5. B. Salamat, A. Gal, T. Jackson, K. Manivannan, G. Wagner, and M. Franz, "Multi-variant Program Execution: Using Multi-core Systems to Defuse Buffer-Overflow Vulnerabilities," Proceedings of the IEEE International Conference on Complex, Intelligent and Software Intensive Systems, 2008, pp. 843–848.

6. Boyd, Stephen, and Angelos Keromytis. "SQLrand: Preventing SQL injection attacks." In Applied Cryptography and Network Security, pp. 292-302. Springer Berlin/Heidelberg, 2004.

7. H. Okhravi, J. Riordan, and K. Carter, "Quantitative Evaluation of Dynamic Platform Techniques as a Defensive Mechanism," pp. 405-425 in Research in Attacks, Intrusions and Defenses, Lecture Notes in Computer Science, A. Stavrou, H. Bos, and G. Portokalidis eds. Cham, Switzerland: Springer International Publishing, 2014.

8. PaX Team, "PaX address space layout randomization (ASLR)," 2003, available at https://pax.grsecurity.net/docs/aslr.txt.

9. H. Shacham, "The Geometry of Innocent Flesh on the Bone: Return-into-libc without Function Calls (on the x86)," Proceedings of the 14th ACM Conference on Computer and Communications Security, 2007, pp. 552–561.

10. M. Franz, "E Unibus Pluram: Massive-Scale Software Diversity as a Defense Mechanism," Proceedings of the 2010 Workshop on New Security Paradigms, 2010, pp. 7–16.

11. J. Seibert, H. Okhravi, and E. Söderström, "Information Leaks Without Memory Disclosures: Remote Side Channel Attacks on Diversified Code," Proceedings of the 21st ACM SIGSAC Conference on Computer and Communications Security, 2014, pp. 54–65.

12. D. Bigelow, T. Hobson, R. Rudd, W. Streilein, and H. Okhravi, "Timely Rerandomization for Mitigating Memory Disclosures," Proceedings of the 22nd ACM SIGSAC Conference on Computer and Communications Security, 2015, pp. 268–279.

Hobson, Thomas, Hamed Okhravi, David Bigelow, Robert Rudd, and William Streilein. "On the challenges of effective movement." In Proceedings of the First ACM Workshop on Moving Target Defense, pp. 41-50. ACM, 2014.

SECTION III

SYSTEMS

CHAPTER 10

Who's Afraid of
the Dark Web?

Harry Halpin

INTRODUCTION: A TECHNO-LEGAL PRIMER ON PRIVACY
AND ANONYMITY

Despite the hysteria in the popular press, the "Dark Web" is simply the part
of the Web where information can be accessed and shared anonymously.
Indeed, the Dark Web does let reporters mail-order illegal drugs over the
Web via the successors of Silk Road, which are likely safer than their local
drug-dealer.[1] Yet, this Dark Web does indeed enable anonymous whistle-
blowing via sites like Wikileaks, and even possibly a new phase of cyberwar
powered by impossible-to-detect hackers. Paradoxically, the self-same
technologies that power anonymity on the Dark Web also can guarantee
the privacy of governments, corporations, and even ordinary users against
cyber-threats such as malicious, targeted attacks and mass surveillance.
These *privacy-enhancing technologies* not only power the Dark Web, but are
also the technical means to guarantee fundamental rights such as freedom of
expression and the right to a private life, as enshrined by the United Nations.[2]
In fact, these technologies can do more than simply power the next phase of
cyberwar: they can also provide the foundation for effective defense.

Privacy in the United States of America

Anonymity can be considered an extreme form of privacy. Privacy is a fairly
new concept in the law, but given the rise of big data and the ever-increasing
frequency of hacking incidents, privacy has become a rather timely topic in
the digital age. The origin of privacy in US law was provoked by the impact
of technological development on society of the newly invented mass market
camera, well before the advent of the Internet. At the end of the 19th century,
Judge Samuel Warren became disturbed by the newfound popularization
of photographic technology on his family; he was shocked to find intimate
details, including photographs, of his family in local Boston newspapers.[3] In
response, both he and Brandeis looked at several cases of case-law and

formulated the concept of privacy as "The Right to be Left Alone" in their masterpiece "The Right to Privacy."[4]

Although not a fundamental right as enshrined by the Bill of Rights, this legal formulation of privacy nonetheless had huge impact on the government, in particular the Federal Information Processing Standards (FIPS). FIPS is a set of principles for data-processing now implemented by the Department of Commerce and the Department of Homeland Security,[5] as well as Health Insurance and Accountability Act of 1995 (HIPPA) that applies to personal medical data.[6] The case-law based approach to privacy allows the United States rapid permissionless innovation, but also leads to privacy violations via terms-of-service that ordinary users cannot understand, and so unwittingly many users sign away the rights to their data. This allows companies to process data in ways that ordinary users do not predict, and so may anger users when they realize that their personal data is being used to empower invasive tracking and surveillance—or even sold for a profit. Furthermore, much of the gathering of data on people is done outside of a legal framework, and everything from user profile photos to passwords can be found for sale, likely illegally, on the Dark Web.[7]

Data Protection in the European Union

In contrast, the European approach has been to consider privacy to be a fundamental right. This right was originated by with the "Convention for the Protection of Individuals with regard to Automatic Processing of Personal Data" in 1981, coming from the long memory in Europe to prevent in the future the kind of automatic data-processing that enabled the Holocaust.[8] The general idea was that ordinary people should have rights over their data, and that control over the data about an individual was necessary for autonomy. For example, the right to request what data is being held about an individual and ask that data to be removed are enshrined in Europe as fundamental rights, even if the exact technical deployment and range of these rights is difficult to ascertain. The term "data protection" tends to be used rather than "privacy" insofar as it then became the duty of the European government to enforce the rights over their citizens around data. These rights were eventually given a solid foundation by Directive 95/46/EC Data Protection Act in 1998,[9] and so harmonized via binding legislation over the nation-state. Data Protection was most recently updated in the General Data Protection Regulation in 2016,[10] further strengthening the role of the state in protecting citizen data in Europe.

Good intentions do not make necessarily good legal frameworks. It has been very hard, if not impossible, to enforce these data rights via court cases such as the infamous "Right to be Forgotten" 2014 court case against Google.[11] While in Europe, the state has been trusted to enforce privacy, in the United States the right to privacy has been generally entrusted to corporations to enforce. In Europe, the state has been unable to actually enforce rights over data due to transnational data flows, and similarly in the United States, gathering data is the prerequisite for "knowing your customer" in the digital age. So users routinely lose control of their data due to the complex terms-of-service common law contracts that come with even free services, such as those of Google. As personal data is transforming from something that is merely incidentally produced by behavior to a valuable asset in its own right, as outlined in the work led by Alex "Sandy" Pentland at the World Economic Forum,[12] the legal framework around privacy crafted in both the United States and Europe has been stretched to its breaking point. It seems dubious at best that traditional state-based legal frameworks and pre-digital institutions are capable of enforcing privacy, much less handling the effects of anonymity and the Dark Web.

From Privacy by Design to Privacy-Enhancing Technologies

Can privacy be guaranteed by technology rather than by the state? The approach put forward by *privacy by design* is to enable a user's privacy by embedding privacy itself in the software. Therefore, software should maximize user privacy as a default setting and implement end-to-end security at every stage of data processing. The goal of privacy by design is to enable the full capacities of the software while minimizing the collection of data. Such *privacy-enhancing technologies* (often abbreviated as "PETS") would preserve the security of the data itself via the usage of cryptography and more advanced techniques from computer science. Privacy by design advocates envisioned that they could legislate the increased usage of privacy-enhanced technologies in society.

The Seven Foundational Principles of Privacy by Design

Ann Cavoukian developed seven principles in the 1990s in her role as Information and Privacy Commissioner in Canada.[13] These principles have been the foundation for privacy-enhancing technologies, and have been foundational in determining how privacy is engineered into technologies, including those technologies like Tor, which powers the Dark Web:

1. Proactive not reactive; preventative not remedial
2. Privacy as the default setting
3. Privacy embedded into design
4. Full functionality—positive-sum, not zero-sum
5. End-to-end security—full lifecycle protection
6. Visibility and transparency—keep it open
7. Respect for user privacy—keep it user-centric

What if privacy by design could create software that could not only preserve privacy, but also give users new capabilities they didn't have before?

In particular, the property of anonymity was not built into the Internet, which by design revealed the origin and destination of every packet. However, the cryptographer David Chaum threw down the gauntlet in several papers in the 1980s, showing that cryptography could enable actual digital anonymity, in order "to make Big Brother obsolete."[14]

The Origin of the Politics of Anonymity on the Net

Spreading beyond academia, a grassroots group of hackers called cypherpunks took up the gospel that cryptography could empower a new form of society based on anonymity, ranging from anonymous digital currency to anonymous online markets. But these included even assassination markets, where the assassination of government officials could be bought and sold. Indeed, in an e-mail list, the young Julian Assange imagined anonymous leaking as a non-violent alternative to assassination markets.[15]

Not surprisingly, this new kind of anonymity is still viewed as a source of danger and confusion by law enforcement and other existing state regimes. Generally, law enforcement is historically based on states with geographically bound territories and clearly identifiable citizens. Although many have declared John Perry Barlow's "Declaration of the Independence of Cyberspace" to be hopelessly naïve in a world now dominated by behavioral advertising by a few large companies and pervasive surveillance by nation-states, anonymous technologies have renewed Barlow's promise to create new kinds of post-national institutions.[16] The principle of anonymity defies pre-Internet legal regimes to approximate a realm of absolute freedom where nothing is forbidden and everything is permitted: from state-sponsored espionage to freedom of speech that even the most authoritarian of regimes has trouble crushing.

DEFINING ANONYMITY AND PRIVACY

While it's intuitive that if one is anonymous then one can't be identified, can we define anonymity with more precision? Are there types of anonymity or ranges of anonymity? Answering this kind of question is necessary to determine if a given design actually provides the property of anonymity to its a user. The question of how to define anonymity has historically been understudied, and unlike the security properties provided by cryptography, the properties actually given by privacy-enhanced systems have proven much harder to nail down with formal certitude.

Cryptographic Definitions of Security

Cryptography gives us the ability to encrypt a message so that an adversary cannot read the contents of an encrypted message, a property called *confidentiality*. In addition, we can create systems where such an adversary cannot pretend to have created a message—a property called *authentication*. Both authentication and confidentiality can be defined with mathematical precision. A particular cryptographic scheme can be rigorously shown to preserve security properties, such as the confidentiality and authentication of messages against adversaries of well-defined complexity and power.[17]

This ends up being no academic exercise, as the competitions by NIST to define the SHA hash functions and AES ciphersuites led to the standardization of algorithms that are expected to meet these properties, and in some cases can even be formally proved to be secure. Although academia and industry understands cryptography reasonably well, with several textbooks starting with Schneier's seminal *Applied Cryptography* being widely available, privacy lacks a widely accepted formal definition, and no textbook yet exists.[18]

Privacy Is Social

The reasons may be foundational, as privacy seems to be, by nature, embedded in social context. Expectations of privacy seem to vary wildly depending on who is involved. For example, if I'm sending a private e-mail to my spouse, it would seem reasonable that only he or she could read that message and even know it was sent. However, a status update over Twitter that includes commentary on current events obviously is going to be read by many people, as Twitter—by design—acts as a medium for broadcasting messages to the whole world. For people trying to maintain their privacy over Twitter, it's unclear how much, if any, anonymity is afforded by using a false name. However, there seems to be a reasonable expectation of privacy for e-mail, even if the underlying protocol does not use encryption or even authenticate the sender and receiver.

Privacy may also depend on what kind of adversaries are expected to violate the privacy of users, and in what ways. Am I worried that the government will know that I am sending messages to my spouse, or that Twitter itself knows that the "fake name" being used by a human rights activist can be linked to their Twitter account that is using their real name, as all messages from both their real and "fake" Twitter account are originating from the same IP address? Would I be worried knowing that the NSA knows exactly when I am communicating to my spouse?

Different users have different expectations, and sometimes this is a matter of life and death. Would a human rights activist be worried knowing that the time and contents of his tweets are known not only by Twitter, but by a local brutal dictator who is monitoring all information coming in and out of Twitter, as the regime controls all the Internet connections at the local IXP (Internet eXchange Point)? What if the dictator could only tell it was someone in his group that was sending the message to the Twitter account? Would it matter if the group was a hundred people, or only three? While breaking the encryption scheme is a black or white operation that either transforms encrypted ciphertext into human-readable plaintext or not, anonymity comes in shades of gray.

Anonymity Requires Hiding Metadata

In terms of being able to build a secure system that can survive powerful cybersecurity threats, just encrypting a message using conventional cryptography is just the tip of a much larger problem. The most valuable part of any conversation is often not the message itself, but who is talking to whom. As shown by Pentland's research on *social physics,* the behavior of an agent can be predicted by its social connections. With every message sent, valuable metadata is leaked, such as sender and recipient of the message, as well as information such as the time the message was sent and the size of the message.[19]

Privacy-enhanced technologies attempt to prevent this information from being leaked to the adversary. So, while in traditional cryptography we assume an attacker can intercept, replay, and create messages in an attempt to break a crypto-system, in privacy we also have to anticipate new kinds of threat models with different kinds of goals, such as attempting to discover the social network (also called the "social graph") of those sending messages.

Social graph analysis is the heart of everything, from identifying the most influential customers to the most influential terrorists, and the exact messages that are being sent are secondary to the value of the connections themselves. So privacy must deal with new kinds of threat models, ranging from a honest, but curious, server that observes metadata, but cannot read the messages itself, to a malicious server that sends fake messages in addition to observing metadata, to a network adversary that controls the entire network that can fake aspects of the communication such as the time a message was sent.

In terms of privacy and anonymity, the whole system counts—and the weakest part of the design that leaks information can lead to de-anonymizing the whole system. In terms of privacy, one may never know what information a determined adversary might already possess or link to supposedly "private" information. Simply "anonymizing" data by removing the identifiers, such as done to the names of reviewers by Netflix in their movie database, may not be enough; simply linking that database to another available database such as IMDB is enough to identify reviewers.[20] The same result has been shown by MIT Media Lab, as big data demonstrates that only four points in time and space can de-anonymize 90% of people in a credit card database of over 1 million.[21]

Luckily, progress has been made in formalizing privacy in terms of *differential privacy*, which formalizes how much random noise must be added to queries to a private dataset to mathematically prove that the anonymity of a user is maintained.[22] However, this kind of provable privacy is still in its early days, and the process of anonymizing data-sets is easy, compared to the harder task of building anonymous systems.

From Pseudonyms to Anonymity

For most purposes, distinguishing between anonymity and simple *pseudonymity* may be enough. A pseudonym is an identifier of an entity that isn't the entity's real name. Everything from the venerable tradition of "hacker names" to the substitution of names in a database with a hash of the name (replacing the name "Harry" with the seemingly random string "23a0b5e4fb6c6e8280940920212ecd563859cb3c") are all examples of pseudonyms—and even the use of a cryptographic key as an identifier in Bitcoin. However, pseudonyms are easily de-anonymized with enough observations of metadata over time, and these observations can easily be put into a machine-learning system that makes de-anonymization of pseudonyms trivial.

Anonymity is much more stringent, requiring the entity to be unidentifiable within a set of entities, the *anonymity* set. To take a simple example, imagine that there are four people in the database: Harry, Alex, Joy, and Chelsea. If all four people had their names replaced by a zero, then they would have an anonymity set of four. If only females were anonymized, then the anonymity set would only be two. Of course, if only Chelsea's name was replaced by a zero, it would be a simple pseudonym, and so would have an anonymity set of one and thus the pseudonym would still uniquely identify Chelsea.

The important thing to remember is that one is never strictly anonymous, but only anonymous in relationship to a "crowd" of other entities, with the maximum amount of anonymity being given if every member of the "crowd" cannot be distinguished. Anonymity loves company! Not only do we want entities to be anonymous, but we also want to make their relationship to their actions be anonymized as well, such as whether or not an entity sent a particular message or visited a particular webpage. In other words, we want to *unlink* the message and the entity. Entities are *unlinkable* if an attacker cannot determine if two entities are related or an entity and its action is related.

Even more extreme is the idea of unobservability, or whether or not an entity even exists. For example, if I cannot tell if a message was ever sent by a particular person because it cannot be distinguished from random noise, then it's unobservable. The most widely accepted informal definitions of anonymity, discussed briefly in this section, come from the seminal

"Consolidated proposal for terminology" by Andreas Pfitzman,[23] while further research has grounded anonymity in information theory.[24]

HOW DOES THE DARK WEB WORK?

While the "Dark Web" is an ambiguous term at best in the popular press, the intuition behind the term is that there is a secret (and thus, "dark") part of the Web that cannot be accessed by ordinary users. Within this presumed Dark Web, all sorts of criminality is imagined to flourish in the most lurid of terms, ranging from marketplaces for illegal weapons to the sharing of all kinds of deviant pornography. While the claims are not entirely false, they are also incredibly simplistic and overly salacious. The reality is much more complex, and while it is true that all sorts of terrifying behavior happens on the Dark Web, the underlying technical infrastructure of the Dark Web has been used for everything from WikiLeaks to CIA agents operating overseas to hide their "digital footprint" and so use the Web anonymously.

In this section, we'll explain technically the infrastructure that powers the Dark Web: the Tor network.

How an IP Address Reveals Location

Tor stands for the "The Onion Router," and it is the name for the entire infrastructure for anonymity online built on top of onion-routing.[25] Tor provides the strongest realworld anonymity that can be provided at this moment. While it does not provide unobservability—i.e., in the general case—it can be detected if you are using Tor. The project was born out of what appears to be a philosophical question: How can a group of untrusted strangers deliver an anonymous message while still being trusted not to read the message? And not surprisingly, a philosopher Paul Syvenson invented an answer: onion-routing.

Before delving into onion-routing, we need to understand how normal routing works on the Internet. Anonymity is difficult by design on the Internet, as the TCP/IP (Transport Control Protocol/Internet Protocol) protocol relies on each participant on the Internet having a unique *IP address.* An IP address takes the form as a series of numbers, such as 152.19.134.40. Every participant on the Internet must have an Internet address.

In the early days of the Internet, ranges of IP addresses were assigned to major participants in the Internet—and that's how MIT ended up with more IP addresses than China. *Dynamic IP addresses* are then distributed by the Internet Service Providers (ISPs) to end-users via their router—and therefore, the IP address almost always geolocates a user to the geographical area covered by the ISP. Although some *static IP addresses* are assigned permanently to a single entity, the vast majority of IP addresses are dynamically assigned, but nonetheless can identify a user down to a very specific area, such as city or even neighborhood, and almost always a nation-state.

If a user is searching the Web, the IP addresses can be retained by the user's ISP and by the server of the website the user is visiting. Due to the popularity of IP address logs, IP addresses tend to be used to track down users by everyone from the police to the mafia. Often in court cases, there is a demand for an IP address log, and criminals can even set up "honeypot" sites to collect IP addresses maliciously. Although browser connections to the Web are often encrypted using Transport Layer Security (TLS), which causes a "lock" to appear in the browser window, the encrypted connection does not hide the IP address.[26]

How Tor Disguises IP Addresses on the Internet

Strangely enough for a philosopher, Paul Syvenson was working for the United States government's Office of Naval Research, from whom he procured by a contract to fund the development of a realworld onion-routing system. Two young hackers from MIT, Roger Dingledine and Nick Mathewson, worked with Dr. Syvenson to build the system, which eventually became Tor.[27]

Tor is similar to many corporate VPNs, but with a few crucial differences. When one uses a VPN, the IP address the server and any intermediaries between the VPN and the site see is the IP address of the VPN. The crucial difference is that while a VPN ships data between only itself and the resource (such as a website) the user wants to access, Tor sends the data between a group of servers (at least three) called the *circuit.*

As illustrated by figure 10.1, the first server in the circuit is called the *entry guard.* When a user sends a TCP/IP packet to the entry guard, the entry guard sends the message inside the Tor network, where a message is sent from one Tor relay to another for a pre-determined number of hops. Entering the Tor network, the message is encrypted as normal using TLS. As a message goes into the Tor network, the message is encrypted with another layer, including the destination IP address, and this layer of encryption is added to disguise the content of the message from the entry guard and the intermediary relay in the Tor network. The new destination address of the encrypted packet is just the next "hop" to a relay. When the next relay receives the message, it is decrypted, and a new layer of encryption is added with another hop. Only when the message reaches the exit relay is the final level of encryption removed and the destination IP address is revealed. Therefore, only the IP address of the Tor exit relay is revealed to the final destination server and anyone in between. This technique of adding layers of encryption to a message (and then "unpealing" to reveal the message) gives onion-routing its name: The encryption is like the layers of an onion.

The Dark Web of Tor Hidden Services

One problem with onion-routing in terms of anonymity is that if a powerful adversary is watching all the traffic going into Tor and all the traffic going out of the Tor exit nodes, they can correlate the messages via statistical traffic analysis. What if the destination of the message was *inside* the Tor network? This kind of hidden server would then be impossible to observe. Tor allows this exact kind of secret server via Tor Hidden Services:[28] traffic goes into the Tor network and then meets with the hidden service, who constructs a *destination point* inside the network itself, where the destination point's name is given by a hash followed by the special ending of ".onion" as in "23a0b5e4fb6c6e8280940920212ecd563859cb3c.onion". These are the names of the Tor Hidden Services, and they can only be accessed via the Tor browser, a high-security browser made specially to work with the Tor network.

Tor Hidden Services are the secret sauce behind the Dark Web. In fact, the best definition of the Dark Web is that the Dark Web is actually only those websites that can be accessed via the Tor network. Everything from WikiLeaks to the Silk Road are technically Tor Hidden Services. WikiLeaks allows anonymous whistle-blowing via its use of a Tor Hidden Service, and it was accessing this Tor Hidden Service via the Tor Browser that allowed Chelsea Manning to send the State Department cables to Julian Assange, while he remained anonymous even from the US military.[29] Chelsea Manning was only caught when Assange discussed his actions with Adrian Lamo, not due to the anonymous whistle-blowing technology of Tor being attacked.[30]

In the same vein, the infamous Silk Road marketplace allowed illegal goods, ranging from drugs to even solicitations for murder, to be bought using Bitcoin, and the identity of Silk Road was itself hidden by the fact that it could only be accessed using Tor. It was a combination of posting to a known website and good-old-fashioned sleuthing that likely allowed Ross Ulbrecht to be caught by the FBI, although some would argue that actually Tor was de-anonymized by the NSA and there was a "parallel construction" to let the evidence be admissible in court.[31]

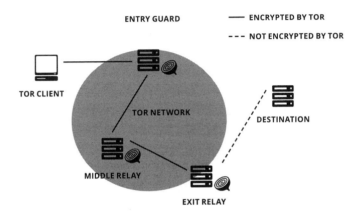

Figure 10.1 The Tor Network (Illustration from the Tor Project, https://torproject.org).

The Users of the Dark Web

What kinds of people use the Dark Web? It ends up being a surprisingly large range of people, including not only criminals and human rights activists, but also governments. On one hand, anonymity allows for people to engage in all sorts of deranged behaviors. Although some such behaviors are fairly harmless, such as the purchasing of marijuana over the Dark Web at the various successor sites to Silk Road, the dark side of the Dark Web is quite terrifying. Perhaps the most atrocious use of the Dark Web is the infamous "Red Room", where the Dark Web was being used to share snuff films featuring children.[32] On the other hand, Tor is also a vital part of defending human rights and is used by human rights activists in repressive countries such as Turkey and Iran, allowing them to access websites that would otherwise be censored by their government.

Although there is no doubt that the Dark Web is also used by child pornographers and drug-dealers and enables other kinds of undesirable behavior, it is also a mission-critical infrastructure for governments, journalists, human-rights activists—and possibly soon corporations. Currently, software called "SecureDrop" allows one to easily deploy Tor Hidden Services to enable anonymous whistle-blowing websites.[33] The municipal government of Barcelona has started using this software to bootstrap Tor Hidden Services to enable anonymous whistle-blowing on government corruption.[34] Although WikiLeaks was the first to allow anonymous leaking via the Dark Web, today Forbes, the *New York Times,* and other major media sites also rely on Tor Hidden Services to allow anonymous leaks to their journalists.

The Advantages of Using Tor

One reason the US government funded Tor was precisely because undercover agents operating in hostile nations would need to hide their identities. After all, not only could a human-rights activist get in trouble by sharing news of an arrest, but an agent of the United States operating in China would get in considerable trouble if discovered accessing a government *.gov* or *.mil* website from China. With Tor, they could now disguise their traffic, although eventually the Chinese government started blocking Tor. Tor is now increasingly easy to use, particularly the Tor Browser that features much better privacy than any so-called "private" browsing mode. For those that want to really cover their tracks with the same security of Snowden, the Tails distribution allows high-security and anonymous use of the Internet by booting from a USB drive.[35]

The NSA revelations have shown that now corporations are also targets of cybersecurity attacks by government actors, including the governments of not only the United States, but China and Russia. One can only assume that other governments, and even corporations, will gain these types of surveillance and hacking powers against their corporate competitors. Strong anonymity via tools like Tor should become part of the everyday operations of any normal corporation concerned with being attacked by their competitors and criminals. After all, if Tor is good enough for WikiLeaks and the U.S. Navy, it should be good enough for most corporations. It's also important to defend yourself as an ordinary user using tools like Tor, as you never know when you may have something to hide. Or as put by Moxie Marlinspike, we should all have something to hide.[36]

CAN THE DARK WEB BEAT EVEN THE NSA?

The problem with privacy-enhancing technologies is that it's a diverse and ever-evolving space: Tor and I2P for IP connections, Signal and Off-the-Record Messaging for messaging, TumbleBit and Zerocash for anonymized crypto-currencies. While this invisible Internet does appear to have "gone dark" to most companies, local police, and the FBI, do these applications actually successfully hide data from both skilled hackers and even nation-state level actors such as the NSA? Furthermore, what is the future of this arms-race over privacy and anonymity, and how will this impact the future of the Dark Web? Is the Dark Web here to stay, enveloping more and more of the Web and the larger Internet, or will it disappear due to the growth of surveillance powers?

From Quantum Computing to Crypto-Currencies

One of the largest weaknesses of the Dark Web is that it does not protect against traffic analysis, the ability of adversaries to monitor traffic to and from various servers to determine who is talking to whom. Although we have no evidence from any of the NSA leaks that any current cryptography is broken, to be fair, the possible advent of *quantum* computers can break most deployed existing cryptography based on Diffie-Hellman key exchange, RSA public key cryptography, or elliptic curve cryptography.[37] Nonetheless, such developments in quantum computing are still far off in the future, and already cryptographers are creating *post-quantum cryptography* that can defeat quantum computers. In the mean-time, we have evidence that the NSA and other intelligence agencies are simply recording all encrypted data to be decrypted later.

Yet, why wait for the future, when you can de-anonymize users now? The real action in de-anonymizing users is discovering who their friends are. The *metadata* of who knows whom can be determined by simply figuring out who is talking to whom. This social graph is important information, often more important than the content of the (encrypted) message itself, as it reveals the social hierarchies and communication pattern of the entire network: As said by General Michael Hayden, former director of the NSA and the CIA, "We kill people based on metadata."[38] Even if the NSA or CIA are doing the right thing, what's important is to remember that many other countries, such as Russia and China, have equivalent agencies and are developing the same capabilities to capture communications metadata—otherwise known as "signals intelligence."

This kind of information is revealed by the very architecture of Internet protocols like TCP/IP and UDP, which do little to defend anonymity to achieve high reliability and throughput over the Internet. Therefore, even encrypted messaging applications, such as Signal, reveal who is talking to whom;

as all an adversary has to do is look at the traffic coming in and out of the single centralized Signal server to de-anonymize a user based on their social network of Signal friends. The same kind of attack could even easily be done on "decentralized" Jabber servers used by encrypted chat programs such as Off-the-Record Messaging, as there are limited numbers of servers.

Bitcoin and other related crypto-currencies make this privacy even more difficult; an immutable public log, shared in a decentralized manner, is an easy subject for data-mining and so de-anonymizing crypto-currency transactions. While recent attempts to create a more privacy-preserving blockchain by using ring signatures with Monero or zero-knowledge proofs with ZeroCash generally may correctly hide who gets what amount of crypto-currency, they do not hide, over the long-term, who is using which key.

The Arms-Race of Privacy Enhancing Technologies

With enough data, even small amounts of signal can be detected in the noise—and that's usually enough to de-anonymize users. In fact, this applies even to the most advanced privacy-enhancing technology we have today, Tor. Can the NSA break Tor by observing metadata?

The answer is that powerful adversaries, such as the NSA, are likely in theory capable of beating Tor, but there is also software that is in theory resistant even to the most powerful mass surveillance. In general, privacy is a much larger problem than the rather well-defined problems of encryption, and also requires hiding the timing and size of messages, as well as hopefully making even the participation in the Dark Web hard to discover. Currently, Tor maintains a list of entry and exit nodes by IP address (in order for users to verify that they are indeed using the Tor network, as well as for law enforcement to know if someone is running a Tor entry or exit node), although in countries that censor Tor, these IP addresses are easy enough to add to a blacklist.

Proxy bridges are "private" un-listed Tor entry nodes, and these are maintained so that activists in countries that block the listed Tor IP addresses can use Tor. Deep packet inspection (DPI) can simply tell if a computer is using Tor by looking at the network traffic itself. Tor then offers "Pluggable Transports" that disguises Tor networks as other kinds of traffic using stenography, which hides the Tor traffic amongst network traffic that appears to be ordinary network traffic in the same way that a small secret message can be hidden inside a large image file. However, it has become an arms-race, and powerful machine-learning techniques are increasingly able to defeat even Tor Pluggable Transports. Regardless, all that a not-so-powerful adversary can do is view a user entering the Tor network, but it will not be able to tell to which particular website the user is going to.

Defeating the Dark Web Using Machine-Learning

Yet, not everything is shrouded in mystery. Very powerful adversaries, such as the NSA, who deploy many more resources than a hacker monitoring a WiFi network connection. Rather than monitor a single connection, a powerful adversary can monitor *all* the connections to the Tor entry nodes. Furthermore, an adversary that powerful can also monitor *all* the connections to the Tor exit nodes. This kind of observation of Tor network traffic can in theory be easily done by an agency such as the NSA. Of course, if the NSA can watch both the traffic in and the traffic out of the Tor network, then the NSA can simply watch the inputs and outputs of the Tor network, and determine via the size and time of the packets sent to disclose who is visiting which website over Tor using statistics, i.e., the statistical *disclosure attack*.[39] Although more difficult, due to the large amount of Tor relays and possible Tor hidden services, this attack could theoretically be done to de-anonymize Tor Hidden services.[40]

While these attacks on Tor seem simple, they do require a fairly large investment in monitoring Tor and machine-learning, and although researchers have shown they are possible on the budget of Microsoft Research, in practice from the Snowden revelation it appears that the NSA (at least as of 2013) does not actually do active statistical disclosure attacks. Instead, to de-anonymize users of the Tor network, the NSA found it simpler to attack unfixed bugs in Mozilla via the bizarrely named "Egotistical Giraffe" attack.[41] Yet looking into the future, there is no reason to suspect that all traffic in and out of the Tor network is not being captured for eventual analysis by powerful actors.

Beyond Tor: Mix Networking

Prior to Snowden's NSA revelations, *global passive adversary* was considered to be too far-fetched to be realistic, and thus was not taken into account by USA-based projects like Tor. In fact, it is now obvious that such an adversary is not only possible, but real. Today, it is all too easy to imagine situations where realworld powerful adversaries want to break privacy properties of secure messaging by gathering metadata or foil the correctness properties of an e-voting system.

To defeat an intelligence agency that is passively monitoring all communications on the network, one has to return to one of the original designs for privacy-enhancing technologies: Mix networking, an idea put forth by cryptographer David Chaum in his 1981 "Untraceable electronic mail, return addresses, and digital pseudonyms."[42] Mix networking is the only technology that is capable of defeating large-scale gathering of metadata by powerful global adversaries, as mix-networking builds computationally strong privacy into the network traffic itself.

Mixing networks, called *mix-nets* for short, are servers that receive messages from multiple senders, shuffle (i.e., mix) the messages, and then send them to their final destinations. The concept of a mix-net is simple: A message is encrypted and then sent into the mix network, where a mix node holds the message. Once the message is held for long enough or enough messages have accumulated at the node, the messages are mixed, and then sent out in a random order to other nodes. This both batches and re-orders the messages, so the metadata of who is communicating with whom is concealed.

Attacks such as statistical disclosure attacks can be defeated by making all the messages the same size by using padding, and by making sure the rate of messages sent is always the same. Dummy messages, also called *cover traffic,* can be generated so that the observer always sees each receiver and sender sending packets at the same rate, and so a global passive adversary cannot distinguish whether or not a user is sending encrypted messages with real content or fake messages. In some mix-net designs, even if an active adversary stops packets and compromises all but one of the mixing nodes in the network, as long as at least one node remains honest, the mix network will remain effective in preserving anonymity.

Despite the potential of mix networking to stop global adversaries like the NSA, there has been little research into the field over the last five years compared to onion-routing like Tor, and only recently have there been attempts to build realworld and general purpose mix-networking systems.[43] Nonetheless, we can be assured that even as adversaries become more powerful in terms of de-anonymizing users on the Dark Web, continued innovation will produce more powerful privacy-enhancing technologies. In this way, the Dark Web will continue to evolve as the arms-race between privacy and surveillance technologies continues.

CONCLUSIONS: SHOULD THE DARK WEB BE ILLEGAL?

The Dark Web is here to stay, and existing legal and technical frameworks need to be updated to take it into account in a realistic manner that minimizes the harm caused by anonymity while maximizing the benefits. Again, the Dark Web is not a bogeyman; it is just the part of the Web where information can be accessed and shared anonymously. Although there has been much focus on the negative aspects, ranging from WikiLeaks to Silk Road, the potential value of privacy-enhancing technologies to offer realistic technical solutions to cybersecurity problems is mostly untapped. In fact, the first individuals, corporations, and even governments that take advantage of privacy-enhancing technologies to protect themselves in an increasingly adversarial online world may hold a tremendous advantage.

Anonymity is not just for "dark social" trolling groups like 4Chan. Anonymity is the strongest possible category of a much more general (and respectable) category of privacy. Although the United States and Europe have vastly differing legal frameworks on privacy, ranging from the "bottom-up" patch-work of individual case-law that defines privacy in the USA to the "top-down" approach of fundamental rights inscribed in the Data Protective Regulation in Europe, both legal frameworks are failing to catch up to technological reality of the widespread use of privacy technologies to create online anonymity. The problem is, thanks to nascent techniques to make even participating in privacy-enhancing technologies unobservable, making anonymity illegal will be difficult: people will continue using these technologies regardless, and it may be difficult to identify these users given they are using privacy-enhancing technologies.

Why not just make the Dark Web illegal? Several large nation-states such as China have made the use of the Dark Web difficult, but the economic damage of making all VPNs and even web-based proxies illegal is very high, as many businesses require them. Even so, China recently passed a law requiring VPNs to register with the government.[44] However, countries such as Pakistan and Bahrain[45] are building their own vast Internet censorship systems, in the hope of maintaining social stability, but are also limiting the ability of their users and companies to communicate and innovate across national boundaries. This is likely damaging their economy in the long-term by removing the valuable network effects of an open Internet taken advantage of by companies like Google and Facebook. Ironically, due to its decentralized nature, the Tor-driven Dark Web is often more effective in resisting censorship than centralized VPNs, and attempts to censor the Internet in countries from Iran to Belarus simply drive users to decentralized alternatives like Tor. For example, before Arab Spring in Egypt in 2011, when the Egyptian government censored Facebook, there was a huge jump in Tor usage.[46] In general, attempts to shut down the Dark Web produce what is called the Streisand Effect: These attempts to censor the Dark Web increase interest and strengthen it.[47]

The alternative is to go on the offensive: To weaponize the Dark Web for hacking. After Podesta's e-mail was hacked due to Podesta falling for a phishing attack, the FBI and DHS launched an investigation called "Grizzly Steppe" into attempts by Russia to influence the 2016 US Election. Of the 876 IP addresses listed that were linked to possible Russian hacking, 42% of them were from the Dark Web, i.e., Tor exit nodes.[48] Was Russia using the Dark Web to hide its attempts to steal the e-mails of the Democratic National Convention? Perhaps, but of course, Tor exit nodes are used for all sorts of things. The root of the problem is that the Dark Web disguises the jurisdiction of criminals just as well as it does human-rights advocates. In response to the Silk Road investigation and other investigations like "Grizzly Steppe," the FBI has asked for broader powers to hack (also called "remote access" by the FBI) into machines overseas in Rule 41(b)(6), so that a warrant can be obtained from any judge in a jurisdiction where "crime may have occurred" to "issue a warrant to use remote access to search electronic storage media and to seize or copy electronically stored information located within or outside that district if...the media or information is located has been concealed through technological means."[49] Although these sort of extra-territorial demands for evidence usually are done via Mutual Legal Assistance Treaties (MLATs), with these broad powers, the FBI can place malware on a computer anywhere and use it to exfiltrate any data they please.

Although the FBI's pleas for help in tracking down criminals to lawmakers claimed that the Web is "going dark" and in turn led to Rule 41(b)(6), the danger of handing this kind of power over to domestic law enforcement, including the FBI, is that the Dark Web is inherently trans-jurisdictional.[50] Surprisingly, hacking then can be considered a declaration of war: Who wants an FBI agent to accidentally trigger World War III while tracking down a criminal through the Dark Web? Let's remember that countries such as Russia and China eschew the prefix "cyber" (in terms of cybersecurity, cyberwarfare, and so on) altogether, but just consider attacks over the Internet to be "information operations" as part of warfare. Although we can and should acknowledge that Dark Web can lead to malevolent uses and the Dark Web's very existence will likely make it more difficult to catch criminals using purely digital means, but this does not justify putting too much power into the hands of law enforcement, who are ill-equipped technologically to deal with the complexities of the Dark Web.

What can be done to counter the increase of criminal and adversarial behavior that originates in the Dark Web? The answer is simple: The best offense is a good defense. In this case, this means taking the fundamental privacy-enhancing technologies that form the foundation of the Dark Web and spreading them throughout society. The logic is that there would be less cybercrime if it wasn't so easy to commit. After all, the level of defense in terms of cybersecurity today is equivalent to leaving one's door unlocked, and being outraged when one's house is robbed. The answer isn't more police or leaving the "digital door" opened; the answer is locking the "digital door" using the same technologies that power the Dark Web.

Rather than make the Dark Web illegal, let's make it legal and spread the technology to enable the kind of world we want. Given that the genie of on-line anonymity is out of the bottle and it is not going back in, if the vast majority of society is fundamentally cooperative and abides by social norms, people will not suddenly transform into trolls or cybercriminals when given privacy and anonymity. The same technologies that have enabled a Dark Web have been vital in protecting at-risk human rights activists throughout the world, and so can protect governments, business, and ordinary citizens if legal and regulatory frameworks catch up to the reality of the technology. Technologies based on encryption and privacy are needed by everyone to defend themselves against attacks, ranging from the loss of control of personal data to securing their data in the cloud. These technologies are also needed to build new privacy-preserving crypto-currencies, smart contracts, and the next generation of machine-learning over sensitive data.

By understanding how the Dark Web works, we can find the parts of it that we want to put into the Web as a whole, and so make the Web more secure and private. This privacy-enhancing upgrade of the fundamentals of the Internet would then allow us to fulfill the vision of Pentland's "New Deal on Data" to allow people control over their own data. This will lead to a whole new round of innovation in the world economy, while simultaneously preventing out-of-control mass surveillance by authoritarian governments— or governments that may become authoritarian in the future.[51] Rather than accept the transparent society we live in today, where all behavior is monitored without self-awareness, let's hand people the knowledge and the tools to preserve privacy via control their own data and so fundamentally allow people to have free control of their own future. The Dark Web is not a threat; it's an opportunity.

Harry Halpin would like to thank the Tor Project for use of their illustrations and for help with finding references. His contribution to this text is based on a lecture he delivered to the Berkman Klein Assembly in January 2017.

NOTES

1. Barlett, Jamie (2016). The Dark Net: Inside the Digital Underworld. Random House.

2. The United Nations enshrines freedom of speech as Article 19 and the right to a private and family life as Article 9 in the United Nations Declaration of Human Rights.

3. Glancy, D.J. (1979). The Invention of the Right to Privacy, The. Arizona Law Review, Vol. 21, No. 1: 1-39.

4. Warren, S. D., and Brandeis, L. D. (1890). The Right to Privacy. Harvard Law Review, pp. 193-220.

5. NIST. FIPS General Information. Accessed April 1st 2017. https://www.nist.gov/information-technology-laboratory/fips- general-information

6. The Health Insurance Portability and Accountability Act of 1996 (HIPAA); Pub.L. 104–191, 110 Stat. 1936, enacted August 21, 1996.

7. Wehinger, F. (2011). The Dark Net: Self-Regulation Dynamics of Illegal Online Markets for Identities and Related Services. In Proceedings of the IEEE European Intelligence and Security Informatics Conference (EISIC), pp. 209-213.

8. The Convention for the Protection of Individuals with Regard to Automatic Processing of Personal Data (1981). ETS No. 108.

9. European Union Directive 95/46/EC (1995). L281, 23/11/1995, pp. 31–50.

10. European Union General Data Protection Regulation (2016). L119, 4/5/2016, pp. 1–88.

11. Costeja González, Mario (2014). Google Spain SL, Google Inc. vs Agencia Española de Protección de Datos, C-131/12, ECLI:EU:C:2014:317.

12. Pentland, Alex (2011). Personal Data: The Emergence of a New Asset Class. World Economic Forum.

13. Cavoukian, Ann. Privacy by Design: The 7 Foundational Principles. Accessed April 1st 2017. https://www.ipc.on.ca/wp-content/uploads/Resources/7foundationalprinciples.pdf

14. Chaum, David (1985). Security without Identification: Transaction Systems to Make Big Brother Obsolete. Communications of the 1030–1044.

15. Greenberg, Andy (2012). This Machine Kills Secrets: How WikiLeakers, Cypherpunks, and Hacktivists Aim to Free the World's Information. Dutton Adult.

16. Barlow, John Perry (1996). A Declaration of the Independence of Cyberspace. Accessed April 1st 2017. https://www.eff.org/cyberspace-independence

17. Goldwasser, S., and Micali, S. (1984). Probabilistic Encryption. Journal of Computer and System Sciences, 270-299.

18. Schneier, Bruce (2007). Applied Cryptography: Protocols, Algorithms, and Source Code in C. John Wiley & Sons.

19. Pentland, Alex. (2014). Social physics: How Good Ideas Spread—The Lessons from a New Science. Penguin.

20. Narayanan, A., and Shmatikov, V. (2008). Robust De-anonymization of Large Sparse Datasets. In Proceedings of IEEE Symposium on Security and Privacy, pp. 111-125

21. De Montjoye, Yves-Alexandre, Radaelli, Laura, and Singh, Vivek Kumar. Unique in the Shopping Mall: On the Reidentifiability of Credit Card Metadata. Science (2015): 536-539.

22. Dwork, C., McSherry, F., Nissim, K., and Smith, A. (2006). Calibrating Noise to Sensitivity in Private Data Analysis. In Proceedings of the Theory of Cryptography Conference, pp. 265-284.

23. Pfitzmann, Andreas (2005). Anonymity, Unlinkability, Unobservability, Pseudonymity, and Identity Management—A Consolidated Proposal for Terminology. Accessed April 1st 2017. https://freehaven.net/anonbib/cache/terminology.pdf

24. Serjantov, Andrei, and Danezis , George (2002). Towards an Information Theoretic Metric for Anonymity. In International Workshop on Privacy

Enhancing Technologies: 41-53.

25. See the Tor Project's web-page. Accessed April 1st 2017. https://www.torproject.org/

26. TLS stands for "Transport Layer Security" and it is the usual protocol used to encrypt HTTP connections. Accessed April 1st 2017. https://tools.ietf.org/html/rfc5246

27. Dingledine, Roger, Mathewson, Nick, and Syverson, Paul. (2004). Tor: The Second-Generation Onion Router. Naval Research Lab, Washington, DC.

28. Tor: Hidden Service Protocol. Accessed April 1st 2017. https://www.torproject.org/docs/hidden-services.html.en

29. Wikileaks Tor Hidden Service. Accessed April 1st 2017. https://www.wikileaks.org/wiki/WikiLeaks:Tor

30. Pilkington, Ed (June 4th 2013). Adrian Lamo Tells Manning Trial about Six Days of Chats with Accused Leaker. The Guardian. Accessed April 1st 2017. https://www.theguardian.com/world/2013/jun/04/adrian-lamo-testifies-bradley- manning

31. Cushing, Tim (October 6 th 2014) Documents Released in Silk Road Case Add More Evidence to the Parallel Construction Theory. Accessed April 1st 2017.

32. Horse, Laze (January 10th 2016). Peter Scully's Red Room Is the Most Disturbing Story You'll Ever Read. Accessed April 1st 2017. http://www.sickchirpse.com/peter-scully-red-rooms-disturbing-story/

33. SecureDrop. Accessed April 1st 2017. https://securedrop.org

34. Xnet (January 17th 2017). A Whistleblowing Platform against Corruption for the City Council of Barcelona. Accessed April 1st 2017. https://www.opendemocracy.net/digitaliberties/xnet/whistleblowing-platform-against-corruption-for-city-council-of-barcelona

35. The Tails Project. Accessed April 1st 2017. https://tails.boum.org/

36. Marlinspike, Moxie (June 13th 2013). We Should All Have Something to Hide. Accessed April 1st 2017. https://moxie.org/blog/we-should-all-

have-something-to-hide/37

37. Simonds, David (June 15th 2015). Quantum Computers: A Little Bit, Better. The Economist. Accessed April 1st 2017. http://www.economist.com/news/science-and-technology/21654566-after-decades-languishing-laboratory-quantum-computers-are-attracting

38. Cole, David (May 10th 2014). We Kill People Based on Metadata. The New York Review of Books. Accessed April 1st 2017. http://www.nybooks.com/daily/2014/05/10/we-kill-people-based-metadata/

39. Danezis, George, Claudia Diaz, and Carmela Troncoso (2007). Two-Sided Statistical Disclosure Attack. International Workshop on Privacy Enhancing Technologies, 30-44.

40. Biryukov, A., Pustogarov, I., and Weinmann, R. P. (2013). Trawling for Tor hidden services: Detection, Measurement, Deanonymization. In Proceedings of IEEE Symposium on Security and Privacy (SP), 80-94.

41. Accessed April 1st 2017. https://www.eff.org/document/2013-10-04-guard-egotistical-giraffe

42. Chaum, David (1983). Untraceable Electronic Mail, Return Addresses, and Digital Pseudonyms. Communications of the ACM Vol. 24, No. 2: 84-90.

43. See the European Commission's Panoramix project: http://panoramix-project.eu/

44. Pham, Sherisse (January 24th 2017). China Fortifies Great Firewall with Crackdown on VPNs. CNN Tech. Accessed April 1st 2017. http://money.cnn.com/2017/01/23/technology/china-vpn-illegal-great-firewall/index.html

45. As of April 2017, the top country using Tor is United Arab Emirates, but it likely is not repressed activists but the country preparing to set up it's own censorship of the internet, and thus using a botnet to explore Tor. For Tor users by country, see https://metrics.torproject.org/userstats-bridge-table.html

46. Dingledine, Roger (2011). Tor and Circumvention: Lessons Learned. Accessed April 1st 2017. https://www.freehaven.net/~arma/crypto2011-tor.pdf

47. What Is the Streisand Effect? April 16th 2013. The Economist. Accessed April 1st 2017. http://www.economist.com/blogs/economist-explains/2013/04/economist-explains-what-streisand-effect

48. Lee, Micah (January 4th 2017). The U.S. Government Thinks Thousands of Russian Hackers Are Reading My Blog. They Aren't. The Intercept. Accessed April 1st 2017. https://theintercept.com/2017/01/04/the-u-s-government-thinks-thousands-of-russian-hackers-are-reading-my-blog-they-arent/

49. Ghappor, Ahmed (2017). Searching Places Unknown. Stanford Law Review, Vol. 69.

50. Valerie Caproni (2011). Going Dark: Lawful Electronic Surveillance in the Face of New Technologies. FBI Statement Before the House Judiciary Committee, Subcommittee on Crime, Terrorism, and Homeland Security. Accessed April 1st 2017. https://archives.fbi.gov/archives/news/testimony/going-dark-lawful-electronic-surveillance-in-the-face-of-new-technologies

51. Pentland, Alex (2014). Saving Big Data from Itself. Scientific American, Vol. 311, No. 2: 64-67.

CHAPTER 11

Social Physics and Cybercrime

Yaniv Altshuler and Alex Pentland

INTRODUCTION

Historically, mathematical and statistical machine learning techniques were developed for "static problems", such as image processing and text recognition. Such problems are dominated by a relatively small number of relatively stable "signals." A trained text recognition model would achieve similar performance when processing the handwritten text of a 2017 MIT student and when analyzing Albert Einstein's personal letters. Similarly, neither Siri nor Google's speech recognition engine would find it difficult to transcribed a high-quality recording of J.F.K's famous "Ich bin ein Berliner" speech.

Human behavior, however, is a different story. Governed by a multitude of "dynamic signals" it is highly dynamic and highly "fractured." A traditional machine learning model trained to detect millennials from credit card purchases rapidly deteriorates in accuracy over time, requiring constant maintenance by a skilled expert, to incorporate new semantics knowledge into it. As millennials' behavior is subject to frequent (and constantly changing) trends, locating this in the data dictates not only a constant re-training of the model, but also the frequent development of new features intended to detect these trends (i.e., complex aggregative behavioral properties that are not part of the raw data). This can only be done through the combined work of a semantics domain expert working side by side with a data expert.

WHY IS SOCIAL PHYSICS NEEDED?

In the information age, companies gather data of all types and from numerous sources about their businesses operations. Data encompasses images and videos, text and tweets, transactions and usage logs. However, the majority of data originates from a single underlying source: People.

Tweets and blog posts are written by humans for humans; purchase transactions and phone call information convey human desires for things and other people; usage and app logs report how people interact with computers and mobile devices.

Data derived from human behavior is "messy": It is dynamic, complex and extremely versatile. Humans' behavior, as recorded in such digital data channels, changes drastically over time, is influenced by underlying complex social networks, and is conveyed in highly multimodal data streams. These characteristics pose significant challenges for companies that wish to analyze, understand, and predict their customers' behavior to improve their business operations.

In recent years, data scientists have started to employ "heavy-weight" statistical methods and machine learning algorithms to try and cope with this complexity. These powerful tools, including the new "deep learning" techniques, collect data and analyze its attributes to classify behavioral patterns, detect anomalies, and predict future trends. However, such tools cannot easily cope with human behavior data: interpreting dynamic, complex, and versatile data streams is at times nearly impossible.

Social physics approaches data from a completely different angle. Instead of deriving patterns from input data itself, it is based on the discovery that all human behavioral data is guaranteed to contain within it a set of common "social behavioral laws"—mathematical relationships that emerge whenever a large enough number of people operate in the same space. These laws govern the way various statistical properties of crowd behavior evolve over time, regardless of the type of data, the demographics of the users who created it, or the data size. Endor.com has integrated these laws into its data analytics engine, which efficiently extracts the underlying social attributes of all people contained in the raw data being provided as input (e.g., phone calls, taxi rides, financial investments).

HOW DOES SOCIAL PHYSICS WORK?

Human reality is composed of many small temporary events and changes. Social physics incorporates the underlying dynamics of human behavior and is, therefore, better equipped to uncover small groups in the population who are likely to behave in a certain way due to recent changes in their social environments. The social physics approach is, therefore, uniquely capable of identifying dynamic signals in human behavior data. This is because without the aid of social physics such signals lack any sort of statistical significance, rendering them indistinguishable from noise for traditional machine learning and deep learning methods.

For many of the most common problems, such as business queries concerning customer behavior, both the machine learning and social physics approaches are viable options. The tables below can help identify the appropriate tool, based on its attributes.

	MACHINE LEARNING IS BETTER FOR	**SOCIAL PHYSICS IS BETTER FOR**	**WHY?**
Type of data	Mechanical / physical - driven data: **Examples:** • Monitoring an oil drill pump's control data to predict malfunction • Face recognition	Human behavior data: **Example:** Analyzing financial transactions to predict who will purchase a premium service	Human behavior is erratic, unpredictable, noisy, complex, and dynamic. Mathematically speaking, human behavior is dominated by a large number of "temporal" signals, each affecting a small group of individuals. Hence, it is very hard to "learn" human data and produce consistent, stable models that represent it.

	TRADITIONAL MACHINE LEARNING	**DEEP LEARNING (W.O. SOCIAL PHYSICS)**	**SOCIAL PHYSICS**	**WHY?**
Small data sets	Able to analyze small data sets, but requires expert data scientists and is a time-consuming process	Requires large amounts of data for every question	Requires very little data to answer any question related to human behavior. The results are generated automatically (no need for data scientists to be involved)	Social physics does not require "big data" to generate results, due to the fact that it already incorporates dynamics of human behavior data, so that accurate predictions are possible even with very small data sets

| Features vs. Raw data | Requires a skilled data scientist and/ or a domain expert to define and select the right features representation of the raw data | Does not need features and can process raw data, but is limited to narrow type of problems | Does not need features and can process raw data, for any type of predictive problem involving (for human behavior) | Machine learning requires a long, often manual, process of transforming raw data into meaningful features. In contrast social physics automatically transforms any raw human behavior data into a canonical form of human behavioral clusters |

In summary, the machine/deep learning and social physics have different strengths. As a consequence, for problems involving human behavior it is often logical to combine the two approaches. Using the canonical social physics representation of data (thus avoiding data cleaning problems) one can use machine or deep learning for analysis. Because the features already encode "universals" of human behavior, the machine/deep learning process is more efficient and powerful than if applied to raw data directly.

EXAMPLE I: CYBER-TERRORISM

As detailed in previous sections the main differentiated capabilities
of social physics is twofold:

- The ability to connect to any structured transactional data streams that
  were created through human activity, with no understanding perquisite
  regarding the semantic nature of the data;

- The ability to detect slight dynamic correlations in crowd data, that
  are manifestations of hidden patterns or undercurrents, or emerging
  patterns that are at the first steps of their appearance.

These advantages make social physics an ideal tool for the analysis of cyber
activity, and, specifically, of hidden threats in the cyber environment. Such
use-cases bring forth the technology's advantages, as follows:

- The ability to connect to structured data streams in a semantics agnostic
  way enabled the social physics engine to efficiently process streams
  written in foreign languages, such as Arabic, Urdu, or Farsi, that many
  mainstream data-analysis tools cannot easily digest;

- Similarly, the use of code-words, evasive behavior or any other attempt
  to mask one's intentions, activity, or social ties by metadata or language
  manipulations—frequent in cyber-terrorism and intelligence use-cases—
  can easily be deciphered (or more accurately, bypassed altogether) using
  social physics.

- Traditional intelligence analysis often resembles a long process of locating
  numerous pieces of a single puzzle and meticulously putting them
  together, unraveling a hidden "story." Using social physics, on the other
  hand, enables the automatization of this process, where analysts are not
  required to know what they are looking for, to analyze it. Using the former
  metaphor, the Social Physics engine receives a "loose thread" from the
  analyst as input, and automatically sifts hundreds of most relevant

- pieces, ready for the analyst to quickly browse through them, and build the complete global picture.

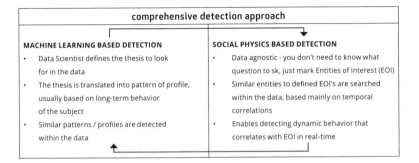

comprehensive detection approach	
MACHINE LEARNING BASED DETECTION	**SOCIAL PHYSICS BASED DETECTION**
• Data Scientist defines the thesis to look for in the data	• Data agnostic - you don't need to know what question to sk, just mark Entities of Interest (EOI)
• The thesis is translated into pattern of profile, usually based on long-term behavior of the subject	• Similar entities to defined EOI's are searched within the data, based mainly on temporal correlations
• Similar patterns / profiles are detected within the data	• Enables detecting dynamic behavior that correlates with EOI in real-time

PERFORMANCE AT DETECTING ISIS ACTIVISTS ON TWITTER

In a recent test, 15 million Tweets' metadata were provided to Endor.com as raw data for analysis. In addition, the customer revealed the identity of 50 Twitter accounts known to be ISIS activists that were contained in the input data, and tested Endor's ability to detect an additional 74 accounts that were hidden within the data. Endor's engine completed the task on a single laptop in only 24 minutes (measured from the time the raw data was introduced into the system until the final results were available), identifying 80 Twitter accounts as "look-alikes" to the provided example, 45 of which (56%) turned out to be part of the list of the 74 hidden accounts. Importantly, this provided an extremely low false alarm rate (35 False Positive results), so that the customer could easily afford to have human experts investigate the identified targets.

EXAMPLE II: DE-ANONYMIZING BITCOIN

For the past half-century futurists have heralded the advent of a cashless society.[1] However, cash is still a competitive and relatively anonymous means of payment. In this sense, Bitcoin, an electronic analog of cash in the online world, is an advanced manifestation of decentralized information thinking: There is no central authority responsible for the issuance of Bitcoins and there is no need to involve a trusted third-party when making online transfers. This makes Bitcoin the payment method of choice for a variety of cybercrime players. In addition, Bitcoin exchange institutes have themselves became targets for cybercriminals that take advantage of the fact that (a) once a large amount of Bitcoin is stolen it is effectively impossible to retrieve it (as Bitcoin transactions are irreversible without the mutual consent of both parties); and (b) as the stolen goods are already in the form of Bitcoins it is very easy for the thief to process, using the anonymity this medium provides.

One aspect of Bitcoin technology that can still be utilized to track down such perpetrators is the fact that the entire history of Bitcoin transactions is publicly available, although each actor's identity is encrypted. Using an appropriate network representation, it is possible to associate many public keys with each other, and with external identifying information. However, this is far from trivial, and requires a long, often manual, and meticulous analysis, that should be performed on a case-by-case basis. An example of such detective-style analysis, uncovering a realworld "sting operation" where an extremely large quantity of Bitcoin was stolen (equivalent to nearly US$30 million in 2017 terms) is presented in a paper on security and privacy in social networks.[1]

As social physics consists of a set of mathematical invariances that are guaranteed to be contained in any "human data," these invariants can be applied to Bitcoin transactions, and used as a prior for automatically extracting "too correlated" groups of Bitcoin accounts. This is done by detecting Bitcoin transactions patterns that social physics dictates are highly unlikely to spontaneously emerge. These behavioral correlations can then be matched against a given set of positive labels (for example, a small set of Bitcoin accounts known to be in possession of stolen Bitcoins) resulting in the detection of behavioral correlations (each representing a "real world commonality") that are associated with the stolen Bitcoins in question.

Social physics can be applied to data from very short periods of time, therefore enabling the detection of temporal signals. These data patterns are indistinguishable from noise without the use of social physics as a prior behavior model, but are key to the deciphering of the identity of the collaborating accounts.

In the Bitcoin theft[2] there were a few Bitcoin accounts known to be part of the collaborative network of Bitcoin accounts that was used to "launder" the funds by propagating them through a large number of fake accounts. For example, the stolen funds were sent to the Bitcoin account *1KPTdMb6p7H3YCwsyFqrEmKGmsHqe1Q3jg*. This was done in close vicinity to another attack, where the identity of the rightful owner of these funds, used for deposits of new funds, was changed to *15iUDqk6nLmav3B1xUHPQivDpfMruVsu9f* – effectively redirecting all new deposits to the thief. As these two attacks are likely to be done by the same group, we can use the identity of these two accounts as an example enabling Endor's social physics engine to analyze the Bitcoin transactions, looking for "look-alikes"—e.g., to find the collaborative accounts.

This result of this process is the uncovering of many of the accounts who are members of the money laundering network. However, unlike the manual, tedious manual process required to achieve this goal using a more traditional approach, this is done completely automatically, and in minutes.

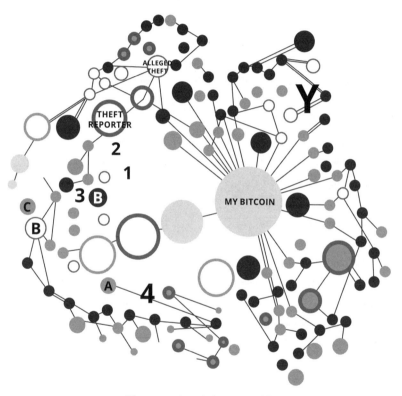

The money laundering network.[2]

NOTES

1. A. Anderson, D. Cannell, T. Gibbons, G. Grote, J. Henn, J. Kennedy, M. Muir, N. Potter, and R. Whitby. An Electronic Cash and Credit System. American Management Association, 1966.

2. Altshuler, Y., Elovici, Y., Cremers, A.B., Aharony, N. and Pentland, A. eds., 2012. Security and privacy in social networks. (pp. 197-223). Springer Science & Business Media.

CHAPTER 12

Behavioral Biometrics

David Shrier, Thomas Hardjono,
and Alex Pentland

The computing and data revolutions have come at a cost of ever easier cybercrime. Computer security has thus far been insufficient to the task. One of the major points of attack is user access control. Systems today remain reliant on a password or some combination of a password and a second factor, perhaps a security token. Efforts to improve on this model, such as biophysical biometrics (like fingerprint or iris scan), have quickly been hacked. Behavioral biometrics—keeping track of the user's behavior, and being more careful when atypical behavior is observed—offers a powerful yet effortless tool in the computer security arsenal that can augment or replace other methods, improving overall security.

SEEKING BETTER ACCESS CONTROL

Electronic user access control began in the early 1960's[1] at MIT with the introduction of the first password by computer science professor Fernando Corbató, to manage usage of the Compatible Time-Sharing System (CTSS) (progenitor of such core elements of computing systems as e-mail and file-sharing). CTSS password control was quickly followed, in 1962, by the first documented case of password theft: MIT PhD Allan Scherr needed more than his allotted time, so he printed out the password file to enable him to log in as other users.[1] Ever since then, there has been an arms race between computer security professionals seeking to provide better protection and bad actors seeking to penetrate systems, complicated by the need to make security as unobtrusive as possible for the user.

The problem of usability is a major driver of weak access control. According to Keeper,[2] an IT security firm, when it analyzed over 10 million passwords in 2016, it found that 17% of passwords are some variation of "123456." SplashData provided similar results from an analysis of over 5 million leaked passwords.[3] TeleSign reveals that 73% of people use the same password for multiple accounts.[4] More entropy is needed, without requiring the user to memorize a random string of 96 characters.

The 10 most popular passwords of 2016

1	123456
2	123456789
3	qwerty
4	12345678
5	111111
6	1234567890
7	1234567
8	password
9	123123
10	987654321

Source: Keeper

Two-factor authentication began to gain currency in the 1980's with the patenting of what has become RSA's keyfob token SecurID, with a secure generated number incorporated into a password of the user's choosing.[5] More recent efforts have included texting of a unique passcode to a user's mobile phone. The flaw is apparent: If you're on my phone, and can get it to trigger a text to my phone, you only need one and not two codes to access my systems. And RSA's keyfob has proven vulnerable itself; a 2011 phishing attack at parent company EMC resulted in a compromise of the RSA token system.[6]

Hollywood has had a long love affair with biometrics as a more secure access control mechanism, such as in the 1971 James Bond film *Diamonds Are Forever*. And for just as long, Hollywood has also shown spies and hackers defeating these systems (Bond uses a fake fingerprint to defeat the scanner). While in reality it's a bit more difficult to hack into biometrically defended systems, biometrics are hardly the panacea that device manufacturers and some security firms present them to be.

Behavioral biometrics offer a more robust means of highly secure, difficult-to-spoof identity validation: a signal passively acquired without the user needing take specific actions. The signal is continuous—meaning that once someone has logged into a computer system, the door hasn't been left open for others to access it—and allows the user to enjoy the benefits of being "in the background."

DEFINING BIOMETRICS

We can categorize biometric security in three broad classifications:
- **Biophysical** e.g., iris, fingerprint
- **Biomechanical** e.g., gait, keystroke analytics
- **Behavioral** e.g., patterns of movement, patterns of usage

When evaluating a security scheme, we suggest that the following criteria are used:
- Uniqueness
- Difficulty to duplicate
- Ease of use
- Ease of continuous verification
- Invariance (stability)

We will briefly review biophysical and biomechanical biometrics for completeness, and focus on behavioral biometrics.

Biophysical

Biophysical techniques are increasingly ubiquitous—for example, most popular smartphones, such as those made by Samsung, Apple, Google Pixel, LG and Xiaomi, have fingerprint scanners.[7] Biophysical techniques have the advantage of being relatively easy for the user, and they are relatively unique. Security groups and hackers, unfortunately, have shown that these easily can be spoofed, or fraudulently validated—for example, Chaos Computing Club of Germany replicated Apple's TouchID within 48 hours using a high-resolution photo of a user's fingerprint on the phone's surface that they 3D printed into a fingertip simulacrum.[8]

Facial recognition emerged in systems that involved identity cards or badges, allowing the persons's face to be automatically compared to the face on the identity card and the face logged in the database.[9] Work by Turk and Pentland established the ability to algorithmically extract facial patterns from video images using "eigenfaces,"[10] leading ultimately to the formation of a biometric security company Viisage (now L-1 Identity Solutions). Today, basic facial recognition capabilities are built into everyday computer systems such as the Alienware laptop and even the latest version of Windows.[11] However, facial recognition factors can be obfuscated by mood, lighting conditions, and other factors.

Next-generation phones, planned by the major handset manufacturers, are reported to have iris scanners built in. While this may introduce a "coolness" factor, they likewise suffer from being readily hacked. They also can be duplicated, and if your fingerprint file is stolen, it's not exactly easy to get a new set of fingerprints.

Biomechanical

Biomechanical techniques are harder to defeat. The unique interactions of muscles, the skeletal system, and the nervous system create a set of patterns that can not only identify an individual, but also potentially provide for continuous authentication instead of one-time. Human-Computer Interface (HCI) techniques, for example, such as combining eye movement and mouse usage, have been explored as a means of uniquely identifying individuals.[12]

Today's smart phones have a series of sophisticated sensors built in that can be used to identify users. By examining from a haptic interface the "dwell time" (how long someone's finger rests on a particular digit) and "flight time" (the speed between keystrokes), perhaps in conjunction with pressure applied, keystroke dynamics can provide a unique identification of a user.[13] A "hold and sign" system has been proposed that generated a 95% acceptance rate and 3% false acceptance rate, ignoring the actual signature generated and only looking at micro-movements detected from the accelerometer and haptic sensors.[14] As wearables become more ubiquitous, other forms of biomechanical security become possible. Researchers have been exploring continuous authentication with computerized glasses—showing a 93% to 99% detection rate and 0.5% to 3% false alarm rate on Google Glass.[15]

Several researchers have shown that fine-grained analysis of an accelerator pedal, brake pedal, and steering, for example, can uniquely identify the driver of a car.[16]

However, biomechanical techniques can face issues due to aging, disease, injury, and other confounding factors.

Behavioral

Behavioral biometrics are an emerging field which explores patterns of user behavior as a means of uniquely identifying a user. Our belief is that behavioral biometrics can be significantly enhanced through the application of the emerging computational social science discipline of *social physics*, as we will explain in the next section.

Behavioral biometrics have several advantages, such as flexibility, convenience for users,[17] and the ability to provide for continuous authentication (instead of only authenticating one time or at intervals). For example, in accessing computer systems, patterns of behavior extracted from file access and application usage can form a behavioral "fingerprint" of the individual that can terminate system access even after someone has logged in, if inappropriate actions are detected.[18] Given that about half of data loss is believed to arise from insiders (employees),[19] a better understanding of behavioral biometric factors can provide a "suspenders and belt" security system.

Behavioral systems have a great advantage of unobtrusiveness, in addition to being difficult to forge. "A well-implemented biometric solution will fit naturally into the regular flow of user behavior," says biometrics executive Tinna Hung.[20]

BEHAVIORAL BIOMETRICS AND SOCIAL PHYSICS

Patterns of human behavior form a unique digital fingerprint of an individual, and are much harder to replicate by someone who is not the individual in question. Validating data can be continuously passively acquired, rather than requiring active intervention by the user.

The computational social science discipline of "social physics" emerged out of the nascence of wearable computing. In the mid 1990s, a team at the

MIT Media Lab under Professor Alex "Sandy" Pentland began exploring the potential of ever-smaller computers working in tandem with human beings to understand the world around them.

With these new sensing devices accompanying people in their everyday lives, new signals began to emerge about human behavior that were much richer than previously available data sources. The discipline of understanding these signals has been named social physics. While patterns of e-mail or text messages, as well as file access log, could provide some glimpses of human behavior, the addition of mobile phone data offers up patterns of how people move around in a neighborhood, town, or city ("geospatial temporal" data streams).

MIT researchers have shown that with only four points of geospatial temporal data, a supposedly anonymized individual can be reidentified.[21] Conversely, a small number of data points can be used to uniquely validate a user.

Primitive forms of social physics are used by financial services companies, particularly credit card companies, to identify potential fraud. Is the type of store and location of charge consistent with the user's typical behaviors? In the event that there is a mismatch, the credit card company is able to mitigate risk by checking with the consumer to see if these are valid transactions. But date/time/location data is only the beginning of the potential for understanding movement patterns.

Geospatial temporal patterns are highly unique to an individual. In our work, the MIT team has identified over 1,400 behavioral indicators that can be extracted from mobile communications data. We constructed an open-source code library, Bandicoot, to enable extraction and analysis of these indicators from mobile data streams.[22]

IMPLEMENTING BEHAVIORAL BIOMETRICS

There are a number of practical challenges in the implementation
and deployment of behavioral biometrics today. Key challenges include
the following:

- **Accurate and authentic data collection:** Endpoints for sources
  of data (e.g., sensors, cameras, access points) must be identified and
  managed in a secure manner as these represent core assets to the
  behavioral biometric systems as a whole. A sufficient number of endpoint
  sources must be deployed, allowing for downtime for some of them. For
  enterprise deployments, these endpoints and the data they generate
  must be must be managed securely under the same policy regime as
  other devices and networks within the corporate boundary.

- **Accurate behavioral "templates"**: Depending on the specific
  behavioral biometric system, some systems (e.g., fingerprint based
  systems) may operate on the basis of "templates" which are created for
  each individual being authenticated by the system. These templates
  must have a high degree of accuracy, and may have to be recalibrated
  at frequent intervals. These templates themselves may carry enough
  information whose loss could aid attackers in providing inferential
  information. As such, these must be protected as an important security
  asset for the organization.

- **Integration into existing security infrastructures:** Most medium
  to large enterprises today already possess security infrastructures of
  varying degrees of complexity. One key challenge in the introduction
  of new or advanced behavioral biometric systems lies in the coherent
  integration with these existing infrastructures, under the same
  organizational security policy regime.

- **Workflows and user experience:** The acceptance of a new or
  advanced behavioral biometric systems (or any security systems) into
  an organization such as an enterprise requires seamless integration into

the user's daily workflow. Altering employees' workflows for improved security should be done as infrequently as possible, preferably never. This aspect should be one of the gating factors in an organization's decision to adopt behavioral biometric systems across the entire organizations. A sufficient number of deployment pilots should be conducted for small groups of employees across a period of time, before any solution be deployed corporate wide.

The best security systems will incorporate multimodal techniques for verification and continuous authentication, incorporating biomechanical and behavioral techniques in conjunction with knowledge-based challenge-and-query. One can envision defining a set of 30 behavioral characteristics, combined with biomechanical technologies, used in rotations of three (such as geospatial patterns, phone tilt, and keystroke flight-time). For each behavior biometric dimension used, we believe there would be a significant improvement in security. Further research is required to quantify this improvement, and should provide a productive area for further investigation.

NOTES

1. McMillan R (2012) "The World's First Computer Password? It Was Useless Too" Wired. https://www.wired.com/2012/01/computer-password/

2. https://blog.keepersecurity.com/2017/01/13/most-common-passwords-of-2016-research-study/

3. SplashData (2017) "Announcing our Worst Passwords of 2016" https://www.teamsid.com/worst-passwords-2016/

4. TeleSign (2015) "TeleSign Consumer Account Security Report" https://www.telesign.com/resources/research-and-reports/telesign-consumer-account-security-report/

5. Jones B (2017) "Two-factor security is the best lock for your digital life, but it's not perfect" Digital http://www.digitaltrends.com/computing/why-2-factor-security-is-flawed/

6. Zetter K (2011) "Researchers Uncover RSA Phishing Attack, Hiding in Plain Sight" *Wired* https://www.wired.com/2011/08/how-rsa-got-hacked/

7. http://webcusp.com/list-of-all-fingerprint-scanner-enabled-smartphones/

8. Mattise N (2013) "Chaos Computer Club hackers trick Apple's TouchID security feature" *ArsTechnica* https://arstechnica.com/apple/2013/09/chaos-computer-club-hackers-trick-apples-touchid-security-feature/

9. Phillips PJ, Wechsler H, Huang J, Rauss RJ "The FERET database and evaluation procedure for face-recognition algorithms" *Image and Vision Computing* 16: 5, 27 April 1998, pp. 295-306.

10. Turk MA, Pentland AP "Face Recognition Using Eigenfaces" *Proc. Of IEEE Conf. on Computer Vision and Pattern Recognition*, pp. 586-591, June 1991

11. http://www.windowscentral.com/how-set-windows-hello-facial-recognition-windows-10

12. Lu H, Rose J, Liu Y, Awad A, Hou L (2017) "Combining Mouse and Eye Movement Biometrics for User Authentication" Traore et al. (eds) *Information Security Practices* Cham, Switz: Ch 5.

13. Awad A (2017) "Collective Framework for Fraud Detection Using Behavioral Biometrics" Traore I e. al. (eds) *Information Security Practices* Cham, Switz: Ch 3.

14. Buriro A, Crispo B, Filippo D, Wrona K (2016) "Hold & Sign: A Novel Behavioral Biometrics for Smartphone User Authentication," 2016 IEEE Security and Privacy Workshops.

15. Peng G, Zhou G, Nguyen DT, Qi X, Yang Q, Wang S (2016) "Continuous Authentication With Touch Behavioral Biometrics and Voice on Wearable Glasses" IEEE Transactions on Human-Machine Systems, p. 99.

16. Yampolskiy R, Govindaraju G (2008) "Behavioural biometrics: a survey and classification" *Int. J. Biometrics*, Vol. 1, No. 1, 2008.

17. Clarke N, Li Fudong, Alruban A, Furnell S (2017) "Insider Misuse Identification Using Transparent Biometrics" *Proc. Of the 50th Hawaii Intl Conference on System Sciences.*

18. Leonard LC (2017) "Web-Based Behavioral Modeling for Continuous User Authentication (CUA)" *Advances in Computers*, Vol. 105: Ch 1.

19. Cisco (2014) "Data Leakage Worldwide: Common Risks and Mistakes Employees Make" Whitepaper accessed 07 Apr 2017 https://www.cisco.com/c/en/us/solutions/collateral/enterprise-networks/data-loss-prevention/white_paper_c11-499060.pdf

20. Meinert M (2017) "Better Security Through Biometrics" *ABA Banking Journal*, January/February 2017.

21. DeMontjoye Y, Hidalgo C, Verleysen M, Blondel V (2015) "Unique in the Crowd: The privacy bounds of human mobility," *Nature,* Scientific Reports 3, article number: 1376.

22. http://bandicoot.mit.edu/

CHAPTER 13

Data Security and Privacy in the Age of IoT

Thomas Hardjono, Alex Pentland,
and David Shrier

INTRODUCTION: DEVICES, CLOUDS, AND THE IOT BIG DATA PROBLEM

The broad area of the Internet of Things represents an important milestone in the history of the Internet because for the first time it brings a host of technological advances data communications together with large-scale advances in data analytics, the combination of which has the potential to shape the future data-driven society.

The IoT revolution itself is not so much about new networks and systems that enable the collection and management of data from diverse sources, but instead it is about increased access to data as the foundation of the future data-driven society. As such, the various aspects of the supply chain of data—from the devices to the applications in the cloud—require rigorous protection from the various possible attacks.[1,2]

Two keys aspects that make the current IoT revolution somewhat different from prior technological advances on the Internet is the potential *speed* for data availability and the potential *breadth* of data types that may become available.

The lessons of big data from the past decade has taught us that *data increases in value when it is shared.*[6] There are numerous circumstances and use-cases today where data sharing would help communities and cities in finding solutions to societal challenges (e.g., the spread of diseases; urban planning; climate change). However, there are a number of challenges in the sharing of data—many of which have become more acute and pressing in the face of the current pace of IoT technology developments:

- **Tension between data sharing and privacy:** There is an apparent tension or conflict between the needs of data sharing and the need for preserving the privacy of the owner or source of the data.

- **Limited scalability of current distributed processing platforms:**
  The rise of big data analytics has ushered in new distributed storage
  and distributed processing platforms, such as Hadoop[9] and Spark,[10] which
  require all relevant raw data sets to be available. We believe this approach
  inherently does not scale for data sharing.[3]

- **Limitations imposed by regulatory requirements:** Different
  legal jurisdictions have placed different regulations regarding
  cross-organization data sharing and cross-border data flows.[4]

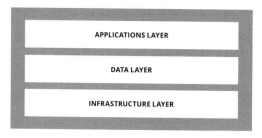

Figure 13.1 Layers of Abstraction within the IoT Ecosystems.

Since data can be generated by different devices within diverse networks,
domains, and verticals, it is often useful to create an abstraction of functions
and services independent of any specific use-case or specific domains.
Figure 13.1 shows a simple abstraction of the IoT ecosystem as the basis
for the ensuing discussions:

- **Infrastructures layer:** This layer represents the functions and services
  that are implemented through various computing and network systems,
  independent of the type of data that may be collected and exchanged
  through these systems, and independent of the specific applications that
  may use the data.

- **Data layer:** This layer represents the various syntax and semantics
  of data originating from the various sources in the IoT ecosystem,
  independent of the specific technology used to collect, collat, and manage

the data within a given storage. The data layer also includes the various data-aggregation services, which together may constitute the future "data market" for IoT data.

- **Applications layer:** The numerous data-driven applications are typically agnostic to the specific technologies within the infrastructures layer. Some applications may be developed for specific data types within a given domain or vertical. In all cases, an application needs assurance that data is (i) source-authentic, that it has (ii) strong provenance, and that it has been (iii) integrity-protected (optionally with confidentiality protection) while the data traversed the IoT supply chain.

TOWARDS A PRACTICAL IOT ARCHITECTURE

In seeking to understand the challenges around IoT data security and privacy, we propose the use of a high-level architecture (figure 13.2) that provides a representation of the entities and their role within the IoT ecosystem, following the industry model proposed by the Open Connectivity Foundation (OCF).[13,14] The purpose of this architecture is to aid in the identification and categorization of different security and privacy challenges across the landscape, from the source IoT devices to the applications that finally make use of the data.

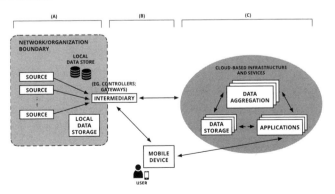

Figure 13.2 High Level IoT Architecture.[13]

The entities within the high-level architecture of figure 13.2 are as follows (left to right):

- **IoT data sources:** These are the various end-point IoT sources of raw data, across the various organizational use cases and verticals. For example, in the consumer sector the IoT devices include smart-home devices (e.g., smart appliances, metering sensors, personal health devices). In the corporate sector, these devices include, for example, building sensors (e.g., heat sensor, alarms), personnel devices (e.g., smart badges), and others. Examples from the industrial sector include smart-grid sensors in industrial plants, devices and sensors in managed buildings (e.g., warehouses, leased offices and apartments), and others.

- **Local Data Storage:** In some deployment use-cases raw data reported from local IoT data sources may be stored locally, depending on specific requirements. For example, for scalability reasons it may not be efficient for low-powered source devices to stream data to storage services located in external networks (e.g., in the cloud). In other deployment scenarios, the local data storage may facilitate curating and cleaning of raw data before it is uploaded to cloud-based storage.

- **Intermediary devices/services:** These are devices whose function it is to manage end-point devices that generate IoT data and to transfer proxy data to a destination repository. In many situations, it may not be efficient for end-point devices to communicate directly to data stores and applications that reside outside the network or organizational boundary (e.g., in a cloud). This architectural design decision may be driven by security concerns or by scalability requirements. In many cases, end-point devices simply may not have the functional capability to interact with remote services (e.g., simple/cheap sensor).

In these scenarios, an intermediate device is deployed that interacts with multiple local end-point devices which report data to the intermediate device.

Examples of these intermediate devices include domain controllers, home gateway boxes, home panels, PC computers, content devices (e.g., Set Top Boxes), and other user friendly devices (e.g., Amazon Echo).

- **Cloud-based data storage services:** Cloud-based storage services offer a practical solution for IoT data storage from the manageability perspective. These storage services range from "public cloud storage" (e.g., for consumer devices) to private clouds for enterprise data. In the area of consumer personal health, for example, many vendors of personal devices offer an accompanying cloud-based storage service for the devices together with some form of personal analytics application.

- **Data Aggregation Services:** Several service providers may provide value-add to raw data by combining data from various sources and aggregating them into packages directed at specific segments of the data market. Data from the growing number of IoT devices may provide new sources of raw-data and therefore new revenue possibilities for these aggregation services.

- **Applications:** Increasingly, cloud-based web applications provide the most economical solution to the problem of voluminous data storage, and multiple vendors today offer these types of services. Applications may range from simple data management functions to more sophisticated AI-based machine learning tools that provide analytics on the IoT data in the cloud.

- **User Mobile Device:** As mentioned previously, there are some deployment scenarios that provide the end-user with mobile applications on their smartphones to provide the user with better control and insight into their data. These mobile applications range from personal heath analytics apps to home-security apps that can be accessed by the user remotely.

The in the next section, we use this IoT architecture as the backdrop to identify the sets of challenges pertaining to IoT data security and privacy.

DATA SECURITY & PRIVACY: CHALLENGES AREAS

In looking at the challenges around IoT data security and privacy, it is useful to break down the broader set of issues into components based on the flow of data and the intended computing applications. This approach is also useful because there are multiple IoT deployment scenarios, ranging from the consumer use-cases to industrial use-cases. As such, a general architecture such as that in figure 13.2 is useful for identifying security challenges that are common to many of these use-cases.

From an ecosystem and infrastructure perspective, we divide the IoT landscape into the following areas of challenges (see figure 13.2):

a.   **Local infrastructure security:** This set of issues pertains to the local infrastructure within the organizational or network boundary. This boundary may range from the simple home network boundary in the consumer scenario, to the larger and more complex enterprise or industrial scenarios.

b.   **Transport infrastructure security:** This set of issues pertains to the security of the transport mechanism from the local organizational/network boundary to the cloud infrastructure boundary.

c.   **Cloud infrastructure security:** This set of issues pertains not only to data-at-rest protection within the cloud infrastructure, but also to the access of data and to privacy-preserving computation challenges.

Additionally, since IoT data concerns citizens in the larger context of society, it is necessary to overlay the following sets of challenges atop the IoT infrastructure security issues:

d.   **User Privacy:** Since the value of IoT data lies in its ability to provide insight into human behaviors and systems behavior, the issues around data privacy—both for individuals and organizations—come to the forefront as a major social concern for future data-driven societies.

e.   **Data Manageability:** Beyond the need for IoT data for special applications (e.g., analytics), there is also the need for ease of manageability of data from the user's perspective—independent of the type of data being collected and the location of the data source and storage. Levels of abstraction above raw data need to be presented to the user, to provide the user with an accurate view of the state of the IoT data.

IOT INFRASTRUCTURE SECURITY

The security of data is only as good as the security of the infrastructure handling the data—namely the infrastructure supporting all aspects of the lifecycle of data, including the collection, distribution, storage, and management of the data. For many modern IT organizations today, network and computing resources represent assets that are core to the survival of the organization. As such, many IT organizations today have already deployed solutions to address the various security challenges in the organizations (e.g., corporate identity management, access control, directory services, remote access, data loss prevention, etc.). New IoT data security solutions should integrate seamlessly—or at least tightly interoperate—with these existing IT security infrastructures.

The advent of cloud computing in the past few years has added another dimension of complexity to the management of IT infrastructure, where corporate assets located in the cloud must be managed as an extension of the existing IT management infrastructure. The infrastructure underlying these cloud services is legally owned and operated by a third party, and, as such, brings other security risk-benefit factors that must be considered by the organization.

For many mature IT organizations, which have already deployed security solutions—both on-premise and in the cloud—the addition of IoT devices may not necessarily impose burdensome challenges as many of these organizations have already deployed thousands to hundreds of thousands of user-centric devices, such as network PC computers, laptops, Wi-Fi access points, and other devices. Most of these existing devices differ from new IoT devices (such as sensors) in their specific functions and in their degree of availability.

From the infrastructure security perspective, IoT computing introduces the dimension of being "always on," always reporting data or measurements at regular intervals, and, in some cases, always alerting the organization to changes. This notion of "always on" is true across the various domains and verticals of IoT computing (e.g., consumer health device, heat sensor in power plant, security camera in corporate offices). It is this aspect that distinguishes IoT infrastructure management from existing traditional IT management.

Some of the security-specific challenges to the IoT infrastructure are as follows:

- **Device identity management:** Each IoT device in the ecosystem must be uniquely identifiable and addressable.[14] For some types of IoT devices, their very existence should not be discoverable by unauthorized entities (e.g., other devices, people, computers). Authenticating a device and associating access policies to these devices are core functions in the IoT infrastructure.

- **Device interactions management:** In some deployment scenarios, it is a requirement for IoT devices to interact only with other authorized IoT devices or endpoints. This requirement stems particularly from a data leakage concern. Device authentication and authorization are core functions in many deployment environments (e.g., industrial, healthcare).

- **Policy management:** Today, many enterprises have adopted a policy-driven approach to managing assets (e.g., files, devices, services) within their organizational boundary. This approach should be extended to IoT devices within the organization, with tighter policy controls over those critical IoT devices (e.g., critical sensors and reporting agents).

- **Device key management:** IoT devices that collect and report data must be able to do so without interference and report data with source-authenticity.[18] This allows the recipient of the data to obtain assurance regarding the integrity of the data, from the sending IoT device to the recipient (e.g., controller device, or storage device). The use of cryptographic techniques for source-authenticity necessitates the use of cryptographic keys, which, in turn, requires careful and methodical management. The issue of key management is also important in the consumer IoT space, beyond the usual issues of local channel security (i.e., 802.11 WiFi systems).

- **Storage security management:** Attacks to data—such as data theft or intentional data corruption or poisoning—is perhaps cost-effective for attackers when directed to the few data stores instead of many IoT device endpoints. As such, protecting data in these repositories is core to the value-proposition of the Internet of Things.

- **Audit Management:** Monitoring data deliveries (e.g., from IoT device to destination), and tracking data access within repositories, are just two of the many tasks related to audit management. This aspect of the IoT ecosystem may be driven not only by business needs, but also by regulatory compliance requirements.

- **Cloud services management:** In organizations that deploy part (or all) of their infrastructure in the cloud, there will be additional security challenges that are cloud-specific and which may not appear in the on-premise counterpart of their infrastructure. These cloud-specific issues include the security of the compute units (e.g., virtual containers) and storage units, key management for multi-tenant configurations, and others.

The above list of infrastructure challenges is by no means exhaustive or detailed, and is intended to be a starting point to begin addressing new security and privacy issues accompanying the uptake of IoT technologies, both in the consumer space and within the organizational space (e.g., enterprise and industrial).

IOT DATA-IN-MOTION SECURITY

The term "data-in-motion" refers to the flow of data from one point in a network (e.g., source sensor) to its intended destination (e.g., another device, storage, etc.) located either in the same network or in a different network. Given the projected scale of IoT deployments in the future, the security issues around data-in-motion takes on an even more significant importance compared to traditional use-cases.

Different IoT deployment use-cases will require differing types of security solutions, possibly with differing levels of assurance. However, the following list provides several common functions that can be applied to address issues around data-in-motion:

- **Source authentication:** The authenticity of the identity of the source (sender) and recipient of an IoT data transfer (e.g., small streams or bulk transfers) is a crucial factor to the value of the data itself. Without this assurance regarding a data's source and recipient, the economic value of a given data-set may come into question. Cryptographic techniques such as mutual authentication protocols and digital signatures on data payloads can be used to provide a foundation to begin addressing this issue.

- **Contents confidentiality:** In some IoT deployment scenarios, data being sent from a source (e.g., heat sensor in nuclear plant) to a recipient (e.g., operations center) must be maintained private due to the nature of the data itself. In these cases, additional cryptographic functions for confidentiality (e.g., encryption) may be applied.

- **Key management:** When cryptographic techniques are introduced—both asymmetric key and symmetric key cryptographic techniques—for authentication and confidentiality, there comes with it the often overlooked need (and cost) to manage keys. For example, many sensor devices do not have sufficient power to perform public key (asymmetric key) cryptographic computations on large amount of data.[18] As such, they must employ symmetric key cryptographic techniques (e.g., block ciphers or stream ciphers). However, this necessitates the management of the keys that these devices employ to protect the data.

- **Non-repudiability:** There are some use-cases that require non-repudiation of the delivery of data, from one endpoint (e.g., IoT device) to another endpoint (e.g., data repository). For example, in the healthcare domain there are situations where a medical device implanted in a patient must report data at regular intervals for the purposes of the patient's health, and potentially for life support and survivability. In these scenarios, both the source device and the destination recipient must not be able to repudiate (e.g., for legal purposes) the occurrence of the data transmittal event or repudiate the data that was transmitted. This feature is also at the heart of trusted computing[19] where a device must be able to generate trustworthy remote attestations[20] regarding its internal state, without manipulation, interference, or hindrance.

DATA-AT-REST SECURITY: SECURING DATA REPOSITORIES

With the emergence of big data computing in recent years there has been increasing concern regarding the security and integrity of data stored within large repositories. There are various kinds of attacks that can be performed on data stored within repositories, ranging from passive data theft (i.e., copying) to highly sophisticated data modifications or manipulations that are designed to be hard to detect (i.e., "poisoning" raw data). As such, with IoT data the problem of "data loss prevention" (DLP) today encompasses a larger set of problems, including detecting unauthorized modifications that may be gradual and cumulative over time, and which may not be solved using traditional data backup solutions.

In many deployment scenarios, data encryption may be used to protect data-at-rest in storage, both in physical drives and in cloud-based storage. Several standards have been developed to address the various lifecycle phases of data storage encryption.[21] While data storage encryption techniques provide security for data on disk or in archive, they do not solve potential attack scenarios targeted at data when it leaves storage and moves into the computation units (e.g., containers in the cloud). More recently, solutions based on advanced cryptographic techniques—such as homomorphic encryption[22]—have been proposed to provide a way to perform computation on encrypted data without having to decrypt it first. These advanced cryptographic techniques require further research and development.

The following provides a short summary of techniques to protect data-at-rest in storage:

- **Full-Drive Encryption (FDE):** Encryption processes can be incorporated into the physical disk drive (e.g., in hardware or firmware).[19] This approach is often referred to as full-drive encryption or *Self-Encrypting Drives* (SED) because the disk drive always encrypts data blocks prior to writing into its internal physical media. This specialized approach is attractive to many deployment scenarios because cryptography is applied below the file system level, and as such it is opaque to the file system. The file system sees no change to its usual operations. If a physical disk drive is lost or stolen, the contents remain encrypted. Often this technical solution is paired with other tamper-resistant hardware solutions for key storage, such as the TPM hardware.[19]

- **File encryption:** Encryption processes can also be applied at the file system level, incorporated into the file system software. The advantage is that all data streams written to disk drives will be encrypted, and ordinary disk drives (non-FDE drives) can be used. The disadvantage includes the need to manage cryptographic keys as part of the file system, which may increase the complexity of the file system itself.

- **Database encryption:** Several database systems today offer the capability to protect data using encryption techniques. These may be applied at the column or row level, and also to entire tables within the database. The advantages and disadvantages from a security management perspective are similar to file level encryption solutions (e.g., key management). Additionally, the performance of the database itself may be affected by the need to perform cryptographic operations as part of the database access.

- **Homomorphic encryption:** Homomorphic encryption offers the promise of computing over encrypted data. *CryptDB*[23] is one such system developed at MIT that encrypts data in a database using homomorphic encryption techniques. It executes SQL queries over encrypted data using a collection of efficient SQL-aware encryption schemes. CryptDB works by intercepting all SQL queries in a database proxy, which rewrites queries to execute on encrypted data. The proxy encrypts and decrypts all data, and changes some query operators, while preserving the semantics of the query. The DBMS server never receives decryption keys to the plaintext so it never sees sensitive data, ensuring that a curious database administrator cannot gain access to private information.

- **MPC Encryption:** Related to homomorphic encryption is a different family of encryption algorithms called *multi-party computation* (MPC).[24] The notion is that a group of mutually distrustful entities could collectively perform some computation without revealing raw data to each other and where all parties are happy that certain features have been satisfied (e.g., cheaters are detected; computation cycle has been fully completed). Although the practical applications of MPC type algorithms still require further research and development, some advances have been made recently. One recent proposal is called *MIT Enigma*[12] where MPC is combined with peer-to-peer (P2P) networks and blockchain technology, such that data is broken up into shares and the shares are dispersed on the P2P network. Nodes must then collectively perform MPC computations on the encrypted shares (without needing to decrypt). Stronger resilience against attacks may be achieved because data is not kept within a monolithic repository, but instead dispersed as encrypted data-shares throughout the P2P network of nodes.

- **Open Algorithms:** The MIT Open Algorithms (OPAL)[3] approach proposes a new paradigm for sharing data. Rather than moving data towards a centralized query location, the query is instead broken down into sub-queries and delivered to the data repositories containing the data-sets of interest. Each of the sub-queries would then be executed by the relevant repository, with the results being reported back to the querier— who would merge the results into a meaningful analysis. In this new OPAL paradigm, raw data never leaves its physical location or the control of its owner. Security and privacy become more manageable in this paradigm because each repository controls its own data store, and monitors the privacy entropy of released answers. As part of access control and policy management, a user whose data resides at a repository has the ability to tune-up or tune-down the granularity of the responses to each query in which their data-sets are used.

One or more of the above techniques can be deployed together, although the additional complexity introduced may need to be weighed against the cost of managing complex IT infrastructures and the degree of risk-mitigation they afford.

DECENTRALIZED ARCHITECTURES FOR OWNER-CENTRIC CONTROL OF DATA

A core design principle in achieving scalable sharing of data is to never release raw data from its repository.[3] Placing control in the hands of the data owner will create a sustainable data environment in which data owners will be incentivized to share data and consequently data uses will be more aligned with the public interest. This principle also combats the dangers of big brother surveillance, and provides the data owner with the ability to control the granularity of the query responses being released by the database.

In this distributed and decentralized data repository architecture, different kinds of data should be stored separately. This reduces the risk associated with a data breach. The external or remote human querier (or query operator) needs to deploy tools that allow queries or sub-queries to be routed to the correct repository. Depending on the implementation, the query-response model for data processing can be performed in real-time over these distributed repositories.

Distributing data across multiple repositories aids in enforcing individual privacy, because it makes possible the tracking of the patterns of communications between each repository and the human operators/ queriers. This capability arises from the observation that each category of data-analysis operation—whether it is searching for a particular item or computing some statistic—has its own characteristic pattern of communication. We refer to this pattern or signature as *metadata about metadata*, and it allows data owners to monitor the overall patterns of otherwise private communications.[11]

In this context of distributed data repositories and privacy, the notion of decentralization refers to the control (by the data owners, co-owners or custodians) of the computing operations that may be performed on the data. Decentralization of control has several possible interpretations and manifestations:[26]

- **Decentralization of services:** At the infrastructure level, decentralization of service means enabling a choice in the selection of the service providers that will provide the best control over the data.
- **Portability of data and services:** At the data level, decentralization of control means the freedom to change or switch service providers at any moment in time.[8] As such, portability of data stores and interoperability of services across providers is crucial to retain independence from any specific service provider. Interoperability is best achieved through good standards, with public participation and review.

One recent ground-breaking initiative towards owner-centric control is the *User Managed Access* (UMA) architecture and specifications,[27] which extends the popular OAuth2.0 framework for authorization.[25] The UMA architecture was designed to address the need for the data owner ("resource owner") to control the permissions and access policies to the various repositories of their data (called "resources") that are dispersed across various services providers on the Internet.

One fundamental concept underlying the UMA architecture is the need to empower data owners (resource owners) with the relevant interoperable standards to share resources, such as data or analytics results, in a scalable manner. The querier (called the Requesting Party) must obtain the consent of the data owner, and will obtain a *consent receipt*—that may be legally binding—which clearly states the purposes and limitations of the data usage, duration of use, the legal obligations of the querier, and so on.

The UMA architecture provides some solutions for the consumer IoT data challenges, notably in the need for consumers to have better control of their IoT data (e.g., household IoT devices and sensors), which can be highly sensitive from the privacy perspective.

SUMMARY AND CONCLUSIONS

We believe that the IoT revolution itself is not so much about new household electronics, new networks, and systems, but rather about the future of the data-driven society. We propose viewing the vast set of problems under the abstract division along the lines of the *infrastructure* layer, the *data* layer, and the *application* layer. Most deployment use-cases of IoT technologies and access to IoT data cut across these three layers.

The future IoT infrastructure shares much in terms of designs, architectures, and protocols with the current network and security infrastructure technologies. However, the world of IoT brings with it additional security and privacy challenges with regards to the data it produces. As such, it is useful to also view these challenges from the *state* of data. This includes security issues surrounding data-in-motion (e.g., streams of raw data from IoT sensors) and data-at-rest.

Once data reaches its intended destination (e.g., a local repository or storage in the cloud), in addition to data-at-rest protection, additional privacy-preserving techniques must be employed to prevent data access or queries that compromise privacy. Thus, although new cryptographic techniques can be used to allow computation on encrypted data (e.g., homomorphic encryption; multi-party computation) additional privacy-preservation techniques must be deployed atop these encryption solutions.

NOTES

1. Mercury News, Groups call for $500 million initiative to prepare for 'deluge of data' from Internet of Things, Mercury News, 9/1/2015. http://www.mercurynews.com/2015/08/31/ groups-call-for-500-million-initiative-to-prepare-for-deluge-of-data-from-internet-of-things/

2. Wall Street Journal, Anthem: Hacked Database Included 78.8 Million People, 24 February 2015, http://www.wsj.com/articles/anthem-hacked-database-included-78-8-million-people-1424807364

3. A. Pentland, T. Reid, and T. Heibeck, *Big data and Health - Revolutionizing medicine and Public Health: Report of the Big Data and Health Working Group 2013,* World Innovation Summit for Health, Qatar Foundation. http://www.wish-qatar.org/app/media/382.

4. Hadoop, Apache Foundation. http://hadoop.apache.org

5. Spark, Apache Foundation. http://spark.apache.org

6. T.Hardjono, D. Shrier and A. Pentland, *Trust::Data: A New Framework for Identity and Data Sharing,* Visionary Future, 2016.

7. European Commission (2016), *The General Data Protection Regulation (GDPR) (Regulation (EU) 2016/679).*

8. Open Connectivity Foundation (OCF), *OIC Core Specification* V1.1.1, Published Specifications, OCF, 2016. https://openconnectivity.org/specs/OIC_Core_Specification_v1.1.1.pdf

9. Open Connectivity Foundation (OCF), *OIC Security Specification* V1.1.1, Published Specifications, OCF, 2017. https://openconnectivity.org/specs/OIC_Security_Specification_v1.1.1.pdf

10. T. Hardjono and N. Smith, *Simplified Key Exchange for IoT Constrained Environments*, Internet Engineering Task Force (IETF), June 2016, https://datatracker.ietf.org/doc/draft-hardjono-ace-fluffy/

11. Trusted Computing Group. *TPM Main Specification Version 1.2.* TCG Published Specification, TCG, October 2003.

12. T. Hardjono and N. Smith (Eds). *TCG Infrastructure Reference Architecture for Interoperability* (Part 1) Specification Version 1.0 Rev 1.0, June 2005. http://www.trustedcomputinggroup.org/ resources.

13. Trusted Computing Group (TCG), *TCG Storage Architecture Core Specification,* Version 2.00. TCG 2010 Published Specifications.

14. M. van Dijk, C. Gentry, S. Halevi and V. Vaikuntanathan. *Fully Homomorphic Encryption over the Integers.* Proceedings of EUROCRYPT 2010. Springer.

15. Raluca Ada Popa, Catherine M. S. Redfield, Nickolai Zeldovich, and Hari Balakrishnan. *CryptDB: Protecting Confidentiality with Encrypted Query Processing.* In Proceedings of the 23rd ACM Symposium on Operating systems Principles (SOSP), Cascais, Portugal, October 2011.

16. D. Chaum, C. Crepeau & I. Damgard. "Multiparty unconditionally secure protocols". ACM Symposium on Theory of Computation (STOC) 1987.

17. G. Zyskind, G., O. Nathan, and A. Pentland. *Decentralizing privacy: Using blockchain to protect personal data.* In Proceedings of 2015 IEEE Symposium on Security and Privacy Workshops, 180-184.

18. A. Pentland, "Saving Big Data from Itself", *Scientific American,* No. 311, pp.64-67. August 2014.

19. T. Hardjono, *Decentralized Service Architecture for OAuth2.0*, Internet Engineering Task Force (IETF), February 2017. https://tools.ietf.org/html/draft-hardjono-oauth-decentralized-00

20. T. Hardjono, D. Greenwood and S. Pentland, *Towards a Trustworthy Digital Infrastructure for Core Identities and Personal Data Stores,* ID360 Conference on Identity, University of Texas at Austin, May 2013.

21. T. Hardjono, E. Maler, M. Machulak and D. Catalano, *User-Managed Access (UMA) Profile of OAuth 2.0*, Kantara Initiative, Published Specifications., April 2015. https://docs.kantarainitiative.org/ uma/rec-uma-core-v1_0.html

22. D. Hardt (ed), *The OAuth2.0 Authorization Framework*, Internet Engineering

Task Force, IETF, RFC6749, October 2010.

23. *World Economic Forum, Personal Data: The Emergence of a New Asset Class, 2011, available on http://www.weforum.org/reports/ personal-data-emergence-new-asset-class.*

24. A. Pentland, D. Shrier, T. Hardjono, and I. Wladawsky-Berger, *Towards an Internet of Trusted Data: A New Framework for Identity and Data Sharing: Input to the Whitehouse Commission on Enhancing National Cybersecurity.* MIT Connection Science. August 2016.

25. T. Hardjono and N. Smith, "Cloud-Based Commissioning of Constrained Devices using Permissioned Blockchains", *Proceedings ACM IoT Privacy, Trust & Security Conference,* 2016 (IoTPTS 2016).

26. IPSO Alliance, http://www.ipso-alliance.org

27. Industrial Internet Consortium, http://www.iiconsortium.org

28. A. Pentland, "Reality Mining of Mobile Communications: Toward a New Deal on Data," in *The Global Information Technology Report 2008-2009: Mobility in a Networked World,* S. Dutta and I. Mia, Eds. World Economic Forum, 2009, pp. 75–80, available on http://hd.media.mit.edu/wef_globalit.pdf.

29. Y. A. de Montjoye, S. S. Wang, and A. Pentland, "*On the trusted use of large-scale personal data,*" IEEE Data Eng. Bull., vol. 35, no. 4, pp. 5–8, 2012.

30. Y. A. de Montjoye, J. Quoidbach, F. Robic, and A. Pentland, "Predicting personality using novel mobile phone-based metrics," in *Social Computing, Behavioral-Cultural Modeling and Prediction* (LCNS Vol. 7812). Springer, 2013, pp. 48–55.

31. Y. A. de Montjoye, E. Shmueli, S. Wang, and A. Pentland, "*openPDS: Regaining ownership and privacy of personal data,*" 2013.

CHAPTER 14

Owner Centric Access Management for IoT Data

Incentivizing Data Owners to Share Data into the Data Markets

Thomas Hardjono

INTRODUCTION: SCALABLE ACCESS AND CONSENT MANAGEMENT FOR IOT DATA

Data sharing is about creating data-driven communities and societies: Participants and stakeholders taking-on the various roles required to realize a full ecosystem where decision-making at every level is data-driven. The ecology of identity, trust and data calls out the need for several types of new roles or entities: data collectors, data aggregators, data brokers, data markets, and so on. This vision of a big data ecosystem also calls out for new systems and platforms to be designed and developed as a core part of the future Internet infrastructure. Data is indeed a new class of asset, "fuel" for the next generation of research, products and services.[1,2,3]

In the Internet of Things (IoT) space, the introduction of next generation "smart things" into people's lives (e.g., smart meters, smart appliance, IoT in vehicles, etc.) promises the opportunity to obtain more data regarding peoples' lives. The data-driven society promises greater insight into communities and societies, allowing governments and individuals to improve planning:[4]

- **Data has more value when combined across disciplines:** Although seemingly self-evident, the weight or impact of this assertion comes to the forefront when we see analytics results (using multi-discipline sourced data) that give us insights into things that were previously unknown or unimagined.
- **Data increases in value when it is shared:** The WISH report[4] on big data in health identifies data sharing as key to solving the world's health problems (e.g., arising from the spread of diseases due to increased human mobility).

Individuals today are more aware of the value of their personal data to improve their lives and the lives of others in the community. However, they are also wary of the negative potential of unregulated collections of personal data:[5]

- **Quantified self:** Increasingly people are becoming aware that their daily lives generated data about themselves, and that these data streams (when correctly analyzed) may present opportunities to better their lives. This is particularly notable today in health-related areas (e.g., WiFi weight scales, smart watches, wireless enabled heart pacers).

- **Economic incentives to share:** Corresponding to this awareness (about personally generated data) is the awareness of the potential value of personal data stores when combined and analyzed. However, there is a need for new economic models for personal data sharing that incentivizes the individual into contributing a richer set of data on an on-going basis.

- **Consent:** A crucial part of incentivizing the end-user is the need to empower them to make decisions regarding their personal data. That is, the user needs to be in the "front-channel" of consent when data about them seeks to be accessed and analyzed by third parties.

An important aspect to reducing this tension between privacy and the utilization of IoT data for the betterment of society is the availability of a user-friendly method for *access and consent management* over data—both data that an individual self-generates (e.g., personal devices) and data generated by other parties (e.g., transaction data) in the course of the individual interacting with other users and services.

ACCESS MANAGEMENT FOR IOT DATA: CHALLENGES

Data is crucial not only to the operational function of businesses and governments, but it is also core to the very definition of an individual in today's society—namely the individual's *core identity*.[6,7,8] Since data gains value when it is applied to solve certain problems, the issues surrounding the privacy-preserving sharing of data—namely *access management to data*—have also become an important challenge to solve, both technologically and legally.

Access management to data for the purposes of sharing includes not only the protection of the data (e.g., from data theft or data corruption), but also includes the mechanisms to implement policies over the usage of data:

- **Access policy administration:** Providing the data-owner(s) with semantically meaningful methods to determine access and usage policies for their data. In organizations this typically means access policies and authorizations that are consistent with the overall organizational policies. For data co-owned by an individual and an organization, this translates to providing a user-centric approach to setting meaningful policies.
- **Access policy enforcement:** Implementing the access policies using mechanisms that enforce those policies consistently, without ambiguity and without any resulting data loss.
- **Access policy tracking & accountability:** Providing the data-owners and policy administrators with method and mechanisms to track, record, audit, and reconcile data-access events in a semantically correct and consistent manner.

These general requirements should apply independent of the location of the data, either in local data repositories or in remote (e.g., cloud) data repositories and independent to the type/domain of the data.

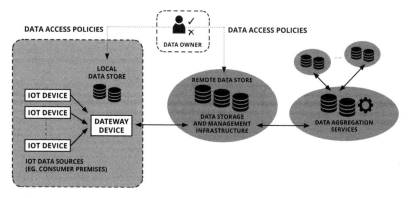

Figure 14.1 Overview of Access Management for IoT Data.[13,14]

AN OWNER CENTRIC ACCESS MANAGEMENT ARCHITECTURE

In this section, we describe the access management features of the MIT *Open Algorithms* (OPAL) platform, which is built by extending the OAuth2.0[17] and UMA1.0[18] standards for authorizations management. Key to the proposition of MIT OPAL is the sharing of data across organizations in a privacy-preserving and policy-consistent manner.[10,11,12]

The MIT OPAL design (figure 14.2) allows for data stores to be created independent of the size of the data-sets and the nature of the deployment situation (e.g., individual personal data store; organizational data store). As such, the MIT OPAL design can be used for IoT data stores for consumer data (e.g., home data server; hosted IoT data account) as well as for industrial or enterprise IoT data repositories.

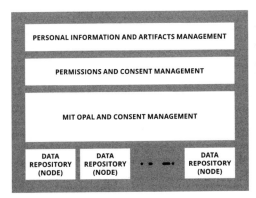

PERSONAL INFORMATION AND ARTIFACTS MANAGEMENT	• Personal data, claims, attributes, anonymous identities/credentials • Vetted algorithms/queries
PERMISSIONS AND CONSENT MANAGEMENT	• Policies, scopes, rules • Consent issuance, receipts, revocations
MIT OPAL AND CONSENT MANAGEMENT	• Algorithm validation and execution • Safe answers • Blockchain client • Decentralized repositories management
DATA REPOSITORY (NODE) **DATA REPOSITORY (NODE)** • • —• **DATA REPOSITORY (NODE)**	• P2P node discovery, acquisition and management • Service smart contracts

Figure 14.2 The MIT OPAL Layers.

In recent years, the increasing prominence of web-services offered through RESTful Web APIs has necessitated the introduction of a new authorization standard for access to these APIs. The OAuth2.0 authorization framework has become the industry standard for a user to authorize applications to access resources (e.g., files) through these RESTful Web APIs. Similarly, the new User Manager Access (UMA1.0) standard is quickly being adopted by organizations that seek to manage protected resources (e.g., data) using the RESTful paradigm.

Authorization in Web Applications Today: OAuth2.0

The OAuth2.0 framework historically arose from the need for users to connect (or "authorize") web applications operated by a service provider to access the user's resources (e.g., data, photos, calendar) located under another service provider. This authorization allows these two applications to regularly connect and synchronize with each other without the user needing to be present online at all times.[19] Depending on the exact applications, this connection or authorization may last for a long time, until the user revokes it. The OAuth2.0 protocol can also be used for mobile (native) applications following the same protocol pattern (e.g., user authorizes

an app on his or her device to access a resource located at a remote
service provider).

Using the terminology of OAuth2.0, the framework defines the basic
interaction between a client (e.g., web application), authorization server
(AS), a resource server (data server), and the resource owner (i.e., the user).
Authorization information is delivered within an OAuth2.0 token (expressed
as a JSON Web Token), which also contains the client identity information.
Using the token, a resource owner (e.g., Alice) can grant the client (e.g.,
calendar application) access to resources (e.g., itinerary) located at the
resource server (e.g., Airlines) without Alice needing to be present online
continuously. As such, OAuth2.0 has also referred to as an "application
delegation" scheme.

There are number of inherent limitations of the OAuth2.0 design, which have
subsequently been addressed in the more recent UMA1.0 standard:[18]

- **Scalability:** In OAuth2.0, Alice (the resource owner) must keep track of
  the various authorizations that she established pair-wise between the
  client (i.e., web applications such as calendar app) and resource server
  (i.e., airline application containing travel itinerary). Even if the resource
  server and authorization server are co-located or operated by the same
  service provider, Alice still has the responsibility of keeping track of the
  authorizations she has granted to the various clients.
- **Limited Roles:** The OAuth2.0 framework does not recognize the
  difference between a user and the entity providing the web application
  which the user drives. As such it does not lend itself sufficiently to be a
  technical foundation of a legal trust framework that defines "user control"
  in the hands of Alice as the resource owner. For most of the OAuth2.0
  deployments today, the main goal is simply to link Alice's account at the
  client web app (operated by a service provider) to her other account at

a resource server (operated by a second service provider). The OAuth2.0 framework fails to recognize that the two service providers are in reality legal entities in the real world, and as such have legal obligations. Thus, in reality, Alice is not the legal co-owner of data that she generated as part of using these services, or which she volunteered to both entities (e.g., personal address information) in return for free services. Alice has no true control over her accounts, and therefore to her data.

It is worthwhile to note that OAuth2.0 is not an identity management system, and the specification itself is very limited—almost to the point of being barely deployable as written. The OpenID-Connect 1.0 standard[20] extends the OAuth2.0 framework for the purposes of identity federation. As such, it is more accurate to state that identity providers today deploy OpenID-Connect 1.0 (OIDC1.0) that wraps additional functionality around the OAuth2.0 specification. However, the two terms (OAuth2.0 and OpenID-Connect 1.0) are often used interchangeably in non-technical literature.

The User Managed Access (UMA) Standard

The goal of the User Managed Access (UMA) v1.0 standard[18] is to develop specifications for technologies that would enable a user to manage the authorizations (based on OAuth2.0 tokens) that he or she has issued, to revoke authorizations efficiently, and to allow access policies to be set by the user as the data owner or co-owner. The UMA1.0 standard builds atop both OAuth2.0 and OpenID-Connect 1.0, and extends these by recognizing that the service providers who operate web applications and resource servers are third parties that have legal obligations to the user as the resource owner.

UMA1.0 also addresses the broader set of use-cases involving two users (or entities) sharing a resource (e.g., data). This is often referred to in semi-technical language as the "Alice-to-Bob" sharing in UMA1.0; whereas

OAuth2.0 is often referred to as "Alice-to-Alice" sharing, where Alice is limited to simply enabling one of her web applications to have access to her resources located at another application or service. As such, for cross-entity data sharing (e.g., IoT data), the UMA1.0 paradigm is more realistic and reflects the true situation of data/resource access in the real world.

The architecture of UMA is designed to allow different technologies or solutions to be deployed to achieve UMA's vision of a data owner having true control in a data-sharing scenario:

- **Single Policy Administration Point (PAP):** The resource owner (e.g., Alice) should be presented with one place to set access policies and grant/revoke authorizations for all the resources (e.g., data) she owns throughout the Internet at different data repositories. The current reality of users having to manage multiple credentials (e.g., passwords) for the various accounts and resources on the Internet does not scale, and presents numerous security and privacy issues. In UMA1.0 this single PAP point is referred to in technical language as the *UMA Authorization Server* (UMA-AS) which incorporates a policy setting interface as well as access token issuance, among its many functions.

- **Enable distributed logging and audit:** The data owner should be provided with information regarding access (and attempted access) to their data located at various distributed repositories on the Internet. When a data owner (e.g., Alice) grants authorization to another person (e.g., Bob) or to a service provider to access her protected resource, then Alice should be able to see if and when that access-grant is exercised.

- **Facilitate Usage Terms:** The resource/data owner should be provided with tools to enable them to set their own legal terms of usage (aka Terms of Service) for their data or other resources. Ideally, the data owner could simply choose from one or more standardized terms of use, much in the way that copyright notices have been standardized within the Copyright

Commons[22] initiative and within the Kantara Initiative organization.[23]

- **Distributed legal trust frameworks for data sharing:** With
  the rise of decentralized peer-to-peer networks and "smart contracts,"
  a new paradigm for the exchange data as a digital asset is needed. New
  economic models are also needed that view data sharing along the lines
  of Ostrom's "common pool" resources[24] and one based on sharing
  of risks and liabilities. We refer to this emerging area as *distributed legal
  trust frameworks*. The UMA1.0 design is better aligned to the notion
  of a distributed legal trust framework, and entities defined by UMA1.0
  corresponds to the entities involved in realworld data sharing. As such,
  this allows trust frameworks for data sharing to be developed jointly
  by legal and technical experts more readily.[24]

ACCESS MANAGEMENT IN MIT OPAL

The MIT Open Algorithms (OPAL) project uses the UMA1.0 standard for
managing authorizations, and extends it to support a privacy-preserving
paradigm to share data.[10,26] OPAL is agnostic to the type of data stored within
its data services, and, as such, can be suitably deployed for managing IoT
data in different industry verticals.

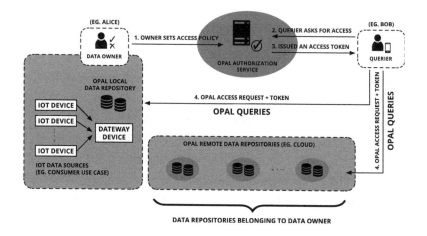

Figure 14.3 Access Management to Data in MIT OPAL.

In MIT OPAL when a querier (e.g., Bob) seeks to access data located within one or more data repositories belonging to a data owner (e.g., Alice), the querier must first obtain the relevant permission from the data owner. This permission takes the form of an access token that is compliant to the UMA1.0 standard. This token is needed regardless of whether the data owner permits access to fixed/static data (e.g., person's unchanging attributes, such as their birth date), signed assertions,[33] or access to safe answers through the open algorithms (OPAL) interface (i.e., sending queries). This access token is necessary because the token carries information about the duration of the granted permission and the type of actions permitted.

An overview of the authorization steps in MIT OPAL is shown in Figure 14.3:

- **Step 1**: The data owner (i.e., Alice) logs in into the UMA Authorization Server within her OPAL instance and sets access policies and authorization for the following:

  - Her IoT devices to have write-access to one or more of her data repositories (e.g., local or remote data repositories).
  - The querier (i.e., the requesting party called Bob) and his web application to have read-access to one or more of Alice's data repositories.

- **Step 2**: The querier (i.e., Bob) requests an access token from Alice's designated authorization server, identifying the specific data sets located at one or more of Alice's data repositories.

- **Step 3**: Alice's authorization server returns an access token to the querier, clearly stating the identity of the person (e.g., Bob) or legal entity that is being granted access. The access token also indicates the OPAL queries (or smart contracts) that the querier is permitted to use. Within the OPAL paradigm, only vetted queries are accepted by data repositories. These vetted queries are created by the data owner as "query templates" which the querier must use to obtain a response from the data repository. OPAL envisages that multiple vetted query-templates would be created according to the type/domain of the data. The responses are aggregate answers only. It is a fundamental OPAL principle that *raw-data never leaves its repository.*[10]

- **Step 4**: The querier selects one or more query-templates available (for the target data), completes the query (e.g., inserts identity of querier; digital signature; payments), and sends the completed query, together with the querier's access token, to the destination data repository. The data repository will validate both the query and the access token that accompanies the query. The data repository will then return a response (safe answers) following the OPAL paradigm.

In the above work flow, the UMA access token plays an important role in providing the building block for identity validation as well as access management policy enforcement. The UMA access token itself is a digitally signed data structure (JSON web token standard[27,28]) issued by the data owner's UMA Authorization Server.

ACCESS MANAGEMENT IN A DATA SHARING CONSORTIUM

The access management architecture in MIT OPAL lends itself by design to deployment in a data sharing consortium model. We define an *OPAL data sharing consortium* for a given data domain (e.g., IoT data) as having at least the following characteristics:

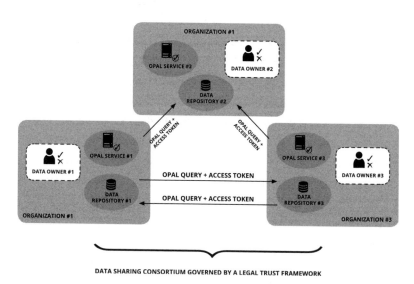

Figure 14.4 OPAL Data Sharing Consortium based on a common and interoperable access management protocols.

- **Collective authoring of OPAL query-templates:** Key to the social and legal acceptance of data sharing (for a given data domain) is the agreed set of allowable queries that the members can send to one another. The basic concept is simple: Individuals and organizations will be more open to sharing information if they are able to see ahead of time the "pre-fabricated" queries that will be executed by them in their data repositories.

- **Interoperability based on the OPAL concept, common specifications and APIs:** Systems have a higher chance of being interoperable if they implement a common set of services accessible over well-defined APIs (Application Programming Interfaces). The OPAL notion of sending queries to data repositories requires that the queries and query-templates be based on standards, and that the data repositories expose access APIs that are well designed and protected. UMA1.0 Protected-APIs should be accessible only by using access tokens whose fields and parameters are defined by the data sharing consortium.

- **Common policy expression framework:** A key operational requirement for a data sharing consortium is the use of a common policy expression framework—one that has no semantic or syntactic ambiguities, and which allows each member to define access policies (to their respective data repositories) which conform to their own internal organizational data access policies.

- **Common legal framework for operational governance:** As mentioned previously, a common legal framework must be created that clearly enunciates the legal obligations and liabilities of members of the consortium. It must also define the operational requirements that are practical and achievable by each member. Examples of trust frameworks exist in the identity federation space[29,30,31,32] for sharing identity-related attributes, and which may be expanded to cover OPAL queries.

SUMMARY AND CONCLUSIONS

As the future data-driven society increasingly depends on accurate and source-authentic IoT data, providing owner-centric access and consent management to this IoT data becomes an imperative—one that may determine the success or failure of the entire IoT revolution.

The MIT OPAL architecture for privacy-preserving data sharing establishes a base-level standard for access and consent management using the UMA1.0 standard. The UMA1.0 design recognizes upfront that the service providers who operate web applications and data/resource servers may be third-party legal entities.

As such, the UMA1.0 design is better suited for providing the technical foundations for access management in a data sharing consortium, because UMA1.0 entities corresponds more realistically to entities in the real world. This, in turn, allows distributed legal trust frameworks for data sharing to be developed in a consortium model, jointly by legal and technical experts from members of the consortium.

NOTES

1. World Economic Forum, *Personal Data: The Emergence of a New Asset Class*, 2011, available on http://www.weforum.org/reports/ personal-data-emergence-new-asset-class.

2. A. Pentland, "Reality Mining of Mobile Communications: Toward a New Deal on Data," in *The Global Information Technology Report 2008-2009: Mobility in a Networked World*, S. Dutta and I. Mia, Eds. World Economic Forum, 2009, pp. 75–80, available on http://hd.media.mit.edu/wef_globalit.pdf.

3. European Commission (2016), *The General Data Protection Regulation* (GDPR) (Regulation (EU) 2016/679).

4. A. Pentland, T. Reid, and T. Heibeck, *Big data and Health - Revolutionizing medicine and Public Health: Report of the Big Data and Health Working Group 2013,* World Innovation Summit for Health, Qatar Foundation. http://www.wish-qatar.org/app/media/382.

5. A. Pentland, "Saving Big Data from Itself", *Scientific American,* No. 311, pp.64-67. August 2014.

6. A. Pentland, D. Shrier, T. Hardjono, and I. Wladawsky-Berger, *Towards an Internet of Trusted Data: A New Framework for Identity and Data Sharing: Input to the Whitehouse Commission on Enhancing National Cybersecurity.* MIT Connection Science. August 2016.

7. T. Hardjono, D. Shrier and A. Pentland, "Core Identities for Future Transaction Systems", in *Trust::Data: A New Framework for Identity and Data Sharing*, Visionary Future, 2016.

8. T. Hardjono, D. Greenwood and S. Pentland, *Towards a Trustworthy Digital Infrastructure for Core Identities and Personal Data Stores,* ID360 Conference on Identity, University of Texas at Austin, May 2013.

9. Y. A. de Montjoye, S. S. Wang, and A. Pentland, "*On the trusted use of large-scale personal data*," IEEE Data Eng. Bull., vol. 35, no. 4, pp. 5–8, 2012.

10. Y. A. de Montoye, T. Hardjono, and A. Pentland, "OPAL/Enigma", in *Trust::Data: A New Framework for Identity and Data Sharing,* Visionary Future, 2016.

11. Y. A. de Montjoye, E. Shmueli, S. Wang, and A. Pentland, *"MIT openPDS: Regaining ownership and privacy of personal data,"* 2013.

12. T. Hardjono & J. Seberry, *Strongboxes for Electronic Commerce,* Proceedings of the Second USENIX Workshop on Electronic Commerce, Oakland, CA, November 1996.

13. Open Connectivity Foundation (OCF), *OIC Core Specification* V1.1.1, Published Specifications, OCF, 2016. https://openconnectivity.org/specs/OIC_Core_Specification_v1.1.1.pdf

14. Open Connectivity Foundation (OCF), *OIC Security Specification* V1.1.1, Published Specifications, OCF, 2017. https://openconnectivity.org/specs/OIC_Security_Specification_v1.1.1.pdf

15. T. Hardjono and N. Smith, "Cloud-Based Commissioning of Constrained Devices using Permissioned Blockchains", *Proceedings ACM IoT Privacy, Trust & Security Conference,* May 2016.

16. T. Hardjono and N. Smith, *Simplified Key Exchange for IoT Constrained Environments,* Internet Engineering Task Force (IETF), June 2016, https://datatracker.ietf.org/doc/draft-hardjono-ace-fluffy/

17. D. Hardt (ed), *The OAuth2.0 Authorization Framework,* Internet Engineering Task Force, IETF, RFC6749, October 2010.

18. T. Hardjono, E. Maler, M. Machulak and D. Catalano, User-Managed Access (UMA) Profile of OAuth 2.0, Kantara Initiative, Published Specifications. April 2015. https://docs. kantarainitiative.org/ uma/rec-uma-core-v1_0.html

19. T. Hardjono, *OAuth 2.0 support for the Kerberos V5 Authentication Protocol,* Internet Engineering Task Force (IETF), December 2010. https://tools.ietf.org/html/draft-hardjono-oauth-kerberos-01

20. OpenID Foundation, *OpenID Connect Core 1.0 Specifications,* Published

Specifications, November 2014. http://openid.net/specs/openid-connect-core-1_0.html

21. T. Hardjono, *Decentralized Service Architecture for OAuth2.0*, Internet Engineering Task Force (IETF), February 2017. https://tools.ietf.org/html/draft-hardjono-oauth-decentralized-00

22. Creative Commons, https://creativecommons.org

23. Kantara Initiative, *Consent & Information Sharing Work Group* (CISWG), http://kantarainitiative.org/confluence/display/infosharing/Home

24. Kantara Initiative, *UMA Legal Subgroup (UMA WG)*, https://kantarainitiative.org/groups/user-managed-access-work-group/

25. E. Ostrom, "Beyond Markets and States: Polycentric Governance of Complex Economic Systems," 2009, Nobel Prize Lecture, December 8, 2009. Available on http://www.nobelprize.org.

26. G. Zyskind, G., O. Nathan, and A. Pentland. *Decentralizing privacy: Using blockchain to protect personal data.* In Proceedings of 2015 IEEE Symposium on Security and Privacy Workshops, 180-184.

27. RFC7519, *JSON Web Tokens,* Internet Engineering Task Force, Published Specifications, May 2015.

28. RFC7515, *JSON Web Signatures,* Internet Engineering Task Force, Published Specifications, May 2015.

29. American Bar Association, Overview of Identity Management, ABA Identity Management Legal Task Force, May 2012, available on http://meetings.abanet.org/ webupload/commupload/ CL320041/ relatedresources/ ABA-Submission-to-UNCITRAL.pdf.

30. OIX, OpenID Exchange, http://openidentityexchange.org

31. FICAM, U.S. Federal Identity, Credential and Access Management (FICAM) Program, http://info.idmanagement.gov

32. SAFE-BioPharma Association, Trust Framework Provider Services, http://www.safe-biopharma.org/SAFE_Trust_Framework.htm

33. OASIS, "Assertions and Protocols for the OASIS Security Assertion

Markup Language (SAML) V2.0," http://docs.oasisopen. org/security/ saml/v2.0/saml-core-2.0-os.pdf, March 2005.

34. OASIS, "Glossary for the OASIS Security Assertion Markup Language (SAML) V2.0," http://docs.oasis-open.org/security/saml/v2.0/ samlglossary- 2.0-os.pdf, March 2005.

CHAPTER 15

Enigma: Decentralized Computation Platform with Guaranteed Privacy

Guy Zyskind and Alex Pentland

ABSTRACT

A peer-to-peer network enables different parties to jointly store and run computations on data while keeping the data completely private. Enigma's computational model is based on a highly optimized version of secure multi-party computation, guaranteed by a verifiable secret-sharing scheme. For storage, we use a modified distributed hashtable for holding secret-shared data. An external blockchain is utilized as the controller of the network, which manages access control and identities and serves as a tamper-proof log of events. Security deposits and fees incentivize operation, correctness, and fairness of the system. Similar to Bitcoin, Enigma removes the need for a trusted third party, enabling autonomous control of personal data. For the first time, users are able to share their data with cryptographic guarantees regarding their privacy.

MOTIVATION

Since early human history, centralization has been a major competitive advantage. Societies with centralized governance were able to develop more advanced technology, accumulate more resources, and increase their population faster.[1] As societies evolved, the negative effects of centralization of power were revealed: corruption, inequality, preservation of the status quo and abuse of power. As it turns out, some separation of power[2] is necessary. In modern times, we strive to find a balance between the models while maximizing output and efficiency with centralized control; checks and balances guard decentralized governance.

The original narrative of the web is one of radical decentralization and freedom.[3] During the last decade, the web's incredible growth was coupled with increased centralization. Few large companies now own important junctures—and, consequently, a lot of the data created—online. The lack of transparency and control over these organizations reveals the negative aspects of centralization once again: manipulation,[4] surveillance,[5] and frequent data breaches.[6]

Bitcoin[9] and other blockchains[10] (e.g., Ethereum) promise a new future. Internet applications can now be built with a decentralized architecture, where no single party has absolute power and control. The public nature of the blockchain guarantees transparency over how applications work and leaves an irrefutable record of activities, providing strong incentives for honest behavior. Bitcoin, the currency, was the first such application, initiating a new paradigm to the web.

The intense verification and public nature of the blockchain limits potential use-cases, however. Modern applications use huge amounts of data, and run extensive analysis on that data. This restriction means that only fiduciary code can run on the blockchain.[7] The problem is that the most sensitive parts of modern applications generally require heavy processing on private data. In their current design, blockchains cannot handle privacy at all. Furthermore, they are not well suited for heavy computations. Their public nature means private data would flow through every full node on the blockchain, fully exposed.

There is a strange contradiction in this setup. The most sensitive, private data can only be stored and processed in the centralized, less transparent, and insecure model. We have seen this paradigm lead to catastrophic data leaks and the systematic lack of privacy we are currently forced to accept in our online lives.

ENIGMA

Enigma is a decentralized computation platform with guaranteed privacy. Our goal is to enable developers to build "privacy by design," end-to-end decentralized applications, without a trusted third party.

Enigma is private

Using secure *multi-party computation* (sMPC or MPC), data queries are computed in a distributed way without a trusted third party. Data is split between different nodes, and they compute functions together without leaking information to other nodes. Specifically, no single party ever has access to data in its entirety; instead, every party has a meaningless (i.e., seemingly random) piece of it.

Enigma is scalable

Unlike blockchains, computations and data storage are not replicated by every node in the network. Only a small subset performs each computation over different parts of the data. The decreased redundancy in storage and computations enables more demanding computations.

The key new utility Enigma brings to the table is the ability to run computations on data, without having access to the raw data itself. For example, a group of people can provide access to their salary, and together compute the average wage of the group. Each participant learns their relative position in the group, but learns nothing about other members' salaries. It should be made clear that this is only a motivating example. In practice, any program can be securely evaluated while maintaining the secrecy of its inputs.

Today, sharing data is an irreversible process; once data is sent, there is no way to take it back or limit how it is used. Allowing access to data for secure computations is reversible and controllable, since no one but the original data owner(s) ever sees the raw data. This presents a fundamental change in current approaches to data analysis.

DESIGN OVERVIEW

Enigma is designed to connect to an existing blockchain and off-load private and intensive computations to an off-chain network. All transactions are facilitated by the blockchain, which enforces access control based on digital signatures and programmable permissions.

Code is executed both on the blockchain (public parts) and on Enigma (private or computationally intensive parts). Enigma's execution ensures both privacy and correctness, whereas a blockchain alone can only ensure the latter. Proofs of correct execution are stored on the blockchain and can be audited. We supply a scripting language for designing end-to-end decentralized applications using *private contracts*, which are a more powerful variation of *smart contracts* that can handle private information (i.e., their state is not strictly public).

The scripting language is also turing-complete, but this is not as important as its scalability. Code execution in blockchains is decentralized but not distributed, so every node redundantly executes the same code and maintains the same public state. In Enigma, the computational work is efficiently distributed across the network. An interpreter breaks down the execution of a private contract, as illustrated in figure 15.1, resulting in improved run-time while maintaining both privacy and verifiability.

The off-chain network solves the following issues that blockchain technology alone cannot handle:

1. **Storage:** Blockchains are not general-purpose databases. Enigma has decentralized off-chain distributed hashtable (or DHT) that is accessible

through the blockchain, which stores references to the data but not the data itself. Private data should be encrypted on the client-side before storage and access-control protocols are programmed into the blockchain. Enigma provides simple APIs for these tasks in the scripting language.

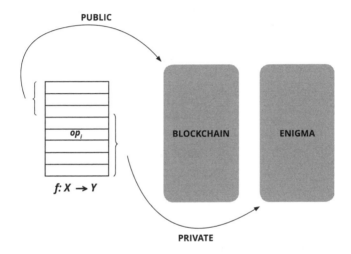

Figure 15.1 Code execution model.

2. **Privacy-enforcing computation:** Enigma's network can execute code without leaking the raw data to any of the nodes, while ensuring correct execution. This is key in replacing current centralized solutions and trusted overlay networks that process sensitive business logic in a way that negates the benefits of a blockchain. The computational model is described in detail in the section on privacy-enforcing computation.
3. **Heavy processing:** Even when privacy is not a concern, the blockchain cannot scale to clearing many complex transactions. The same off-chain computational network is used to run heavy publicly verifiable computations that are broadcast through the blockchain.

OFF-CHAIN STORAGE

Off-chain nodes construct a distributed database. Each node has a distinct view of shares and encrypted data so that the computation process is guaranteed to be privacy-preserving and fault tolerant. It is also possible to store large public data (e.g., files) unencrypted and link them to the blockchain. Figure 15.2 illustrates the database view of a single node.

| SHARES |
| ENCRYPTED DATA |
| PUBLIC DATA |

Figure 15.2 A node's local view of the off-chain data.

On a network level, the distributed storage is based on a modified Kademlia DHT protocol[11] with added persistence and secure point-to-point channels, simulated using a broadcast channel and public-key encryption. This protocol assists in distributing the shares in an efficient manner. When storing shares, the original Kademlia distance metric is modified to take into account the preferential probability of a node.

PRIVACY-ENFORCING COMPUTATION

In this section, we describe Enigma's computational model. We begin with a brief introduction to publicly verifiable secure MPC based on state-of-the-art advances in cryptography. Then, we describe a series of performance improvements to secure MPC that makes the technology practical, even when the network is large: hierarchical secure MPC, network reduction, and adaptable circuits.

To use Enigma, developers write high-level code, where public parts are executed on the blockchain and private parts are run off-chain, on Enigma's platform. We call these *private contracts*, since they are smart contracts that can handle private information.

Overview of Secure Multi-Party Computation

Privacy (Passive Adversaries)

Yao introduced the first solution to secure two-party computation protocols in 1982.[12] In the same paper, Yao suggested the popular *millionaire problem*, describing two millionaires interested in knowing which was richer, without revealing their actual net worths. In the decades since, the two-party problem has been generalized to MPC, which refers to the n-party case. For general-purpose MPC, in which every protocol could be composed from a circuit of elementary MPC gates, two major approaches have been developed over the years: Yao's garbaled (boolean) circuits[13] and MPC based on secret-sharing. The latter has been more commonly used in production systems[14,15] and is our focus as well.

A threshold cryptosystem is defined by $(t + 1, n)$ – *threshold,* where n is the number of parties and $t + 1$ is the minimum number of parties required to decrypt a secret encrypted with threshold encryption. Secret-sharing is an example of a threshold cryptosystem, where a secret s is divided among n, s.t. at least $t+1$ are required to reconstruct s. Any subset of t parties cannot learn anything about the secret. A linear secret-sharing scheme (or LSSS) partitions a secret to shares such that the shares are a linear combination of the secret. Shamir's secret-sharing (or SSS) is an example of a LSSS, which uses polynomial interpolation and is secure under a finite field.[16] Specifically, to share a secret s, we select a random t degree polynomial $q(x)$:

$$q(x) = a_0 + a_1 x + \cdots + a_t x^t,$$
$$a_0 = s, a_i \sim U(0, p-1).$$

The shares are then given by

$$\forall i \in \{1, \cdots, n\} : [s]_{p_i} = q(i).$$

Then, given any $t + 1$ shares, $q(x)$ could be trivially reconstructed using Lagrange interpolation and the secret s recovered using $s = q(0)$. Since SSS is linear, it is also additively homomorphic, so addition and multiplication by a scalar operation could be performed directly on the shares without interaction. Formally:

$$c \times s = reconstruct(\{c[s]_{p_i}\}_{i \in n}^{t+1}),$$
$$s_1 + s_2 = reconstruct(\{[s_1]_{p_i} + [s_2]_{p_i}\}_{i \in n}^{t+1}).$$

Multiplication of two secrets s_1 and s_2 is somewhat more involved. If each party would attempt to locally compute the product of two secrets, they would collectively obtain a polynomial of degree $2t$, requiring a polynomial reduction step ($2t \rightarrow t$). For an information theoretic setting, this result adds an honest majority constraint (i.e., $t < \frac{n}{2}$) on privacy and correctness. If we bound the adversary's computational power, both properties are assured for any number of corrupted parties, but fairness, and deciding on an output, still requires an honest majority.[17]

As to performance, a re-sharing step is required in the degree reduction step, implying all parties must interact with all other parties ($O(n^2)$ communications). This makes MPC impractical for anything larger than a small constant number of parties n. While optimized solutions exist for improving the amortized complexity, they are based on assumptions that restrict functionality in practice. Conversely, we describe a generic solution to this problem for any functionality in Section 5.2, which makes secure MPC feasible for arbitrarily large networks.

Note that, with secure addition and multiplication protocols, we can construct a circuit for any arithmetic function. For turing-completeness, we need to handle control flow as well. For conditional statements involving secret values, this means evaluating both branches and, for dynamic loops, we add randomness to the execution. Our general-purpose MPC interpreter is based on these core concepts and other optimizations presented throughout the paper.

Correctness (Malicious Adversaries)

So far, we have discussed the *privacy* property. *Liveness*, namely that computations will terminate and the system will make progress, is also implied given an honest majority, since it is all that is needed for reconstruction of intermediate and output values. However, in the current framework there are no guarantees about the *correctness* of the output; party *pi* could send an invalid result throughout the computation process, which may invalidate the output. While BGW[17] presented an information-theoretic solution to verifiable MPC, its practical complexity could be as bad as $O(n^8)$, given a naive implementation.

Therefore, our goal is to design an MPC framework that is secure against malicious adversaries but has the same complexity of the semi-honest setting ($O(n^2)$). Later, we would further optimize this.

Very recently, Baum et al. developed a publicly auditable secure MPC system that ensures correctness, even when all computing nodes are covertly malicious, or all but a single node are actively malicious.[18] Their state-of-the-art results are based on a variation of SPDZ (pronounced *speedz*)[19] and depend on a public append-only bulletin board, which stores the trail of each computation. This allows any auditing party to check the output is correct by comparing it to the public ledger's trail of proofs. Our system uses the blockchain as the bulletin board; thus, our overall security is reduced to that of the hosting blockchain.

SPDZ

A protocol secure against malicious adversaries (with dishonest majority), providing correctness guarantees for MPC. In essence, the protocol comprises an expensive offline (pre-processing) step that uses *somewhat homomorphic encryption* (or SHE) to generate shared randomness. Then, in the online stage, the computation is similar to the passive case and there is no expensive public-key cryptography involved. In the online stage, every share is represented by the additive share and its MAC, where a is a fixed secret-shared MAC key and $\langle \cdot \rangle$ denotes the modified secret-sharing scheme, which is also additively homomorphic:

$$\langle s \rangle_{p_i} = ([s]_{p_i}, [\gamma(s)]_{p_i}), \; s.t. \; \gamma(s) = \alpha s,$$

$\langle \cdot \rangle$-sharing works without opening the shares of the global MAC key a, so it can be reused.

As before, multiplication is more involved. Multiplication consumes $\{\langle a\rangle, \langle b\rangle, \langle c\rangle\}$ triplets, s.t. $c=ab$, that are generated in the pre-processing step (many such triplets are generated). Then, given two secrets s_1 and s_2, that are shared using $\langle\cdot\rangle$-sharing, secret-sharing the product $s = s_1 s_2$ is achieved by consuming a triplet as follows:

$$\langle s\rangle = \langle c\rangle + \epsilon\langle b\rangle + \delta\langle a\rangle + \epsilon\delta,$$
$$\epsilon = \langle s_1\rangle - \langle a\rangle, \ \delta = \langle s_2\rangle - \langle b\rangle.$$

As mentioned, generating the triplets is an expensive process based on SHE.[18] Verification is achieved by solving:

$$\gamma - \alpha s = 0,$$

s is the secret that, without loss of generality, can be the reconstructed result of any secure computation. Intuitively, this is just a comparison of the computation over the MAC, against the computed result times the secret MAC key. The reason we are not performing actual comparison is so that α remains secret and can be reused.

We can now see that $\langle\cdot\rangle$-sharing has similar properties to SSS, namely that it is additively homomorphic and requires a re-sharing round for multiplication ($O(n^2)$ communication complexity), but, in addition, it ensures correctness against up to n 1 active adversaries. The offline round is easily amortized over many computations and can be computed in parallel while other computations are running, so it does not significantly affect the overall efficiency.

Publicly verifiable SPDZ

In the publicly verifiable case, MACs and commitments are stored on the blockchain, therefore making the scheme secure even if all n computing parties are malicious. We follow the representation,[18] which defines $\|\cdot\|$-sharing, as:

$$[\![s]\!] = (\langle s \rangle, \langle r \rangle, \langle g^s h^r \rangle),$$

s is the secret, r is a random value, and $c = g^s h^r$ is the Pedersen commitment, with g, h serving as generators. $\|\cdot\|$-sharing preserves additive homomorphic properties, and with a slightly modified multiplication protocol, we can reuse the same idea of generating triplets ($\{\|a\|, \|b\|, \|c\|\}$) offline.

A key observation here is that the nodes only need to compute over $\|\cdot\|$-shared values and not over the commitments. These are stored on the blockchain and could later be addressed by any public validator that has the output. Even if a single node has broken its commitment, it would be evident to the auditor.

Hierarchical secure MPC

Information-theoretic results show that secure MPC protocols require each computing node to interact with all other nodes ($O(n^2)$ communication complexity) and a constant number of rounds. In the case of an LSSS, this computational complexity applies to every multiplication operation, whereas addition operations can be computed in parallel, without intercommunication. As previously mentioned, secure addition and multiplication protocols are sufficient to construct a general-purpose interpreter that securely evaluates any code.[17]

Cohen et al.[20] recently proposed a method of simulating an n-party secure protocol using a log-depth formula of constant-size MPC gates, as illustrated in figure 15.3. We extend their result to LSSS and are able to reduce the communication-complexity of multiplication from quadratic to linear, at the cost of increased computation complexity, which is parallelized. Figure 15.4 illustrates how vanilla MPC is limited by the number of parties, while our implementation scales up to arbitrarily large networks.

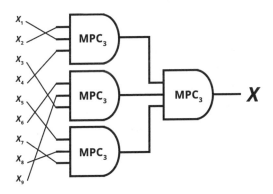

Figure 15.3 Hierarchical Formula Builder.

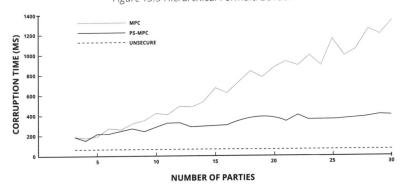

Figure 15.4 Simulated performance comparison of our optimized secure MPC variant compared to classical MPC.

Network reduction

To maximize the computational power of the network, we introduce a network reduction technique, where a random subset of the entire network is selected to perform a computation. The random process preferentially selects nodes based on load-balancing requirements and accumulated reputation, as is measured by their publicly validated actions. This ensures that the network is fully utilized at any given point.

Adaptable circuits

Code evaluated in our system is guaranteed not to leak any information unless a dishonest majority colludes ($t \geq \frac{n}{2}$). This is true for the inputs, as well as for any interim variables computed while the code is evaluated. An observant reader would notice that as a function is evaluated from inputs to outputs, the interim results generally become less descriptive and more aggregative.

For simple functions or functions involving very few inputs, this may not hold true, but since these functions are fast to compute, no additional steps are needed.

However, for computationally expensive functions, involving many lines of code and a large number of inputs, we can dynamically reduce the number computing nodes as we progress instead of having a fixed n for the entire function evaluation process. Specifically, we design a feed-forward network (figure 15.5) that propagates results from inputs to outputs. The original code is reorganized so that we process addition gates on the inputs first, followed by processing multiplication gates. The interim results are then secret-shared with $\frac{N}{c}$ nodes, and the process is repeated recursively.

Scripting

As previously mentioned, end-to-end decentralized apps are developed using private contracts, which are further partitioned to on-chain and off-chain execution. Off-chain code returns results privately, while sending correctness proofs to the blockchain. For simplicity, the scripting language is similar in syntax to well-known programming languages.

There are two major additions to the scripting language that require more detail.

Private data types

Developers should use the private keyword to specify private objects. This automatically ensures that any computation involving those objects remains secure and private. When working with private objects, the data themselves are not locally available, but rather a reference of them.

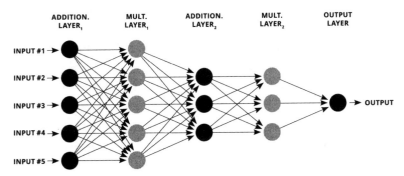

Figure 15.5 Feed forward flow of the secure code evaluation.

Data access

There are three distinct decentralized databases living in the system, each accessible through a global singleton dictionary:

1. **Public ledger:** The blockchain's public ledger can be accessed and manipulated using L. For example, $L[k] \leftarrow 1$ would update key k for all nodes. Since the ledger is completely public and append-only, the entire history is stored as well and (read-only) accessible using $L.get(k, t)$.

2. **DHT:** Off-chain data are stored on the DHT and accessible in the same way the public ledger is. By default, data are encrypted locally before transmission and only the signing entity can request the data back. Otherwise, using $DHT.set(k, v, p)$, where k is the key, v is the value, and p is a predicate, namely, $p : X \rightarrow \{0, 1\}$, sets v to be accessible through k if and only if p is satisfied. We supply several built-in predicates in the language, such as limiting access to a list of public keys. If encryption is turned off, the default predicate is $\forall x\, p(x) = 1$, so the data is public but distributed off-chain.

3. **MPC:** Syntactically, using MPC is equivalent to DHT, but the underlying process differs. In particular, executing $MPC.set(k, v, p)$ secret-shares v. The shares are distributed to potential computing parties that store their shares in their local view. Now p can be used to specify who can reference the data for computation using $v_{ref} \leftarrow MPC[k]$, without revealing v. By default, only the original dealer can ask for the raw data back by running $v \leftarrow MPC.declassify(k)$, which is similar to the sharing process, and collect shares from the various parties to reconstruct the secret value locally. In addition, any other entities belonging to the same shared identity can reference the data for computation. See the next section for details about shared identities.

Note that for simplicity, we addressed all keys in *L, DHT,* and *MPC* dictionaries as using a single namespace, whereas in practice, finer granularity is available, so that they can be segmented to databases, tables, and finer hierarchies.

BLOCKCHAIN INTEROPERABILITY

In this section, we show how Enigma interoperates with a blockchain. Specifically, we detail how complex identities are formed using digital signatures, which are automatically compatible with blockchains. We then continue to describe, in detail, the core protocols linking Enigma's off-chain storage and computation to a blockchain.

Identity Management

A recent survey paper divided blockchain-inspired technologies into two groups: fully decentralized permissionless ledgers (e.g., Bitcoin, Ethereum) and semi-centralized permissioned ledgers (e.g., Ripple).[21] In the paper, the author argues that there is an inherent trade-off between having a pseudo-anonymous system, where no one is trusted and all information must remain public, and having a somewhat centralized system with trusted nodes that can verify true underlying identities. With an off-chain technology linked to a blockchain, this trade-off can be avoided while the network remains fully decentralized.

For this to work, we define an extended version of identities that captures shared identities across multiple entities and their semantic meaning. Formally, the pseudo-anonymous portion of a *shared identity* is a (2*n* + 1)-tuple:

$$SharedIdentity_P = (addr_P, pk_{sig}^{(p_1)}, pk_{sig}^{(p_2)}, \cdots, pk_{sig}^{(p_n)})$$

n denotes the number of parties. It should be clear that for $n = 1$ we revert to the special pseudo-identity case.

To complete our definition of shared identities, we incorporate the idea of metadata. Metadata encapsulates the underlying semantic meaning of an identity. Primarily, these include public access-control rules defined by the same predicates mentioned earlier, which the network uses to moderate access-control, along with any other relevant public or private data.

For example, Alice may want to share her height with Bob, but not her weight. Alternatively, she may not even want to tell Bob her exact height, but will allow him to use her height in aggregate computations. In this case, Alice and Bob can establish a shared identity for this purpose. Alice invokes a private contract that shares her height using *MPC[0alice height0] = alice height*, which Bob can reference for computations, without accessing Alice's height value directly.

The default MPC predicate establishes that Alice's pseudonym is the owner of the shared information and that Bob has restricted access to it. The predicate, shared identity's list of addresses, and a reference to the data are stored on the blockchain and collectively define the public metadata. In other words, this information related to the identity is not sensitive but should be used to publicly verify access rights. Any additional metadata that is private (in other words that only Alice, Bob, and perhaps several others should have access to) could be securely stored off-chain using the DHT.

It should now be clear how our system solves the need for trusted nodes. As always, public transactions are validated through the blockchain. With shared identities and predicates governing access-control stored on the ledger, the blockchain can moderate access to any off-chain resources.

For anything else involving private metadata, the off-chain network can act as a trustless privacy-preserving verifier.

Link protocols

We now discuss the core protocols linking the blockchain to off-chain resources. Specifically, we elaborate on how identities are formed and stored on the ledger and how off-chain storage (DHT) and computation (MPC) requests are routed through the blockchain, conditional on satisfying predicates.

Access control

Protocol 1 describes the process of creating a shared identity, and Protocol 2 implements the publicly verifiable contract for satisfying predicates.

Store and Load

Storing and loading data for direct access via the DHT are shown in Protocol 3. For storing data, write permissions are examined with the given q_{store} predicate. The storing party can provide a custom predicate for verifying who can read the data. This is the underlying process that is abstracted away using the *DHT* singleton object in the scripting language.

Algorithm 1 Generating a shared identity

Input: $P = \{p_i\}_{i=1}^{N}$ parties, $A = \{POLICY_{p_i}\}_{i=1}^{N}$
Output: Ledger L stores reference to the shared identity.
   $addr_P = 0$
   $ACL = \emptyset$
   for $p_i \in P$ **do**
      $(pk_{sig}^{(p_i)}, sk_{sig}^{(p_i)}) \leftarrow \mathcal{G}_{sig}()$
      $addr_P = addr_P \oplus pk_{sig}^{(p_i)}$
      $ACL[pk_{sig}] \leftarrow A[p_i]$
   end for
   $m \leftarrow (addr_P, ACL)$
   send signed tx(m) to the network

   procedure STOREIDENTITY($addr_P, ACL$)
      $L[addr_P] \leftarrow ACL$
   end procedure

Algorithm 2 Permissions check against the blockchain

Input: $pk_{sig}^{(p_i)}$ the requesting party signature, $addr_P$ the shared identity's address, q – a predicate verifying if p_i has sufficient access rights.
Output: $s \in \{0, 1\}$.
   procedure CHECKPERMISSION($pk_{sig}^{(p_i)}, addr_P, q$)
      $s \leftarrow 0$
      if $L[addr_P] \neq \emptyset$ **then**
         $ACL = L[addr_P]$
         if $q(ACL, pk_{sig}^{(p_i)})$ **then**
            $s \leftarrow 1$
         end if
      end if
      return s
   end procedure

Algorithm 3 Storing or Loading Data

Input: $pk_{sig}^{(p_i)}$, $addr_P$, x (data), $q_{read}^{(x)}$ – a predicate for verifying future read access.

Output: if successful, returns a_x – the pointer to the data (predicate), or $\emptyset$ o.w.

    procedure STORE($pk_{sig}^{(p_i)}$, $addr_P$, x, $q_{read}^{(x)}$)

        if $CheckPermission(pk_{sig}^{(p_i)}, addr_P, q_{store}) = \text{True}$ **then**

            $a_x = \mathcal{H}(addr_P \parallel x)$

            $L[a_x] \leftarrow q_{read}^{(x)}$

            $DHT[a_x] \leftarrow x$

            return a_x

        end if

        return $\emptyset$

    end procedure

Input: $pk_{sig}^{(p_i)}$, $addr_P$, a_x – the address of the data (predicate)

Output: if successful, returns the data x, or $\emptyset$ o.w.

    procedure LOAD($pk_{sig}^{(p_i)}$, $addr_P$, a_x)

        $q_{read}^{(x)} \leftarrow L[a_x]$

        if $CheckPermission(pk_{sig}^{(p_i)}, addr_P, q_{read}^{(x)}) = \text{True}$ **then**

            return $DHT[a_x]$

        end if

        return $\emptyset$

    end procedure

Share and Compute

Share and compute, illustrated in Protocol 4, are the MPC equivalents of store and load protocols, since they enable processing. Internally, they store and load shares from the DHT and allow for working with references to the data while keeping the data secure.

Algorithm 4 Secure computation and secret sharing protocols

Input: $pk_{sig}^{(p_i)}$, $addr_P$, x (data), x_{ref} – reference for computation, $q_{compute}^{(x)}$ – predicate verifying computation rights.

Output: if successful, returns pointer to x_{ref} for future computation, or $\emptyset$ o.w.

    procedure SHARE($pk_{sig}^{p_i}$, $addr_P$, x, x_{ref}, $q_{compute}^{(x)}$, n, t)

        $[x]_p \leftarrow VSS(n, t)$

        $peers \leftarrow$ sample n peers

        for $peer \in peers$ **do**

            send $[x]_p^{(peer)}$ to $peer$ on a secure channel

        end for

        return $Store(pk_{sig}^{(p_i)}, addr_P, x_{ref}, q_{compute}^{(x)})$

    end procedure

Input: $pk_{sig}^{(p_i)}$, $addr_P$, $a_{x_{ref}}$ – reference data address, f – unsecure code to be rewritten as a secure protocol.

Output: if successful, returns $f(x)$ without revealing x, or $\emptyset$ o.w.

    procedure COMPUTE($pk_{sig}^{p_i}$, $addr_P$, $a_{x_{ref}}$, f)

        $x_{ref} \leftarrow Load(pk_{sig}^{(p_i)}, addr_P, a_{x_{ref}})$

        if $x_{ref} \neq \emptyset$ **then**

            $f_s \leftarrow$ generate secure computation protocol from f

            return $f_s(x_{ref})$

        end if

        return $\emptyset$

    end procedure

INCENTIVES

Since Enigma is not a cryptocurrency or a blockchain, the incentive scheme is based on fees rather than mining rewards; nodes are compensated for providing computational resources. Full nodes are required to provide a security deposit, making malicious behaviour punishable.

Security Deposits

A possible attack on MPC protocols takes advantage of the lack of guaranteed fairness in the protocol. Under certain conditions, a malicious party can learn the output and abort the protocol before other parties learn the output as well. While this attack cannot be prevented when carried out by a majority, it can be penalized. Using Bitcoin security deposits for punishing malicious nodes in MPC has been investigated by several scholars recently.[22, 23] We use a similar model, and extend it to penalize other malicious behaviors such as breaking correctness, which is validated by the SPDZ protocol.

To participate in the network, store data, perform computations, and receive fees, every full node must first submit a security deposit to a private contract. After each computation is completed, a private contract verifies correctness and fairness were maintained. If a node is found to lie about their outcome or aborts the computation prematurely, it loses the deposit which is split between the other honest nodes. The computation is continued without the malicious node (e.g., by setting its share of the data to 0).

Computation Fees

Every request in the network for storage, data retrieval, or computation has a fixed price, similar to the concept of gas in Ethereum. Unlike Ethereum where every computation is run by every node, in Enigma different nodes execute different parts of each computation and need to be compensated according to their contribution, which is measured in rounds. Recall that every function is reduced to a circuit of addition and multiplication gates, each of which takes one or more rounds. A node participating in a computation is paid the weighted sum of the number of rounds it contributed to and the operations it performed (addition, multiplication).

Since the platform is turing-complete, the exact cost of a request cannot always be pre-calculated. Therefore, once the computation is finalized, the cost of each request is deducted from an account balance each node maintains. A request will not go through unless the account balance is over a minimum threshold.

Storage Fees

Fees for data storage are market based and time limited. The hosting contract is automatically renewed using the owner's account balance. If the balance is too low, access to the data will be restricted, and unless additional funds are deposited, the data will be deleted within a certain amount of time.

APPLICATIONS

Data Marketplace

A data marketplace is a direct consumer-to-business marketplace for data. With guaranteed privacy, autonomous control, and increased security, consumers will sell access to their data. For example, a pharmaceutical company looking for patients for clinical trials can scan genomic databases for candidates. The marketplace would eliminate tremendous amounts of friction, lower costs for customer acquisition, and offer a new income stream for consumers.

Secure Backend

Many companies today store large amounts of customer data to provide personalized services, match individual preferences, target ads and offers, and more. With Enigma, companies can use the data for the same purposes they do today, without actually storing or processing the data on their servers, thereby removing security risks and assuring the privacy of their customers.

Internal Compartmentalization

Large organizations can use Enigma to protect their data and trade secrets from corporate espionage and rogue employees. Employees can still use and analyze data for the benefit of the organization, but won't be able to steal any data. Productivity inside organizations would be improved since more people can have access to more data, and costs on security would be lower.

N-Factor Authentication

Voice, face, and fingerprint recognition are stored and computed on Enigma. Only the user ever has access to these data. Policies for when and if additional keys are required can be set inside a private contract, unexposed to any potential attacker.

Identity

Authenticating and securely storing identities in a fully anonymous, yet provably correct, fashion is trivial on Enigma and requires as little as several lines of code. The process is simple—a user secret-shares her personal information required for authentication. When the user logs in, an authenticating private contract is executed, validating the user and linking her real identity with a public pseudo-identity. The process is completely trustless and privacy-preserving.

IoT

Store, manage, and use (the highly sensitive) data collected by IoT devices in a decentralized, trustless cloud.

Distributed Personal Data Stores

Store and share data with third parties while maintaining control and ownership. Set specific policies for each service with private contracts. Identity is truly protected since the decision to share data is always reversible—services have no access to raw data; all they can do is run secure computations on it.

Crypto Bank

Run a full-service crypto bank without exposing private internal details. Users can take loans, deposit cryptocurrencies, or buy investment products with the autonomous control of the blockchain, without publicly revealing their financial situation.

Blind E-Voting

Allows for voting on anything, from political elections to company board meetings, without exposing anything besides the final outcome. Not only is the privacy of each voter maintained, but even the actual vote-count can also remain private. For example, if the elections require any kind of majority vote, but no details about the distribution, a unanimous decision would be indistinguishable from one decided by a single vote.

Bitcoin Wallet

1. **Decentralized private key generation:** Multiple Enigma nodes locally create a segment of the key, whereas the full key is only ever assembled by the user. No trail of evidence is left anywhere.

2. **Decentralized transaction signing:** Transactions are signed without ever exposing the private key or leaving a trail.

3. **Decentralized controls:** Set spending limits, multi-sig, CHECKLOCKTIMEVERIFY like controls, and more with a private script. Lock time, limits, or number of required signatures are completely invisible to a potential attacker.

NOTES

1. Diamond, Jared, and Germs Guns. *Steel: The fates of human societies.* New York: W. W. Norton,1997.

2. deMontesquieu, Charles. *The spirit of the laws.* Digireads. com Publishing, 2004.

3. Barlow, John Perry. *A Declaration of the Independence of Cyberspace.* Electronic Frontier Foundation 8,1996.

4. Goel, Vindu. *Facebook tinkers with users emotions in news feed experiment, stirring outcry.* The New York Times, 2014.

5. Ball, James. "Nsas prism surveillance program: how it works and what it can do." TheGuardian,2013.

6. Hardekopf, Bill. "The Big Data Breaches of 2014." Forbes,2015.

7. Szabo, Nick."The dawn of trustworthy computing."2014.

8. Szabo, Nick. "The God Protocols."1997.

9. Nakamoto, Satoshi. "Bitcoin: A peer-to-peer electronic cash system." Consulted 1.2012(2008):28.

10. Clark, Joseph Bonneau Andrew Miller Jeremy, Arvind Narayanan Joshua A. Kroll Edward,and W. Felten. "SoK: Research Perspectives and Challenges for Bitcoin and Cryptocurren-cies.",SecurityandPrivacy(SP),2015IEEESymposiumon.IEEE,2015.

11. Maymounkov, Petar, and David Mazieres. "Kademlia: A peer-to-peer information systembased on the xor metric." In Peer-to-Peer Systems, pp. 53-65. Springer Berlin Heidelberg, 2002.

12. Yao, Andrew C. "Protocols for secure computations." 2013 IEEE 54th Annual Symposium on Foundations of Computer Science. IEEE, 1982.

13. Ben-David, Assaf, Noam Nisan, and Benny Pinkas. "FairplayMP: a system for secure multi-party computation." Proceedings of the 15th ACM conference on Computer and communica-tions security. ACM, 2008.

14. Bogdanov, Dan, Sven Laur, and Jan Willemson. "Sharemind: A framework for fast privacy-preserving computations." Computer Security-ESORICS

2008. Springer Berlin Heidelberg, 2008. 192-206.

15. Team, VIFF Developement. "Viff, the virtual ideal functionality framework." 2009.

16. Shamir, Adi. "How to share a secret." Communications of the ACM 22.11 (1979): 612-613.

17. Ben-Or, Michael, Shafi Goldwasser, and Avi Wigderson. "Completeness theorems for non-cryptographic fault-tolerant distributed computation." Proceedings of the twentieth annual ACM symposium on Theory of computing. ACM, 1988.

18. Baum, Carsten, Ivan Damgrd, and Claudio Orlandi. "Publicly auditable secure multi-party computation." Security and Cryptography for Networks. Springer International Publishing, 2014. 175-196.

19. Damgrd, Ivan, et al. "Practical covertly secure MPC for dishonest majorityor: Breaking the SPDZ limits." Computer SecurityESORICS 2013. Springer Berlin Heidelberg, 2013. 1-18.

20. Cohen, Gil, et al. "Efficient multiparty protocols via log-depth threshold formulae." Advances in CryptologyCRYPTO 2013. Springer Berlin Heidelberg, 2013. 185-202.

21. Swanson, Tim. "Consensus-as-a-service: a brief report on the emergence of permissioned, distributed ledger systems," 2015.

22. Bentov, Iddo, and Ranjit Kumaresan." How to use bitcoin to design fair protocols." Advances in CryptologyCRYPTO 2014. Springer Berlin Heidelberg, 2014. 421-439.

23. Andrychowicz, Marcin, et al. "Secure multiparty computations on bitcoin." Security and Pri-vacy (SP), 2014 IEEE Symposium on. IEEE, 201.

CHAPTER 16

The Trust::Data Framework as a Solution to the Cybersecurity Challenge

Thomas Hardjono, David Shrier,
and Alex Pentland

In 2016, government officials from the EU and the US asked Professor Alex Pentland at MIT to gather thought leaders and develop a new cybersecurity framework. A portion of this thinking was adapted to a submission for the Obama White House Commission on Cybersecurity. The working group assembled in summer 2016 led to the creation of the Trust::Data Consortium that seeks to simultaneously make data more secure and more easily shared and used. Interest has been diverse and global, as the problems solved through the Trust::Data Framework span all areas of industry, technology, and society. Concepts in this chapter are expanded in the book from Hardjono, Shrier, and Pentland called "Trust::Data."[1]

As the economy and society move from a world where interactions were physical and based on paper documents, toward a world that is primarily governed by digital data and digital transactions, our existing methods of managing identity and data security are proving inadequate. Large-scale fraud, identity theft, and data breaches are becoming common, and a large fraction of the population has only the most limited digital credentials. Even so, our digital infrastructure is recognized as a critical global which must be resilient to threat. If we can create a system for what we call "Trust::Data," which provides safe, secure access for everyone, then huge societal benefits can be unlocked, including better health, greater financial inclusion, and a population that is more engaged with, and better supported by, its government.

The future of cybersecurity should be supported by Trust::Data to enable both auditable provenance of identity, and the credibility of data in order to enhance economic viability of new technology solutions, policies, and best practices. Simultaneously, Trust::Data must protect the privacy of people; ensure public safety, economic, and national security; and foster public, individual, and business partnerships.

In order to accomplish these goals, thought leaders from government, academia, and private sector organizations must collaborate to deliver this new future.

Elements required for Trust::Data include:

- **Robust digital identity:** Identity, whether personal or organizational, is the key that unlocks all other data and data-sharing functions. Digital identity includes not only having unique and unforgeable credentials that work everywhere, but also the ability to access all the data linked to your identity and the ability to control the "persona" that you present in different situations. The "work you," the "health system you," and the "government you" will typically have different data access associated with them and will be owned and controlled only by the core "biological you." To accomplish this, there needs to be a kind of "internet of identity" to genuinely enable all other sharing functions.

- **Distributed Internet trust authorities:** We have repeatedly seen that centralized system administration is the weakest link in cybersecurity, enabling both insiders and opponents to destroy our system security with a single exploit. The most practical solution to this problem is to have authority distributed among many trusted actors, so that compromise of one or even a few authorities does not destroy the system security consensus. This is already standard practice for the highest security systems: For instance, no single actor can launch nuclear. Now we need to implement this sort of consensus security widely. Examples, such as the blockchain that underlies most digital cryptocurrencies, show that distributed ledgers can provide world-wide security even in very hostile environments.

- **Distributed safe computation:** Our critical systems will suffer increasing rates of damage and compromise, unless we move decisively toward pervasive use of data minimization, more encryption, and distributed computation. Current firewall, event sharing, and attack detection approaches are simply not feasible as long-run solutions for cybersecurity, and we need to adopt an inherently more robust approach.

- **Universal access:** The advantages of secure digital infrastructure are diminished without universal access.

ROBUST DIGITAL IDENTITY

Our mission in suggesting a robust identity framework focuses on connecting the individual with the digital identity while protecting privacy. When we say "robust," we mean reliable, unique, and unforgeable. A robust digital identity is the keystone to cybersecurity and can mitigate the risks seen from recent cyber-breaches.

Identity plays a major role in everyday life. Think about going to an office, getting on an airplane, logging onto a website, or making an online purchase. We generally don't pay much attention to our identity credentials unless something goes wrong, despite the fact that our credentials are all around us. But, it's a highly complex and increasingly important subject.

Whether physical or digital in nature, identity is a collection of individual information or attributes associated with an entity, individual, institution, or device, which is used to determine the transactions in which the entity can rightfully participate.

For individuals, the so-called "identity attributes" fall into three main categories: (i) Inherent attributes are intrinsic to an individual, such as age, height, date of birth, and fingerprints; (ii) assigned attributes are extrinsic to the individual and can change over time, such as e-mail address, login IDs and passwords, telephone number and passport number; and (iii) accumulated attributes are gathered over time, such as health records, job history, and residential addresses.

In general, the attributes needed to validate an identity are isolated within different private and public sector institutions, each using its data for its own purposes. To reach a higher level of privacy and security we need to establish a trusted data ecosystem, which requires the interoperability and sharing of data across the various institutions involved. The more data sources a trusted ecosystem has access to, the higher the probability of detecting fraud and identity theft while reducing false positives.

A robust digital identity ecosystem needs to distinguish between and separate personal data belonging to an individual (referred to as Core-Identity or CoreID)[2] that are long-lived, and the transaction identifiers that are used in daily engagement by that individual. These transaction-identities may be short-lived or ephemeral, and may even provide some degree of anonymity with the purpose of providing just enough information to a relying party (counter-party) to complete a transaction.

Secondly, entities within a robust digital identity ecosystem need to share data regarding individuals, communities, and organizations that are housed in separate data repositories and are quite likely be under distinct legal/jurisdictional domains. As such, a crucial aspect of a future digital identity ecosystem requires addressing the challenges around data sharing: (i) Currently data remains isolated within the organizational boundaries; (ii) data is of a limited type only, belonging to specific domain/verticals (e.g., financial domain; health domain); and (iii) sharing of raw data with parties outside the organization remains unattainable, either due to regulatory constraints or due to business risk exposures and liabilities.

To this end, the MIT Open Algorithms (OPAL) paradigm for data sharing offers a foundational component for the future digital identity ecosystem, using the OPAL model for identity-focused data sharing. The following are key principles of OPAL:[3]

- **Moving the algorithm to the data:** Instead of sending raw data to the location of processing, it is the algorithm that should be sent to the location of the data (i.e., data repository) and be processed there.

- **Raw data must never leave its repository:** A raw set must never be exported, and must always be under the control of its owner or the owner of the data repository.

- **Vetted algorithms:** Algorithms must be studied and vetted by domain-experts to be "safe" from bias, discrimination, privacy violations, and other unintended consequences.

- **Provide only safe answers:** When executing an algorithm on a data-set, the data repository must always provide responses that are deemed "safe" from a privacy perspective.

The OPAL principles become immensely relevant in a digital identity ecosystem when information regarding an individual is needed to complete transactions. The OPAL paradigm can be used by an identity ecosystem to enable richer information sharing among participants in the ecosystem. The key idea is for industry to move from an attributes-based unidirectional model to a richer algorithms-based interaction:[4]

- **Algorithms instead of identity-attributes:** Rather than attribute providers delivering static attributes (e.g., "Joe is over 18") to the relying party, allow instead the relying party to choose one or more vetted algorithms (e.g., from a given data domain) to be executed at the data repository. In this way, the relying party obtains more assurance regarding the individual or organization with whom it is transacting.[4]

- **Trust network for OPAL-based data sharing for identity:** A new set
  of legal rules and system-specific rules must be devised and must clearly
  articulate the required combination of technical standards and systems,
  business processes and procedures, and legal rules that, taken together,
  establish a trustworthy system for information sharing based on the
  OPAL model.

DISTRIBUTED TRUST

Interest in distributed computing and peer-to-peer (P2P) networks has been
rekindled in the past few years due to the emergence of the Bitcoin system.[6]
The Bitcoin digital currency system—albeit limited in transaction type
and throughput—has provided a real working example of a P2P value-
transfer system that does not depend on centralized intermediary entity
(i.e., a bank). This perceived independence from a centralized authority has
raised interest in the possibility for a future Internet of transactions based
on "distributed trust," loosely interpreted to mean an Internet that provides
entities a greater degree of autonomy in conducting transactions (i.e.,
performing computations). We extend this interpretation to also include
the control over data (e.g., for business survivability; for individual privacy),
which also means control over the sharing of data.

The use of distributed sources of trust allows transacting entities to obtain
better assurance through an increased availability of data from various
sources on the P2P network. Here the term "trust" is taken to mean sources
of information of strong provenance, either arrived at through some
computation (local or distributed) or obtained through analysis of accurate
data (e.g., historical transaction data). Entities that are in possession of strong
provenance data regarding a party (e.g., individual, organization, etc.) could
make this information available more generally for transaction assurance
purposes. Transacting entities could make use of this information in decision

making, and new models for a market of trustworthy data could be enabled using blockchain technology and distributed ledger technologies.

Blockchain technology offers a way to anchor this information, or claimed in a common ledger mechanism, allowing the existence of information to be verified. The information or data itself may not need to be recorded on the blockchain system or distributed ledger; instead, only "pointers" to the information are recorded there. This more recent reappraisal of the purpose a blockchain system has effectively turned it into more of a directory system. In fact, some commentators have begun to refer to the blockchain as the information "routing" layer—even though this concept of hash-based routing is at least a decade old and has been at the heart of the *Content Addressed Networking* (CAN) paradigm in the IP networking industry.[7]

In order to create a generalized model for distributed trust with decentralization of control, it is instructive to look at the key features that make the Bitcoin system a successfully running P2P system:

- **Equal access to relevant data:** One key aspect of the Bitcoin system is that nodes in the P2P network have equitable access to the same set of state information (data) regarding the completed/validated transactions and unprocessed transactions. Here, each node can independently select transactions, process them, and report the result in the form of a block of transactions.

- **Independence to compute:** Another key feature of the Bitcoin system is the entities' ability to independently arrive at a consensus regarding the state of the set of validated transactions captured in the chain of blocks. Nodes are not dependent on each other or hindered in any way to complete the mathematical "puzzle" in Bitcoin (also referred to as the proof of work). Furthermore, once consensus is reached it is almost computationally infeasible to reverse the agreement (short of human intervention). This last feature is often referred to as the "immutability" of the ledger or the sequence of validated blocks of transactions. Note that the concept of "unhindered computations" has been a pillar of the trusted computing industry for nearly two decades now.[8]

- **Correct incentives model:** The Bitcoin model of using a combination of processing fees and rewards for the puzzle winner has proven to be sufficient for the specific task for which Bitcoin was created (transferring digital currency). This same fee-based model is currently being used within other systems such as Ethereum.[9] This successful incentives model should be a foundation for future distributed trust systems.

- **Specific task definition:** Another design aspect of the Bitcoin system is its limited programmability and narrow task definition or purpose, namely to move "value" (numbers) from one account (address) to another in a safe manner, which detects cheating (double spending). This specific purpose of the Bitcoin system is built into the system itself, and all its available operations (op-codes) are geared for this singular purpose.

There are several challenges that need to be addressed before a future Internet with distributed trust and decentralization of control can be achieved:

- **Technical trust and legal trust:** Cryptographic techniques combined with computer hardware and software may achieve what is commonly referred to as *technical trust*.[8] This means that a high degree of assurance is achieved by the system, namely assurance that the system performed the computation correctly, without any external interference and with a high degree of accuracy. Distributed trust requires technical mechanisms to achieve technical trust, but this alone does not guarantee the social acceptability of the system by users in the ecosystem. As such, "legal trust" must also underlie the system, by which we mean the use of legal agreements and contracts to define the rights, obligations, and liabilities of all participants in the ecosystem. It is the combined technical-trust with legal underpinnings that allows systems with distributed trust to gain broad social acceptability. It also allows parties to quantify risk in some manner, and therefore allows them to manage risk in the face of uncertain outcomes (e.g., unforeseen events) even with the use of blockchain technology.

- **Equitable access to resources:** In order to attain a degree of distributed trust with decentralization of control, there needs to be autonomy of computing entities with equitable access to the resources needed to complete computations for the specific task at hand. Resources, here, include information about the state of the network (local and global), computing power, bandwidth, power sources (i.e., electricity), and last mile access to the network.

- **Degrees of programmability:** Currently, the term "smart contracts" is most often used to mean a distributed ledger system that provides a greater degree to task-programmability (compared to the narrow task-specific Bitcoin system). The technical view of smart contracts is often combined with a legal view to mean that the result of the execution of the programmed code (smart contract) is legally binding to entities who agree to deploy it and that the outcome has legal enforceability. Note that the Bitcoin system does not presume any legal substrate, and therefore transactions are not legally binding to parties in any way.

  Currently there is no general agreement as to the precise meaning of "smart contracts." In fact, the term today incorporates a broad range of meanings.[10] These range from the "pure code as contract" at one end of the spectrum to that of smart contracts merely as a digital representation of "business logic" that carries no legal weight on its own. As such, for future systems based on smart contracts that are highly programmable, there needs to be a correspondingly high degree of correlation between (i) what is intended in the legal sense of the contract (legal prose) with (ii) what the executable code actually carries out (i.e., what it computes). Furthermore, there needs to be indisputable methods or mechanisms to unambiguously validate this correlation prior to execution.

- **Governance model and operating rules**: Most, if not all, shared systems and infrastructures today operate based on some governance model that dictates in precise terms—both legal and technical—the daily operational rules of all components and entities in the ecosystem. The governance mechanism also represents the interface between the digital system and the real-world external to that digital system.

  A future Internet with distributed trust and decentralization of control must operate with a governance model that not only defines the degree of trust to be offered, but also sets the "rules of the game" to ensure equitable access to resources by all participants in the ecosystem according to their agreed roles. Since there are no perfect computer systems, and since any human and system error will always be present in methods for dispute (despite efforts to reduce them), the governance model must provide for resolution of differences. Note that even the Bitcoin system has a human governance model. The task-specific and consensus-algorithm based approach used in Bitcoin has led some commentators to note—incorrectly—that Bitcoin possesses "self-governance." However, the technical aspects of Bitcoin are "governed" by human programmers and developers who determine the technical features to be added to subsequent revisions of the source code. Their choices affect the Bitcoin system as a whole. Furthermore, their current governance model is not free from controversy.[11]

DISTRIBUTED SAFE COMPUTATION

As we have seen in[1] the MIT Enigma project a combination of some cryptographic techniques with P2P distributed systems offers a promising direction for information sharing in a privacy-preserving manner. More interestingly, it offers an avenue to the notion of *distributed safe computations*, which we define as possessing the following characteristics:

- **Computation execution at the data:** The execution of a joint computation is performed by each party at the respective locations of their data. Parties must never export or exchange raw data to each other.

- **Data encrypted during computation:** New cryptographic techniques—such as secret-sharing and multi-party computation— allow computations to be performed on encrypted data, possibly even in a distributed manner.

- **Safe-response by constrained algorithms:** Algorithms jointly computed by nodes in a distributed fashion must result in safe answers, preserving the privacy of the subjects whose data are included in the joint computation. Vetting of algorithms by experts should be performed prior to execution.

- **Distributed computation and storage units:** The P2P network of nodes underlying current blockchain systems offers an opportunity for these nodes to be utilized to perform sub-computations (as part of a larger distributed safe computation event). On their own their partial results may not be meaningful, but combined their collective compute power provides many opportunities for future transactions.

There are numerous applications of the MIT Enigma model, ranging from finance to health care:

- **Better insight into financial risk exposures:** Distributed safe computation methods and protocols allow entities (e.g., in a group or consortium) to compute the aggregate risk exposures of their membership organizations without affecting the privacy of these respective entities. Examples of computations include those that detect over-concentration in the credit default swaps market, computations to indicate the aggregate leverage of a set of hedge funds, and other similar computations. Furthermore, this approach provides a tool for regulators (and the public) to gauge more accurately and monitor the amount of risk in the financial system at any point in time.

- **Improved visibility in clinical trials:** Distributed safe computations may be used to provide better visibility into the ongoing results of clinical trials (e.g., of new drugs) while preserving the privacy of the participants of the trial (i.e., patients). More specifically, the state of the cohort or group can be measured collectively without pinpointing to specific individuals.

UNIVERSAL ACCESS

A new identity and data framework is meaningless without universal access. Solving a problem for only a few will exacerbate the digital and wealth divides that already have created numerous problems for many societies.

A key aspect of universal access is that of empowerment of the individual.[12] New infrastructures based on distributed safe computations should seek to provide universal access not only to data (e.g., an individual's own personal data), but also access to computing power offered by the P2P nodes. Distributed trust systems based on blockchain technologies should allow traditionally disempowered parties (e.g., an individual) to take part in transactions with counterparties that traditionally hold greater power (e.g., governments and companies).

Universal access through user-centricity is a recurring theme within both the blockchain community and identity management community. In the first, the term "disintermediation" is often used to capture sentiments regarding the need for a better balance of power in transactions. Within the identity management community, "user-centric" management of identity is the concept most often used to denote the need for individuals to have better control over their personal data.

In both these communities, a common thread is that of the need to provide better leverage for the individual as the disempowered party to negotiate terms through new constructs, such as smart contracts. The current dominant model of "take-it-or-leave-it" contract constrains the individual to get a "better deal," notably in large third-party outsourcing of services.

The P2P network offers a glimpse of possible solutions to this dilemma, using the "flat" arrangement of peers with various smart-contracts-based offers as the new market model for services. Distributed trust and distributed safe computation at P2P nodes provides:[13]

- **Greater dynamism in contracts:** Smart contracts introduce greater dynamism between transacting parties, where both parties have greater say in the construction of the smart contract. Furthermore, the duration of contracts may be limited, and renegotiated parameters may be conducted when a new smart contract is about to begin. Thus, rather than being statically locked into a contract for long periods of time without the power to renegotiate terms, an individual is better able to select shorter term smart contracts from the P2P-based market and negotiate parameters at the commencement of each new contract.

- **Broader market choice:** In addition to greater dynamism in contracts negotiation, the P2P model encourages new entrants to the market, providing a broader choice to the individual and to organizations.
- **Improved transparency and accountability:** Transparency in all aspects of a smart contracts fulfilment and settlement is core to the concept of universal access. Smart contracts and blockchain technologies built on distributed safe computation allows transacting parties to view the partial state of the computation of the smart contract. The use of the ledger feature allows post-event analysis to be performed using "evidence" found on the ledger.

A CALL TO ACTION

The frameworks described herein aren't theoretical. We have begun an open source code project, at http://trust.mit.edu, that is translating theory into reality. We are making it open source in the continued MIT tradition of providing technology-driven solutions to humanity's biggest problems.

To successfully turn this vision of a new cybersecure, shareable, universal identity and data sharing system, we need a vibrant community of collaborators around the world. We need corporate partners to commit resources to work with us on adapting these general-purpose frameworks to industry and use-case-specific implementations. We need developers to extend the architecture into viable, scalable, and robust code. And we need entrepreneurs to create a new generation of companies that build widespread adoption of this dynamic new approach to a connected society.

We are at the beginning of our journey. We invite you to contact us and become part of the effort to deploy Trust::Data to the world.

NOTES

1. T. Hardjono, A. Pentland, and D. Shrier, eds., in Trust::Data—A New Framework for Identity and Data Sharing. Visionary Future, 2016.

2. T. Hardjono, D. Greenwood, and S. Pentland," Towards a Trustworthy Digital Infrastructure for Core Identities and Personal Data Stores," ID360 Conference on Identity management, University of Texas, May 2013.

3. A. Pentland, D. Shrier, T. Hardjono, and I. Wladawsky-Berger, "Towards an Internet of Trusted Data: Input to the Whitehouse Commission on Enhancing National Cybersecurity," in *Trust::Data - A New Framework for Identity and Data Sharing,* T. Hardjono, A. Pentland, and D. Shrier, eds. Visionary Future, 2016, pp. 21–49.

4. T. Hardjono and A. Pentland, Open Algorithms for Identity Federation, May 2017. Available at: https://arxiv.org/pdf/1705.10880.pdf

5. T. Hardjono and A. Pentland, On Privacy-Preserving Identity within Future Blockchain Systems, W3C Workshop on Distributed Ledgers on the Web, May 2016.

6. S. Nakamoto, "Bitcoin: A Peer-to-Peer Electronic Cash System." Available at: https://bitcoin.org/bitcoin.pdf

7. I. Stoica, R. Morris, D. Karger, F. Kaashoek, and H. Balakrishnan (2001). "Chord: A scalable peer-to-peer lookup service for internet applications". ACM SIGCOMM Computer Communication Review 31 (4): 149. Available at: http://pdos.lcs.mit.edu/chord/

8. Trusted Computing Group, "TPM Main – Specification Version 1.2," Trusted Computing Group, TCG Published Specification, October 2003, http://www.trustedcomputinggroup.org/ resources/ tpm main specification.

9. V. Buterin, "Ethereum: A Next-Generation Cryptocurrency and Decentralized Application Platform," Bitcoin Magazine, Report, January 2014, https://bitcoinmagazine.com/articles/ ethereum-

next-generationcryptocurrency-decentralized-application-platform-1390528211/.

10. Norton Rose Fulbright, "Can smart contracts be legally binding contracts," Norton Rose Fulbright, Report, November 2016, http://www.nortonrosefulbright.com/knowledge/publications/144559/cansmart-contracts-be-legally-binding-contracts.

11. Oscar Williams-Grut and Rob Price, *A Bitcoin civil war is threatening to tear the digital currency in 2,* Business Insider, March 2017. http://www.businessinsider.com/ bitcoins-hard-fork-bitcoin-unlimited-segregated-witness-explained-2017-3.

12. T. Hardjono, E. Maler, M. Machulak, and D. Catalano, "User-Managed Access (UMA) Profile of OAuth2.0 – Specification Version 1.0," April 2015, https://docs.kantarainitiative.org/uma/rec-uma-core.html.

13. T. Hardjono and E. Maler, eds., Report from the Blockchain and Smart Contracts Discussion Group, Kantara Initiative, June 2017. https://kantarainitiative.org/confluence/display/BSC/Home

Conclusion

Howard Shrobe, David Shrier,
and Alex Pentland

In the fall of 2016, the authors posted an OpEd piece on CNBC.com[1] saying that we were at war and losing badly, due to the inadequate state of cybersecurity. With the benefit of time, it is apparent that we were overly optimistic in our appraisal. In the months following, we have witnessed two major world-wide ransomware attacks that have shut down hospitals and that even caused the shut-down of the computers which monitor the Chernobyl nuclear plant.

Some of the latest generation of cyberattacks have been mediated through IoT devices, such as baby monitors and home webcams. The ever-proliferating IoT infrastructure, forecast to reach over 75 billion connected devices by 2025,[2] offers up a rich set of poorly secured targets.

Autonomous cars? Fantastic. We can reduce traffic fatalities,[3] mitigate greenhouse gas emissions,[4] and improve traffic flow.[5] And we can introduce another flight of weakly protected computer systems for bad actors to exploit.

How did we get to this situation? The first prototype of the Unix operating system was designed in 1969 on a PDP-7 computer, and the first release of Unix in 1971 ran on a PDP-11 that could support 64 kilobytes of main memory. Window-NT, the root of the current Windows systems, was introduced in 1993; in the same year, Intel introduced the Pentium product family. These chips ran at a clock rate of 60 MHz. These are the architectural antecedents of today's commercial processor chips and of the UNIX, Macintosh OSX, and Windows operating systems. Most importantly, the C programming language, and its derivatives were enshrined as the programming language of choice for systems programming in all three families of operating systems.

Moore's law has enabled us to build computers that are much more capable than these, but the key architectural decisions in the design of both the hardware and the software are grounded in the realities that confronted the designers of these earlier systems. The paucity of computing power meant that little mattered as much as squeezing out as much performance as possible; once that performance had been squeezed out, it was used to support new features.

The Internet was not yet a significant presence and most machines were not connected to a network. In this context, security was not seen as important. The Morris worm, accidentally unleashed on the network in 1988, provided the first glimpse of what we were to face. But it failed to be a wake up call; computer architectures continued along the same paths as before.

However, as the Internet has pervaded our lives, it has reduced the time and space between machines to nothing. This has amplified the security vulnerabilities of the computers connected to the network, to the point that a worldwide attack is possible and can be launched in minutes. Yet our technology is still based on inappropriate architectural models, and we are stuck with a legacy of hundreds of millions of lines of code optimized for yesterday's needs while exposing an attack surface of major proportions.

We are now living in a "cyber hell" of our own making, but we need not stay here forever.

We have new cybersecurity tools at the research stage, some of which have been described in this volume. These hardware, software, and methodological systems can help solve the global cyber(in)security crisis. They need additional investment for development and commercialization. However, as long as national governments continue to cut science and technology funding (whether in the US, due to ideology, or in Europe, due to downstream effects of Brexit, or elsewhere, due to economic uncertainty) we will continue to see bigger and bigger impacts from cyberattacks.

We can also offer hope. Awareness of cyber-risk is growing, which may in turn lead to greater effort to solve cybersecurity problems. While quantum computing may put existing systems at risk,[6] we believe it also may reduce the costs of developing new cybersecure systems.

New cryptographic techniques for control of data and computation may limit the damage to the underlying data structures. Evolution in 3D printing may accelerate the creation of hardware prototypes to test theories in practice. We may see enhancements in the efficiency of investment and return for developing the next generation of cybersecurity from these and other developments.

Society is at a crossroads. We cannot afford to wait and hope that cybersecurity will evolve naturally against cyberthreats. Take action. Join the fight.

NOTES

1. http://www.cnbc.com/2016/09/27/the-spiraling-arms-race-of-data-insecurity-commentary.html

2. http://electronics360.globalspec.com/article/6551/75-4-billion-devices-connected-to-the-internet-of-things-by-2025

3. http://www.mckinsey.com/industries/automotive-and-assembly/our-insights/ten-ways-autonomous-driving-could-redefine-the-automotive-world

4. https://www.scientificamerican.com/article/self-driving-cars-could-cut-greenhouse-gas-pollution/

5. https://arxiv.org/abs/1705.01693

6. http://www.networkworld.com/article/3197366/security/how-quantum-computing-increases-cybersecurity-risks.html